GUIDE TO IRISH QUAKER RECORDS
1654—1860

COIMISIÚN LÁIMHSCRÍBHINNÍ NA hÉIREANN

GUIDE TO IRISH QUAKER RECORDS
1654—1860

BY
OLIVE C. GOODBODY

WITH CONTRIBUTION ON
NORTHERN IRELAND RECORDS
BY
B. G. HUTTON

CLEARFIELD

Originally published
Dublin, 1967

Reprinted for
Clearfield Company, Inc. by
Genealogical Publishing Co., Inc.
Baltimore, Maryland
1999

International Standard Book Number: 0-8063-4927-1

Made in the United States of America

CONTENTS

	Page
INTRODUCTION	1
PART I. Quaker archives	25
PART II. Documents in the Historical Library at 6 Eustace Street, Dublin :	
Family Collections	53
Manuscript drafts	117
School records	121
Diaries	122
Genealogical material	135
Will abstracts	136
Deeds and other legal documents	158
Portfolios	169
Maps and plans	171
Miscellaneous	171
Lists, inventories etc. of material available in other sources	174
APPENDIX I. Ulster Province Meeting : records in Friends' Meeting House, Lisburn	179
APPENDIX II. Quaker material in the Public Record Office of Northern Ireland	189
Surnames occurring in Irish Quaker Registers	193
INDEX OF PERSONS AND PLACES	209

INTRODUCTION

ORGANIZATION

George Fox, the founder of the Religious Society of Friends, recognized early that attention to detail was an essential in an organization which had no paid Minister. His own constructive powers included the knowledge that the value of written records could at no time be underestimated.

The worship of the Religious Society has, from its beginning been based on a quiet waiting on God, so that his Spirit may be revealed in the heart of each person. In the disorderly period of the mid-seventeenth century, when any man might speak in church after the conclusion of the Service, such quiet withdrawal in reverent silence must have been helpful to many. Meetings for Worship, the first essential of the Society, were attended by hundreds of people, not all of whom professed to join it in membership, and it does not seem clear when the sharp distinction between well-wishers and those received into formal membership was drawn. (See Rufus Jones, *Later Periods of Quakerism*, Macmillan 1921, I, 108). The early preachers of the Society spoke in market places, open fields, hills and towns, as well as in the quietness of their own homes and places of worship.

Quakerism was but one manifestation of the bewildered groping of men of the seventeenth century for a religion to fit their needs. Minds moulded by Reformation and Counter-reformation to habits of religious thought were ready to seek for truth. Many sects arose, of whom only a few survived. George Fox's doctrine, that God was revealed to man through the life of Christ and through the work of the Holy Spirit in each individual, appealed to minds torn by the dissensions within the orthodox church. Men of every social standing flocked to hear him speak as he moved from place to place during the Civil War and the interregnum.

A deep religious spirit was awakened in England among those who listened to him. Fox realized that without paid ministers some organization was needed to co-ordinate groups which met in widely dispersed areas. Thus his genius for church government evinced itself. It is very important that this systematized approach should not be confused with the religious sense of unity with God which preceded it. The best study of the subject may be found in W. C. Braithwaite's *First Period of Quakerism* and his *Second Period of Quakerism* (Macmillan, 1912 and 1919) and in the introduction of Frederick Tolles to the 2nd edition (Cambridge University Press, 1955 and 1961) of the *Second Period*. The second edition of each volume has valuable annotation and revision by Professor Henry J. Cadbury.

MEETINGS

The word ' Meeting ' as used among Friends has several applications, the most familiar being that for Worship held, not alone on Sunday and at least one other day of the week, but also as a preliminary to many other meetings. This consists usually of periods of silent worship interspersed with vocal prayer or ministry. Meetings for Discipline are those which are responsible for the organization and business of the Society, and are conducted without a paid ministry. The " sense of the Meeting " is the outcome of a quiet deliberation and contribution to the matter in hand, and is arrived at without division or vote. One member, known usually as the clerk of the Meeting, records the wish of the gathering. A system of special or sub-committees often carries out the decisions arrived at, while individual members arrange to do the work of visiting and looking after the sick and the poor, of matters concerning education, and all the various activities of church life.

A pyramid system of Meetings throughout England was evolved gradually to conduct the business of the Church, its pattern being followed in broad outline in Ireland. The base of the pyramid was the National or Yearly Meeting, to which representatives from all parts of the country came. Their main function in the earlier days was to bring news of distant Friends, to record the sufferings to which Friends were exposed for their beliefs, and to give opportunity for a combined meeting for worship. In Ireland each Province was asked to send at least six representatives to these meetings. More were usually present. As time went on Epistles or letters of advice and exhortation were sent to other Meetings of the Provinces, and much later still to America, Europe, the West Indies and other parts of the world. From such Meetings Epistles were also received. Throughout the country representative Meetings for extensive areas were formed, later to be known as Quarterly (in Ireland Province) Meetings. A Six-weeks Meeting was, in the 18th century, usually held between each Province Meeting, transacting nearly the same business as the latter, but differing in different areas. These were discontinued in 1792. Province Meetings were composed of members from the Men's (later Monthly) Meetings of more localized districts. Monthly Meetings were instituted to look after the business affairs of the Church, including essentially the care of the poor. These Meetings were, and still are, composed of members of particular Meetings for Worship in the district most of which hold a Preparative or Business Meeting monthly to conduct local business and to appoint representatives to other Meetings. In 1692 the National Meeting desired that the Province Meeting should include one or two Friends from each particular Meeting " to meet apart and take account of the management of each respective meeting in relation to the Meeting for Worship or concerning Public Friends or Testimonies borne in the Meeting." From this select Province Meeting Elders and Friends in the Ministry were (from the year 1694) appointed to the select, or Chamber, Meeting held before each National Meeting. These select meetings were the forerunners of the present Meetings of Ministers and Elders. For further particulars of the growth of these meetings the book known as the manuscript book of Extracts should be consulted as a guide to the dates needed, before search is made of the appropriate minute books.

Thus the pyramid was complete—Meeting for Worship, with its Preparative or Business Meeting, Monthly Meeting for a district, Quarterly Meeting for a larger area, and finally the National, now known as the Yearly Meeting. In Ireland the Six-Weeks Meeting was actually a part of the Province Meeting. It appears, however, that such a Meeting was held for Tipperary in addition to the Province one for Munster, and included Waterford (see Munster Province Meeting Minutes and also those for Cork, 10th March, 1692). This may be accounted for by the difficulty experienced in travelling throughout the Province. The entry for Cork Six-Weeks Meeting for the 27/7/1690 reads " The siege of Cork happening to be just at that time we had no Meeting."

The main outline of this system was set up in Ireland following the visit of George Fox in 1669. William Edmundson, who in 1654 had become convinced of the soundness of the approach to religion made by Friends, had spent the intervening years in Ireland both preaching and practising the new religion, and it appears from Wight and Rutty's *History of the Rise and Progress of Friends* in Ireland (1st ed. Dublin, I. Jackson, 1751) that Edmundson had already been instrumental in establishing Provincial, and some Monthly Meetings. (The modern spelling of the name Edmundson has been used throughout. In the 17th century it was spelled Edmondson).

The arrival of George Fox coincided with the arrangements being made for the holding of the first National Meeting. His advice and help are acknowledged by William Edmundson in his *Journal* (1st ed. p.51, Dublin, Samuel Fairbrother, 1715). Thus " In the year 1669 George Fox came into Ireland and several Friends in the Ministry with him. He settled Men's and Women's Meetings amongst Friends throughout the Nation, i.e. that faithful men and women should take care in the Government of Church Affairs, which were and are of great Service. I was much eased by it (as I told George Fox at the time) for I had a great concern in those things which had lain heavy upon my spirit for several years before; This gave every faithful Friend a share of the Burthen."

Meetings of Women Friends took place, generally at the same time and place as those of the men, but in a separate room. They had great influence, dealing with the relief of the poor, widows and orphans; the good behaviour of women and girls; enquiries into suitability of marriages; and such matters as the observance of moderation in dress and in the furnishings of houses.

But the Men's Meeting alone had executive authority. It dealt with membership and disownment (often, however, asking for advice from the Women's Meeting); with matters relating to property, including Meeting Houses and burial grounds; and in dealings with the State and with the Established Church. Therefore, it was unnecessary for the Women's Meeting to keep regular detailed minutes. That they did not do so was certainly not due to illiteracy for, from the early women's records that survive from the 17th and early 18th century, we realize that they wrote long Epistles to other Meetings in Ireland and elsewhere. Although we do not obtain much historical information from such, or from the scanty minutes available, it is remarkable that from 1680 onwards women Friends seem to have conducted their own affairs regularly on the three levels of Monthly, Province and National Meetings, though they never assembled at the Autumn Half-year Meeting.

George Fox advised that every Meeting should keep true records of transactions by means of minutes, and emphasized that registers of births, marriages and burials must be kept. In 1669 in an Epistle to Quarterly Meetings he wrote "... And that one or two Friends in every Meeting do take account of all the Births, Marriages and Burials and carry them to the Monthly Meeting and let one or two there be ordered to receive them and record them there in a Book which is to be kept at the Monthly Meetings. And from thence a copy of what is recorded there to be brought to the Quarterly Meetings, and let one or two there be appointed to receive them and to record them all in one Book, which is to be kept for the whole County. And this will be most safe, that if one book should happen to be lost the other may be preserved for the use of such as may have occasion ... " (*Epistles of George Fox*, 1st ed., London, 1698, II no. 264). The National Meeting of 3rd month 1671 held in Dublin added to this by a minute of advice concerning the proper method of recording.

INTRODUCTION 5

RECORDS

As time went on the value of making records of other transactions became evident and resulted in an accumulation of material which, in in Ireland, dates from 1670, though some fragmentary earlier records may be found, for instance Moate Men's Meeting accounts mention a sum sent to London in 1667 " after it was burned." Material recorded may be classified as follows:—

Minute Books occurring in every Meeting, most of which survive.

Membership Records: i.e. Family lists or "Lineage Books," lists of members, and statistics, copies of certificates of Removal from the compass of one Monthly Meeting to another, records of Sufferings, copies of Wills and Inventories.

Finance. This section includes the accounts kept by various Meetings and those scattered throughout Minute Books, a few Poor Account books, ledgers etc.

Education. Books recording the minutes and transactions of committees set up to establish schools under the care of the Religious Society of Friends; also books for recording the internal management of such schools in cases where they are now defunct, or relating to the early period of those still in existence.

Property and deeds. This includes books for copying deeds and transactions relating to property owned by Meetings.

As far as possible the archives in this Guide are arranged under the headings of Meetings which produced them. First Minutes of the National Half-Year Meeting (changed to a Yearly Meeting in 1794) which has met in an unbroken sequence since 1669. Secondly Province Records; Leinster, Munster and Ulster had Province Meetings. Connaught alone had none, though a few isolated Meetings took place within its bounds for which no records remain. Thirdly Monthly Meetings, whose function is noted later and whose records include minutes of Men's and Women's Meetings, oversight of the poor. Books for recording Births, Marriages and Deaths, for recording Sufferings in the area, for copying certificates given to Friends on their removal from or to the compass of a Monthly Meeting, and other records dealing with educational and financial matters. Material for fourteen such Meetings is noted, Bandon and Youghal being included in the Cork section, and Mountrath with Mountmellick. Fourthly Preparative Meetings etc. for particular congregations. Few Minute Books of these have been preserved for the period under review. Where they do exist they are included in the Guide. Local business was transacted by these Meetings, and representatives sent to Monthly Meetings. All these Meetings are still the functional method of organization of the Religious Society of Friends in Ireland. Minutes were kept for every Meeting, generally in folio volumes, very many of which are still extant. The majority are now housed in the strong room of the Meeting House at 6 Eustace Street, Dublin. Northern Ireland retains its own in the Meeting House at Lisburn, Co. Antrim*, and those for Waterford are in the Meeting House of that city.

The Yearly Meeting of Ireland has always been independent of London Yearly Meeting in its constitution. Efforts have always been made to keep Friends of both Meetings united in principles and parallel in habits and customs by inter-visitation and regular exchange of Epistles.

SUFFERINGS

Factual records of the imprisonments, fines, distraint of goods, excommunications and other penalties for religious beliefs were kept from the earliest days of the body. At a meeting in Skipton in Yorkshire in 1653 it was recommended that a Friend be appointed in each Men's Meeting to keep a detailed record of all " Sufferings." The books of Sufferings of a few Monthly Meetings are preserved in Ireland. All such Meetings, however, sent reports to the Province Meetings, which in turn sent them on to the National or Yearly Meeting. Thus we have among the Yearly Meeting records two such books dated 1653-1693 and 1693-1705, and three for the Province of Leinster 1656-1701, 1706-1714 and 1719-1723, in addition to those of Ulster and Munster, neither of which is of an early date. A few early loose papers do, however, exist which have been catalogued in the Library. Joseph Besse, who in 1753 published a two volume folio work entitled *An Abstract of the Sufferings of the People called Quakers*, drew his material from such recorded events throughout England, Scotland, Wales, Ireland, America and Europe. This work covers the period 1650-1689, the year of the Toleration Act of William III. His earliest date for Ireland was 1654 when three English preachers travelled through that country, testifying to their faith. Abraham Fuller of King's County and Thomas Holme of Wexford had previously published in 1672 *A Brief Relation of some part of the People called Quakers* supplemented by William Stockdale's *Great Cry of Oppression* in 1683. In 1731 Thomas Holme and Samuel Fuller, grandson to Abraham, printed in Dublin at Fuller's press *A Compendious View of some of the extraordinary Sufferings of the People called Quakers*. All these books must have had their origin in the manuscript records named above.

---

* See Appendix I by B. G. Hutton, pp. 179-188 *infra*.

One of the most usual causes for complaint against Friends by lay and ecclesiastical authorities alike was their steadfast refusal to pay for the support of the established church, especially in the form of tithe collections. So strong was the feeling against such payments that individual Friends were asked to sign a testimony declaring that he or she has not and will not pay such dues. A number died in prison as a result of hard treatment, bearing such rigours rather than submit to what was considered not only an injustice, but also a direct denial of the belief that the coming of Christ had ended priesthood and church dues. A minute of the National Half-year Meeting of 8/3/1682 reads: " Agreed that William Williamson get a book of six quires of paper bound with clasps, in which he is to record all the testimonies against Tithes against the next half-year, and bring the Book and the original copies to the Provinces of Leinster and Munster, and also that the testimonies against Backsliders be recorded in the latter part of the said Book, giving a place for each Province." That the book was procured we know, for it may still be consulted though rebound. (A.59).

Some of the original papers drawn up by Monthly Meetings for presentation to the Province Meetings, for Sufferings and for Tithes still exist in the strong room at Eustace Street. One such for Sufferings reads:

The Sufferings of Thomas Knight, the year 1711.

Thomas Knight had taken from him by Andrew Vaugh, Tithemonger under Thomas Blewett, Tithemonger, under Richard Goodman, priest of the parish of Ballymodane for one half, and under the Countess of Burlington for Impropriation the other half, two great cocks of hay, fourteen sheaves of pease, two hundred sheaves of english barley and one hundred and forty sheaves of bear barley, all worth about £2 6s. More taken by the same Andrew Vaugh and his assistants about 80 sheaves of wheat worth about 10s.

While the above serves to show the elaboration of methods of persecution it is not fully representative of penalties inflicted which included "fining, whipping, stocking, imprisonment and loss of goods, and for meeting to worship God in their own houses " (see Besse, *Collection of Sufferings*, Vol. II p.462). Many more details of goods distrained etc. are to be found in manuscript than published. Those for towns show costs of commodities such as materials by the yard, clothing, shoes, household utensils which, being distrained, generally had a greater value than the penalty due.

INTRODUCTION

Every Meeting was expected to keep a complete record of Sufferings which were collected from individuals, thus enabling the Meeting to make an accurate assessment, in order that the magistrates and justice of the peace might be approached when occasion seemed to warrant such a step. Such returns also served to help Friends to keep a watchful care on members whose worldly affairs were often reduced to a state of great poverty. There is a uniformity in the drawing up of these papers of Sufferings due to the fact that the National Meeting laid down specific rules at the Meeting of the 3rd month 1671, and again issued six rules for the proper recording of Sufferings in 3rd month 1699. By 1706 the work of reading Sufferings in the National Meeting was found " tedious " on account of the increase and each Provincial Meeting was instructed to keep a Record Book and to bring it to each Half-yearly Meeting, "only signifying to that Meeting the exact sum of each Province Suffering, with such account as may be of any Friends' extraordinary suffering or imprisonment." (Nat. Half-year Meeting 3rd. mo. 1706).

The earliest Meeting record is for the year 1669 when the first National Meeting was held in Dublin. It is contained in a small notebook of Cork Monthly Meeting (Cork 61) and is an alphabetical summary of some of the early minutes of the Half-yearly Meeting, " collected by order of Munster Province Meeting in the year 1704." Only three entries are of 1669, each concerning Sufferings viz. A. Application to Justices of the Peace etc. S. Sufferings, an exact account to be kept. T. Testimonies of Truth to be kept clear against tithes, etc.

REGISTERS

A minute of the National Meeting of the 3rd month 1671 advises that Births, Burials and Marriages be recorded in the Particular and Province Books of Registry. As we have seen, this followed the recommendation of George Fox. The earliest record to be found among Irish Friends' archives pre-dates the establishment of the Society by several years, births being given for those who later joined Friends, one being as early as 1615. These early registers are variously named:—Family Lists, Lineage Books, Registers, or, as in the case of Mountmellick, " Book of Mountmellick Meeting from 1667, Sufferings, Family Lists, Marriage Certificates, Testimonies of Condemnation and about prominent Friends to the middle of the 18th century." (G.17). The early part of this book appears to be in William Edmundson's hand-writing. These books are valuable not only for their genealogical content but for the fact that they show, often, the locality from which Friends had come, where they settled and occasionally the trade or occupation of a man.

Some Quakers had an Irish background, but the majority came as settlers during the Cromwellian period when land was cheap, and tradesmen or skilled artificers badly needed. Others had been soldiers who had left the army after the Battle of Worcester. Yet others served in Ireland under Henry Cromwell and with a resolute courage left that avocation to join Friends, suffering severely for so doing. There are many instances of such convincements to the tenets of the Society in print. The best available source for these and other incidents among Friends is *Quakers in Ireland*, by Isabel Grubb (London, Swarthmore Press Ltd. 1927), who has used throughout documented manuscript material.

From the early registers indexes were made in the last century which contain abstracts of all births, marriages and deaths up to 1859, after which date new books were put into use. They are in the strong room at 6 Eustace Street. There are eleven early "Family Lists," and records of Bandon Meeting families in the back of the Bandon Minute Books (Cork 55 and 56). The care with which these books are compiled is evidence of the importance with which such records were regarded. (See *Beginnings of Quakerism* op. cit. 2nd ed. II, 144, and note p.588).

The registration of births seems to have presented a problem in the early days of the Society. The Women's Meeting of a particular Monthly Meeting was responsible for notifying the men's Meeting concerned, who in turn notified the Province Meeting, an entry then being made in the registers of both Meetings. At some time, however, there must have been a lapse in this duty because a minute of the Men's Meeting of Cork, 1/11/1693, noted neglect in this matter, while that for 5/8/1714 decided that in future a woman was to be paid to send notification of a birth to each Monthly Meeting.

Two men Friends were responsible to the Monthly Meeting for the making of death entries, and no grave-digger might open a grave without a written form from these representatives. See a minute of Dublin Men's Meeting 20/10/1681 saying that Humphrey Smith is to bury none but those for whom he hath a note. In 1680 on the 18th of 11th month the same Humphrey was paid four shillings for four graves and 22*s.* for arrears.

MARRIAGE

In order that no error might creep in which could cause trouble with ecclesiastical or legal authorities the procedure in regard to marriage was stringent. During the Commonwealth Friends' method of marriage was accepted as being legal. By an Irish order in Council of 1653, modified in 1656, no marriage was legal unless public proclamation thereof was made. This proclamation, followed by State registration, to be made in " the public meeting place " or in the market place, and the subsequent marriage performed by a justice of the peace. Friends, following the advice of George Fox, believing that the intervention of magistrate or clergyman is unnecessary, published the intention of marriage in their own Meetings for Worship which were open and public to all. The couple, having obtained the consent of parents and guardians, notified their intention in person to the respective Men's and Women's Meetings to which they belonged. Friends were appointed to visit the parents to find out whether they approved, or whether there was any cause why they should not be married. The couple then appeared before the next Province Meeting for the area (often accompanied by two members of the Women's Meeting). Leave having been given to marry, an " Intention of marriage " was drawn up and they were free to take each other in marriage at a Meeting for Worship. The subsequent ceremony, at which the man and woman took each other, in the sight of God, as man and wife, was witnessed by the congregation of whom at least twelve, generally many more, put their signatures to the prepared certificate. There has been little alteration in the ceremony through the centuries, though the procedure of presentation of the marriage to the Province and Monthly Meetings is much modified. Some of the certificates were recorded directly into the Provinces or the Men's Meeting Books, and to several of these, as well as to the many loose ones preserved, original signatures are written. The Province Meeting was the earliest one to which all marriages were referred and a record of 1671 is shown in the Wexford Men's Meeting Book (F.I.27). Presentation of the marriage had been made in person by the couple, Richard Holcombe and Sarah Holme, to the Province Meeting held at Rosenallis on 25/9/1671, and again at that at Athy on 22/4/1672, with consent of parents. The respective Men's and Women's Meetings found clearness from other marriage entanglements, and the marriage is duly recorded by Wexford Monthly Meeting, and includes as well as the signatures of Richard and Sarah those of eighteen witnesses. A direction was made that this should be recorded in the Province book. By a minute of 12th month 1733 presentation to the Province Meeting was discontinued.

By an Irish statute of 1667 marriages celebrated by civil contract during the Commonwealth were made legal in retrospect. After the Restoration the legality of Quaker marriages was contested, civil registration having been abolished, but a test case appearing at Nottingham assizes the judge pronounced the marriage lawful (Lloyd, *Quaker Social History*, p.51, Longman Green 1950; which see for a clear exposition of the marriage question). In Ireland as in England Friends were subject to attempts to prove their marriages to be illegal, and an interesting comment to the difficulties experienced is provided in a minute of Cork Men's Meeting 3/11/1683:—which informed Friends that the Registrar of the Bishop's Court of Cork had stated to Friends that " observing some favours extended by the Council Table at Dublin towards Papists in reference to their marriages, that though they were not done according to the rules of the English clergy, yet they should be owned as lawful upon causing a record to be made in the Registrar's office of the Bishop's Court, upon which the said Bishop, as the registrar informed John Haman, did say why might not a Quaker marriage to be made lawful that way as the Papists, and withall signified to the registrar his willingness thereunto . . . the most of this Meeting thinking well of it have left it to Francis Rogers and John Haman to go to the said Registrar and further inform themselves thereof, and unless they see something in relation of it that may be non-consistent will treat to close with him for it." Three years later a minute of the same Men's Meeting noted that Friends wishing to register in the Bishop's Court might do so " if certificates are fully recorded." (24/7/1686).

POOR

From a very early date the Society of Friends (sometimes called among themselves " Children of Light," " Friends of Truth " or just " Friends ") assumed responsibility for the care of the poor amongst its members. Evidence of such care appears among the minutes of Men's Meetings as well as in the scanty minutes of Women's Meetings. In 1659 it was advised at a General Meeting at Skipton that " each particular Meeting should be expected to care for its own poor; to find employment for such as want work or cannot follow their former callings for reason of the evil therein . . . and to help parents in the education of their children, that there may not be a beggar amongst us." If a particular Meeting be overburdened the Monthly Meeting should come to its assistance. (Braithwaite, *Beginnings of Quakerism*, 2nd ed. p.330). In Ireland a letter of George Fox was read to the National Half-yearly Meeting of 9th month 1671; he asked all Meetings to be diligent in " setting forth apprentices and fatherless and poor Friends' children and that all the poor and widows be carefully looked after—then all will be well, and all to see that the testimony of Jesus be kept in all things." It was also advised that all documents relating to disbursements for the poor should be cancelled, and no further remembrance thereof be had, " which may beget many offences in future times, but cannot be of any service to the Truth." It is fortunate for the historian that a few escaped the result of this praiseworthy advice. In Ireland Minute Books for the Committee of the Poor have survived only for Cork and for Dublin Monthly Meetings, and in neither case is the date early. Cork has three which include accounts 1780-1799 (Cork 37), 1799-1829 (Cork 38), 1829-1862 (Cork 39), and Dublin two, 1805-1826 (D.36) and 1820-1837 (D.13). In addition there are Poor accounts only for Dublin from 1700-1748. For such essential work as the care of the poor one must search the Province and Monthly Meeting Minute Books, both Men's and Women's. Work of caring for those in need usually fell to the care of the Women's Meeting, but the raising of subscriptions and general oversight was part of the work of the Men's whose accounts show occasional disbursements to the women, who, at times, however, raised their own subscriptions. A study of these minutes shows the great care taken in watching over the needs of members in low circumstances, and give a valuable insight into costs and methods of relief. In cases of hardship the Province Meeting at times helped. The removal of a needy member from the compass of one Monthly Meeting to another needed adjustment and obviously such movements were not encouraged. In 1737 a dispute arose between Limerick and Moate Meetings as to who was responsible for payments for a poor family which had gone to live near Limerick from Moate, to which place they had previously removed from Ulster, (Leinster Province Meeting 18/4/1737). A common form of aid was the purchase of a cow, or cows, whose yield supported a family, the animal remaining the property of the Meeting. Orphan children were boarded out or cared for with Friends' families (see Dublin Monthly Meeting 28/5 and 9/12/1719 for a child of John Kelly, deceased, being cared for by Merrick King at Oldcastle). James Thompson was necessitous and had a pain in his leg in 1683 and the Dublin Meeting cared for him, as it did in the same year for Mary Davis, for whom a surgeon was employed. Money was raised by each Meeting as required, and a careful study of the minute books during and before the period of the Williamite Wars shows a barometric reading of the state of the Society. In 1684 Irish Friends had raised £400 17s. 6d. to help Friends suffering in England, but in 1691 somewhat reluctantly accepted aid from England for those who had suffered large losses here. For an account of Irish Friends' Sufferings in war time see Isabel Grubb, *Quakers in Ireland* p.70, who tells of the distribution of £3,200 sent by England, and of £100 sent by Barbadoes, the letter of thanks for which was captured by a French privateer. This help was at first refused but in the second month 1692 the Province Meeting at Cork proposed to the National Half-year Meeting that "in the event the money was refused by the other Provinces, Cork will feel at liberty to call on it for £200." The Half-yearly Meeting allowed them £275 and Cork was to keep a strict account of disbursement. In the 4th month 1691 an epistle was sent from the National Meeting held in Dublin to the Yearly Meeting in London saying that Irish Friends " notwithstanding their sufferings and exercises have been well supplied by the Lord's power under the same and have yet those to assist them that stand in need."

A complete picture of this period is best seen by reading the London Yearly Meeting Minutes and those for the Meeting for Sufferings in London, as well as the appropriate Irish Minutes. A Minute of the London Meeting for Sufferings of 17/6/1689, for instance, directs that the recording clerk, B. Bealing, is to have a letter from Ireland to D. Charles of Bristol, transcribed, and six copies sent to each meeting in and about London. Another dated 4/8/1689 appoints four Friends to assist " any who are forced to come out of Ireland and are destitute of lodging or subsistence." The same Meeting on the 7th of 12th month (Feb.) 1689, having read a letter from William Williamson of Ballyhagen (Co. Armagh) telling of losses caused by the depredations of the Army, decided to write to the secretary " now about to be appointed to the Duke of Schomberg (Dr. Robert Gorges)."

The application of the Poor Fund (raised by collections) was very wide and ranged from caring for prisoners and their families to giving very practical assistance to those emigrating to England or America, sometimes providing food for the journey, (see Cork Men's Meeting 13/7/1708 et. al.). An interesting comment is that of Cork Province Meeting 21/8/1689, which, in deciding, to help six men and women and nine children of Youghal, gave £3 towards laying in provisions, agreeing that it should be given " now before provisions become too dear." In Dublin in 1770 a " combination among linen weavers prevents Jacob Fuller working as a journeyman," so looms were bought to enable him to set up on his own.

Though a few books of Poor Accounts exist, they do not give further detail than the receipt of collection money and the bare names of those to whom it was disbursed.

CERTIFICATES OF REMOVAL

The archives of every Monthly Meeting have books for recording the certificates given on the removal of persons from the compass of one Meeting to another. Only two of these books date from the 17th century, one for Dublin and one for Carlow. The date of the start of the Dublin one is significant, being 1682, a year after the National Meeting had agreed (in response to a query as to whether persons removing to America should be provided with certificates) " that all Friends who do intend to remove thither or elsewhere do first lay such their intentions before the particular Men's Meeting or Province Meeting to which they belong, and that Friends, after they have advised them concerning their intentions (if they do remove), give them Certificates according as they deserve, according to the best of their Knowledge, Signifying their Unity or Disunity with their Removing; and when young or unmarried people remove into America, Friends do Signifie their clearness in relation to Marriage, having time allowed by such persons to make enquiry concerning them, according to the order of Truth, and that all certificates be entered in a book." (Nat. Meeting, 3rd Mo. 1682).

The Dublin Book has 250 entries of which the first is dated 13/12/1682. It was obviously intended for Certificates to America at a period when numbers of Friends had decided to remove there, and many of the names there recorded are also mentioned with much other detail by the late Albert Cook Myers in his *Immigration of Irish Quakers into Pennsylvania*, 1682-1750. (Swarthmore Pa. 1902). While a special book was officially kept for certificates, their issue was generally recorded as well by the Men's or Province Meeting, sometimes giving detail of circumstances. The dates of issue to America show that often large groups decided to travel together. For instance in 5th month 1729 thirteen certificates are recorded to Pennsylvania, some including families. Such documents became essential for those travelling or removing their place of habitation enabling the bearer to establish himself among Friends in a place to which he was a stranger, without difficulty, and with an assurance of recognition in Meeting and in business. The loss of one could cause difficulty, though in one case where the recipient was saved after shipwreck, losing her possessions, the captain and other passengers testified that they had actually seen the said certificate, so saving her embarrassment. (Dub. Men's Meeting 25/1/1729). A difficulty was caused in another instance when a family removed from Ireland to England and certificates were issued to all except the father. His daughters were much concerned and wrote to their friends that it would have been better if those in Ireland had stated what was wrong, instead of leaving the poor man without any certificate.

The Dublin book to which reference has already been made shows the issue of no certificates between the years 1685 and 1689. That members did leave Ireland during these difficult years is, however, evident from other sources. A minute of London Yearly Meeting on 3/4/1691 reads as follows:—" William Edmondson of Ireland being present acquaints this Meeting that, notwithstanding Friends their great sufferings and losses, care is taken that no Friends need now come from thence for want of a present supply, or without a certificate from Friends of a meeting there."

Friends " travelling in the Ministry " were introduced to the Meetings to which they proposed to pay religious visits by means of certificates, which were handed back to their own Meeting on completion of such service.

By the following century certificates were issued as a matter of course and the attached names of those signing them on behalf of a Meeting are of quite considerable interest. When John Cadwallader, an American minister, was returning home after a religious visit to Ireland he was given a certificate on behalf of the National Meeting which had 65 signatures of Irish Friends, and another one from the Meeting of Ministers and Elders in Dublin with 36 names.

The earliest certificate said to be known seems to have been sent to Ireland on behalf of two early Quaker preachers, Edward Burrough and Francis Howgill, who had met with considerable adverse treatment in Waterford. It was sent by Bristol Friends to try to establish their reputation. (W. C. Braithwaite *op. cit.* I 214).

A typical early certificate reads as follows:—

" From our Men's Meeting in the city of Dublin, Ireland, to all our Friends in Pennsylvania, New Jersie or any other part of America to whom these may come is the Salutation of our Indeared love in the Truth to all the Faithful.

"Whereas our Friend Robert Turner has laid before our Meeting his Intention of removing himself and his Family into America, these are, therefore, to certifie to you and all whom it may concern That the said Robert Turner has been an ancient Friend of this Meeting and of a good conversation as far as we know, and we have nothing against his said removal. And he being a widow man we do not understand, but that he is clear from all women on account of marriage. In Testimoney whereof we have subscribed our hands at our Meeting the 3rd day of the 5th month 1683:—

Anthony Sharp,	John Burnyeat,	Alex Seton,
Thos. Ashton,	Joseph Thomas,	James Taylor,
John Roberts,	George Pope,	Saml. Stoddart,
Daniel Thackrey,	Thos. Breatherick,	John Stevens.
Daniel Weld,	John Tristram."	

WILLS

Abstracts of the contents of five manuscript books for recording copies of Wills and Inventories have already been published by the Irish Manuscripts Commission (Eustace and Goodbody: *Quaker Records, Dublin, Abstracts of Wills*, Ir. Mss. Commission, 1957). These are now supplemented in this volume by the publication of a further 40 abstracts of wills of which copies are filed in the Historical Library in the Friends

Meeting House, Dublin. There is ample evidence throughout the Minutes of the Province and the Monthly Meetings that many more books of wills must have been kept, and their loss may be due to an injunction to keep such documents as private as possible (see Leinster Province Meeting 14/12/1684). In the 9th month 1684 the National Meeting made the following minute:—

" It is desired that each Men's Meeting may appoint such particular Friends as they may think fit to take an account of executors and Trustees yearly concerning their trust; and that the books for recording Wills and Inventories be kept by the said Friends appointed by the Men's Meeting; that the portions of Orphans, etc. may not be made more public than need may require."

Some wills pre-date this instruction, that of Thomas Pearce of Limerick being dated 1664 and bequeathing property in Idstone in Suffolk, his former home.

In addition to the above there are two books of Dublin Monthly Meeting entitled *Affairs and Wills*, dated respectively 1816-1850, and 1851-1855, and an old one lately discovered dated 1704-1772, called on the cover " A book for Friends to Inspect Wills and Inventories, Anno. 1704." These are records of visits paid by a small committee of the Men's Meeting to enquire whether Wills were being made and monetary affairs put into satisfactory order by individual Friends. For other accounts of this service Monthly Meeting minutes should be searched, as even where no special book was kept there is evidence that watchfulness was encouraged by most Meetings so that none might suffer through neglect.

DISUNITY

Nine Monthly Meetings contain books for the recording of certificates (or statements) of disunity with the practices of Friends. There are also several loose bundles of original ones in the Library. These records have been, mistakenly, classified at times under one heading and named " disownments," pre-supposing that all disunity meant separation from the body. They should properly be called Testimonies of Condemnation, Disunion, or Denial. In most cases Friends who had written papers condemning their own faults were not disowned, though attendance at all Meetings except that for worship might be denied to them until they had " shown a spirit of repentance." (See minute of the Half-yearly Meeting for 3rd month 1704). Offences varied very greatly and infinite care was taken by the Men's and by the Women's Meetings to send suitable persons to visit those suspected of having strayed from the high moral code expected. In a large number of cases these visits were effective in persuading persons to acknowledge their faults. These might range from failure to attend Meetings, backbiting or spreading slander, dishonesty in trading or unnecessary debt, to various social and moral defects. Marriage " out " of the Society, that is with one of another faith, or solemnised by a clergyman, accounted for the loss of many members throughout the 18th century, and half of the 19th, as did the unwillingness of young people to conform to a strict discipline which advocated a withdrawal from the fashions of the world.

There are many minutes to be found concerning the prohibition of wearing of wigs or periwigs, obviously a temptation to many young men who wished to be fashionable. Keeping dogs for pleasure was forbidden by Cork Men's Meeting on the 19/7/1715, and we hear no more of Samuel Randall " who goes on the river with guns on First Day morning" (Cork Men's Meeting 3/7/1722).

By the beginning of the 18th century many of the first great body of men and women, who had suffered severely for their faith, were dead and their place had been taken by others, anxious that the beliefs and practices of their predecessors should be maintained.

Statistically " disownment " papers are of little account, but to the genealogist they are valuable, throwing light on names removed from Friends' records yet not appearing elsewhere. The Library is now in process of making alphabetical lists of the loose ones (which are those actually read in Meeting, and often bearing the signature of the person disowned). Those copied into books for the purpose are mostly indexed. To the historical student there is some value attached to certain causes of disownment. For instance, the bearing of arms and the wearing of uniform, which are complained of at intervals, especially during the period of the raising of the Volunteers in the eighteenth century.

PARLIAMENT

In 1698 a select meeting of the National Meeting was set up to ensure that Friends' interests were watched in every session of the Irish Parliament. There are three books of the Minutes of this committee among the records of the Yearly Meeting. They are dated from 1698 to 1797, and are of particular interest in that they provide a chronological picture of the effect of Irish legislation on Friends. Also they show the effect produced by the quiet, orderly resistance of Friends to laws appearing detrimental to the conviction that levies for the upkeep of another church were inconsistent with their testimony. It was felt, too, that penalization for refusal to take an oath was unjust, and that liberty in the matter of conscience should be defended by the legislative system. Much that is good in present law springs from this strong and effective determination to defend belief.

The Parliamentary Committee appointed two or three Friends to examine the heads of Bills about to come before Parliament, and, if any matter appeared which was likely to affect Friends, word was sent to the Men's and Province Meetings warning representatives to be ready to travel. The Committee, having met in Dublin, sent some of its members to attend the Parliament House on College Green, and watch events. These members reported back to the Committee, which often sat at 8 o'clock in the morning and 6 o'clock in the evening of the same day. In addition visits were made by individual Friends to members of both Houses, privately, and almost always granted a quiet discussion. Names of representatives and of members are given throughout the minute books. In 1716 when the Affirmation Bill was in debate, the names of 43 Friends and of 241 Members of the House of Commons are set out.

TESTIMONIES

It seems fitting in a community which deprecates all forms of adulation that records should have been made, after decease, of the lives of those who had borne a living testimony to their faith.

Many of these exist in printed form in such collections as the series of volumes known as Piety Promoted, or as introductions to the lives or journals of well known Friends. They were also used by John Rutty in his *History of Friends* (*op. cit.*) and by Mary Leadbeater in her *Biographical Notices of Friends* (London, Harvey and Darton, 1823).

The Journal of William Edmundson, the pioneer of Irish Quakerism, has no fewer than fourteen appreciations of him following the preface to the first edition (Dublin, 1715). Official testimonies to deceased Friends were made by order of the National Meeting, or, in some cases, by the Province or Monthly Meeting to which the member had belonged. A large number of these are transcribed into a volume (A.19) named " Testimonies to deceased Ministers, 1661-1933." As small biographical vignettes these are valuable, often throwing light on names now lost in obscurity, but they are valuable, too, as records of lives lived quietly but carrying the gospel message of peace, of love, and of integrity in daily life to all among whom the subjects of such testimones had lived.

EDUCATION

From a very early period in their history Friends recognized the importance of a sound education, and Quaker schools in many parts of the world bear witness to the part they have played in this field. For references to 17th century schools and schoolmasters among Friends in Ireland one must search the Minutes of Monthly and Province Meetings, which show the care bestowed on the subject. In *Quakers in Ireland*, (London, Swarthmore Press, 1926) the author, Isabel Grubb, has summarized (pp.90-93) some of the material available for such research, and stresses that " Education in its widest sense, including all that fits a child for what lies before it, was the constant care of Friends." Two articles relating to Quaker education have been published by Dr. Michael Quane in the *Journal of the Royal Society of Antiquaries, Ireland*, " The Friends' Provincial School, Mountmellick," (Vol. LXXXIX, 1959) and " Quaker Schools in Dublin " (XCIV), 1964 the material for which has been mainly taken from manuscript records in the Meeting House, 6 Eustace Street, Dublin.

The earliest established school seems to have been one set up by Mountmellick Friends in that town in 1677, followed by one in Cork in 1678. In Dublin a school was started in 1680, being taught by a Scotsman, Alexander Seaton, in the small Meeting House in Bride's Alley (alias Parson's Lane). This Meeting House was the first built by Friends and lay to the rear of the larger one situated in Bride Street, which was first used in 1669 at the time of the visit of William Penn. (For reference to this school see Dublin Men's Meeting Minutes 5th and 10th months 1680, 7th month 1681, 8th month and 11th month 1682 and 4th month 1683).

Some records are available for the school at Edenderry (1764-1775) and the complete records of the school at Mountmellick (1786-1921) comprising about 90 volumes, noted hereafter, are also in the strong room at Eustace Street. These, together with a few for Newtown School, Waterford, and for Lisburn School, Co. Antrim, are listed under the heading "School Records" in the guide, as well as some references to other material available. There is no series of books for the famous school at Ballitore, owned by the Shackleton family, where Edmund Burke was educated, but a list is appended in Part II of material relating to it which is in the Historical Library. This school was a private one, though very closely connected with Friends. It did not, therefore, come under the auspices of any Provincial Meeting, as did the other schools, hence the lack of records.

Throughout the Men's minutes of most Monthly Meetings constant references are made to the welfare of boys and girls apprenticed to trades, upon whom a watchful care was exercised by the Meeting. On the 28/9/1721 Dublin Men's Meeting asked that a list of apprentices should be called over twice a year, and entered in the minute book. The Book of Extracts gives dates and references from 1680, from which date this care was exercised by the respective Meetings.

From time to time considerable difficulty was experienced in finding satisfactory teachers, and on 15/12/1764 Friends were asked " to look out for any suitable genius " to teach at Edenderry boarding school for girls, just being started. Some meetings of schoolmasters are recorded, viz. National Half-yearly Meeting 8/9/1705.

PEACE

The subject of peace occupies no separate book, no series of positive statements, no accumulation of documents. It is a principle deeply inculcated into the lives of Friends from their earliest rise. Its doctrinal message is a negation of all forms of strife in daily living, rather than the declaration of a creed. In England Quakerism rose first in the midst of civil war. In Ireland its beginnings were in the times of the greatest desolation the country had ever known. Many soldiers joined the sect, only gradually leaving the army for more peaceable vocations as other means of livelihood offered themselves. By 1660 the clarity of the peace conviction became apparent, and in the Acts of Settlement of the Restoration period many names appear of soldiers who settled in groups which later became large centres of Quakerism.

This is particularly evident in Wexford, Cork and parts of the Midlands, where names appearing in State papers and in official and semiofficial letters are found also in the record books of Friends.

The preaching of George Fox's testimony of peace appeared in Ireland as early as 1655, and Cork Men's Meeting, making a search in 1678 for the early history of Friends in Ireland, gives the names of " the first Friends to publish the doctrine of peace in these parts." (Cork Men's Meeting 11/5/1698). These names include those who visited Ireland from 1654.

Family Lists, Testimonies, Sufferings and Minute Books are all sources for the subject, as well as the books and papers of disunity, which during the disturbed period of the 18th century, as well as during the Williamite Wars, reveal the temptations to which young men were subject. It is not, however, under the broad subject of war alone that the peaceful precepts of Quakerism should be sought. Constant care and vigilance was asked for so that no member might pursue any cause of contention. By 1676 this had been embodied in a minute of Advice of the National Meeting which was amplified in 1697. This makes it clear that in the event of a difference between two Friends, the intervention of some "honest" Friends should be sought, and if agreement is not then reached, the help and advice of the Meeting should be obtained, but recourse to Law is, in all events, to be avoided.

PROPERTY

Early books for recording schedules of Meeting Property exist for five Meetings only, but all possess carefully preserved lists, usually appended to the Minute Books of Men's Meetings. In all cases they consist of copies of documents, such as assignments, leases, agreements, statements, and such matter as reports of trustees. From these may be traced the early history of a Meeting, and of the acquiring of the ground on which Meeting Houses were built. It was usual for Friends to buy properties adjoining their places of worship, and in many cases these were let, not only to Friends, but to tradespeople and merchants of other persuasions. The minute books of almost every Men's Meeting have references to the careful preserving of the "writings" of the Meeting, a care usually delegated to two or three members. Unexpected material relevant to burial grounds, houses, lodgers, property owners etc. may be found in these papers. The title deeds of property still owned by Friends are in the custody of officials of the Meeting concerned, those for most of Leinster being at 6 Eustace Street, Dublin. Some are with the clerks of the meetings concerned, Cork having a particularly interesting collection.

Those of purely historical interest are in the Library of 6 Eustace Street, and include, among other relics of value, two deeds signed by William Penn.

It is impossible in a short introduction to describe fully the amount of material available, but the following Guide, which is divided into archival material and historical matter, should serve the student as a pointer to sources.

LIBRARY

The Historical Library of the Yearly Meeting of the Religious Society of Friends in Ireland was started in the year 1908 in order to preserve books and documents relating to Quaker history, principles and practice. Its printed works include most books relating to Irish Friends and a very representative collection of Quaker history, biography, theology and belles-lettres, with a few rare early editions. It is supplemental to the lending library of general works also on the premises of the Society of Friends at 6 Eustace Street, Dublin.

The manuscript collection to which this book is a Guide, has been carefully built up during the last 60 years and is representative of family and commercial life in Ireland throughout three centuries. A very large proportion of documents consists of letters of the 18th and 19th centuries with a few of the 17th century.

The intermarriage of Irish Quaker families through these centuries, coupled with the habit of writing and preserving letters, has led to the accumulation in the library of this enormous amount of correspondence. It is catalogued under the names of correspondents and full lists of contents with individuals' names are placed with each collection of letters and documents. The introductory remarks to each series gives an indication of the value of the collection and of its social background.

In most cases the bulk of the letters is of purely family nature, detailing items of interest to a closely knit community: births, marriages, accounts of those deceased, removals to another part of the country or abroad, letters from and to children away at school, meetings, journeys, trivial happenings of every day, but of deep interest to the recipient. Interspersed, however, with domestic concerns are letters containing valuable social detail for the historian of a period. Here and there one catches glimpses, especially in the later letters, of an intellectual curiosity far beyond the bounds of the inward mystical background of religious thought of early Friends.

This widening of interest shows itself as part of the growth of a people disciplined by inborn habits of restraint, and a waiting on God's power which fulfilled itself in the quiet capacity to deal with social problems and evils with a liberal and efficient outlook. One does not find here material of great political or biographical importance, but the discerning student may well be surprised at the quiet dignity of the few surviving letters from unknown, or little known, Friends in correspondence with the great.

Sometimes the letters refer to family troubles of one kind or another. In reading them one has to remember the sorrow, out of proportion to its reason, brought on many by the defection from one cause or another of a member. Financial embarrassments, if thought to be caused by carelessness, were severely dealt with by the Society, and letters of the early 19th century throw an interesting sidelight on Irish bank failures of the period. Business affairs and fluctuations in prices are frequently mentioned, particularly in letters of Cork and Waterford families. The letters in the Grubb Collection (which has an independent catalogue in the library) contain much material concerning trade between England and Ireland.

Deposited material of the nature of correspondence has usually been classified under the name of the donor, each document being separately indexed. Thus in what is known as the Fennell Collection we get a large proportion of letters of the Shackleton, Leadbeater, Chandlee and kindred families. The Grubb Collection includes collected letters of the Jacob, Lecky, Strangman, Newsom, as well as of various branches of Grubb families. The Lecky collection pertains entirely to the Leckys and Harveys of Youghal and Cork and to those with whom they intermarried.

The method used in the Guide is to detail these large collections as fully as space allows, picking out items which appear to have the greatest importance or interest socially or historically. Much has had to be left out, but it is hoped that the material quoted may serve as a pointer to what can be found. In the smaller collections a brief outline only of the contents is given, though in some cases valuable items of social interest exist.

The largest collection of 17th century manuscripts in the library is the Sharp Collection. This has been noted under *Drafts* as the original intention underlying the amassing, copying and arrangement of these papers early in the following century had been to publish them. This, however, was never fulfilled. They are of considerable interest and are used by students of the period for the picture they give of 17th century Quaker, Irish, and American business and social life.

Testamentary documents consist of 50 wills not before abstracted. These were found in the library among bundles of deposited documents and are now formed into a separate series. The indentures etc. here classified and noted recite back in a few cases to the 17th century, though most are of the 18th. They form the major part of those deposited in the library. Others are among the archives in the strong room. While not necessarily of historical value except to the student of local history, they have in many cases a genealogical content which is helpful.

Among the genealogical material available in the library is the valuable abstract of names and Meetings made by Isabel M. Jones a few years ago. This is probably unique of its kind, enabling a searcher to find at a glance where any name occurs in the Registers of Births, Marriages and Deaths. The Registers are classified under each Monthly Meeting.

Draft material includes the original of the Glossary of the Forth-Bargy dialect of Co. Wexford, made by Jacob Poole early in the last century.

For Quaker material in the Public Record Office of Northern Ireland see Appendix II by B. G. Hutton, p. 189, *infra*.

I am indebted to Isabel Grubb, Phyllis Eason and William Glynn for reading my typescript and for giving me their help and advice, to my grandson, Jonathan, and to Mrs. Norah Draper for their help with the index, and to the office staff at 6 Eustace Street, Dublin, the Quaker Meeting House, for their co-operation, including Mr. Webster who lifted many heavy volumes.

To the late John M. Douglas I want to record my great gratitude for his never failing encouragement.

OLIVE C. GOODBODY

PART I

QUAKER ARCHIVES

NATIONAL HALF-YEARLY AND YEARLY MEETING

1. Early records kept by the National Meeting were those of Sufferings which, apart from their social interest, throw considerable light on the names of persons and of localities in which they lived.

The earliest Minutes deal with these as well as with the spiritual significance of the message contained in epistles and letters to and from Friends and Meetings. From its earliest days changes in organization were referred to the National Meeting. This was a democratic assembly, each Province being asked to send at least six members chosen from its constituent meetings. These acted as representatives, but it is evident that before long isolated Meetings were sending members too, (witness the minutes of the Tipperary Six-weeks Meeting, held in various parts of the county, which nominated persons not only for the province but for the Half-Yearly Meetings). This Half-Yearly National Meeting was abolished in 1797, after which the Yearly Meeting came into being, and a permanent committee was appointed to transact interim business.

Epistles sent from the National Meetings to Provincial and Monthly Meetings provided not only the opportunity of sending advice and help but, after the years 1738, a means of circulating queries to be answered by the subsidiary meetings. The system of submitting queries for the consideration of Meetings dates in Ireland from 1682, and in 1692 every Province Meeting appointed Friends of particular meetings who were to enquire into the affairs and proper conduct of such meetings. These queries were, however, consolidated and recommended for answering by the National Meeting of 1740. Queries were answered by the Monthly to the Province Meeting, and others by the Province to the National Meeting. They were varied from time to time and according to circumstance, but covered every aspect of religious and family life. The present queries are included in the Book of Discipline, first printed 1811 and at subsequent intervals, the last edition being that of 1960 (printed for the Society—6 Eustace Street). In 1861 the Society issued a pamphlet giving a historical account of the queries.

Christian Advices—Books A.15 to 18 are the manuscript books of Extracts already referred to. A.18 does not give the date of the earlier Advices. They summarize in digested form the numerous minutes, epistles, letters and verbal admonitions dealing with every aspect of Christian living. In later years these were printed as part of the Discipline of the Society.

A.14—Occurrences for the Progress of Truth—apparently had a predecessor, now lost, though a few loose pages have come to light, dealing mainly with the 1714. These papers were the result of the appointment of a few Friends to enquire into matters concerning the Discipline of the Society throughout the country, and were used fully by Thomas Wight and John Rutty in the compilation of the History of Quakers in Ireland, Dublin 1751.

The oversight of the printing of all books written by Friends was part of the duty of the National Meeting, and several of its early minutes concern this subject—see Nat. Minutes 8/3/1676 for an agreement with the " printer of Cork to print 1,000 or 1,500 of George Fox's book *A Warning to England*."

The importance of the index to A.19 " Testimonies to Ministers deceased " should be noted.

NATIONAL HALF-YEARLY AND YEARLY MEETING RECORDS

2. MINUTE BOOKS.

Minutes of Half-yearly National
Meeting . . . 5/3/1671 — 9/9/1688 (copy) A.1
8/3/1689 - 8/9/1707   A.2
(Indexed and with queries and epistles)
Minutes of Half-yearly National Meeting   8/3/1708 - 8/5/1757   A.3
1/11/1757 - 3/5/1778   A.4
1/11/1778 - 25/4/1808   A.5
1/5/1809 - 26/4/1852   A.6
25/4/1853 -   1867   A.7
Original Minutes of the Half-yearly National
Meeting . . . . 1671 - 1688 A.13
(After 1867 proceedings were printed).
Minutes of National Meeting of Ministers and
Elders . . . . . 1757 - 1834 A.68
(This also contains copies of Ministers Certificates 1778-1834).

QUAKER ARCHIVES 27

Minutes of National Meeting for Ministers and Elders	1784 - 1885	A.54
	1835 - 1894	A.79
Minutes of Yearly Meeting Committee .	1797 - 1817	A.60
	1817 - 1824	A.61
	1825 - 1834	A.62
	1834 - 1853	A.63
Minutes of the Women's National Meeting	1785 - 1840	A.46
	1840 - 1882	A.49
(Both of the above contain Epistles from Women's National Meeting).		
Minutes of the School Committee	1764 - 1770	A.55
Parliamentary Committee	1698 - 1729	A.56
	1731 - 1778	A.56
	1778 - 1797	A.58

NATIONAL YEARLY MEETING

MEMBERSHIP

Birth and Burial Notes after 1858 only		A.29/35
Testimonies to deceased Ministers (indexed)	1661 - 1933	A.19
Ministers Certificates	1778 - 1834	A.68
National Meeting Record of Sufferings .	1665 - 1693	A.11
	1693 - 1705	A.12
Testimonies against Tythes	17th century	

FINANCE

Treasurer's Accounts	1749 - 1858	A.53
Cash Book	1819 - 1855	A.64
Ledger	1819 - 1858	A.65
Yearly Meeting Accounts	1814 - 1868	A.67

EDUCATION

Ulster School Reports	1792 - 1841	A.51
	1841 - 1847	A.52

MISCELLANEOUS

Christian Advices	to c. 1798	A.15
	1797 -	A.16
	1809 -	A.17
	1779 -	A.18
Occurrences for the Progress of Truth .	1748 - 1849	A.14

NATIONAL AND YEARLY MEETING

Copies of Epistles (devotional) sent and received:—

To and from National Meeting	1708 - 1739	A.20
(includes answers to queries)	1739 - 1760	A.21
	1766 - 1793	A.22
To and from Yearly Meeting	1794 - 1820	A.23
From Yearly Meeting to American and other Meetings	1822 - 1853	A.25
To Yearly Meeting	1821 - 1847	A.34
From	1854 - 1870	A.26
To	1848 - 1854	A.27

Women's Epistles:—

Women's National Meeting Epistle	1676 - 1776	A.43
	1776 - 1799	A.44
	1800 - 1825	A.45
including minutes	1785 - 1840	A.46
Women's National Meeting Epistles	1825 - 1843	A.47
	1844 - 1867	A.48
including minutes	1841 - 1882	A.49
also see Epistles	1724 - 1754	A.71
Women's National Meeting Epistles from London	1671 - 1854	A.72
and from various places	1785 - 1834	A.73
	1778 - 1840	A.74
	1772 - 1828	A.75
	1827 - 1854	A.76
Women's Meeting Epistles	1839 - 1852	A.66
Letter Book of Yearly Meeting Committee	1834 - 1878	A.78
Memorandum Book	1823 - 1916	A.77
Yearly Reports from London and Provincial Meetings, answers to Queries	1822 - 1865	A.28

LEINSTER PROVINCE MEETING

3. A precise dating of the settlement of Provincial Meetings cannot be stated as William Edmundson had already started their establishment before the year 1669. Records of these were probably kept in loose quires but the direction to buy a bound book was not made until 1680 when Laurence Routh was directed to transcribe the old one—now B.I1670 - 1706. From 30/3/1670 the meeting met alternately at Lehinchie (or Lehensie) (near Clara), Rosenallis and Newgarden, Co. Carlow, and in the following year Athy was added to this list; Castledermot appeared later, a Meeting House being built there in

1676. It was usually held in private houses until, in 1682, it was decided to build a Meeting House in Meath Street, Dublin, for the use of the Province. This was done by subscriptions raised throughout the Meetings of the whole country, though Cork Friends protested at being asked to contribute. (Munster Six-weeks Meeting 19/11/1683). Minutes concerning this Meeting House appear through most Monthly Meetings.

The business of the Province included Presentments of Marriage, decisions on disputes, care of the poor, the collection of Sufferings for presentation to the National Meeting, and the answering of the set Queries of the latter, also the periodical sending of Advices to Monthly Meetings. It also included the distribution to the latter of printed books sent from England and the collection of money for the same.

The Provincial School at Mountmellick came under the care of Leinster Provincial Meeting from 1784 - 1922.

The constituent Monthly Meetings of Leinster Province were:— Carlow (formerly Newgarden), Dublin, Edenderry, Moate, Mountmellick Mountrath, Wicklow, Wexford.

The Historical Library owns a valuable typescript made by Peter Skelton detailing the construction and component parts of the Monthly Meetings of Leinster and Ulster. This includes particular Meetings formed in the 19th century which do not appear in this Guide, and should be consulted for variations in the constitution of Monthly Meetings.

It is hoped to do a similar work for Munster.

It is also known from minutes that Meetings took place at irregular intervals at varied places which, while coming under the surveillance of a Monthly Meeting, have left no record except through minutes and the appointments of visitors.

LEINSTER PROVINCE QUARTERLY MEETING

4. MINUTE BOOKS.

Minutes of Province Meeting	. 30/ 3/1670 - 28/ 7/1706	B.1
	6/ 9/1706 - 6/ 5/1760	B.2
	21/ 6/1760 - 28/ 4/1798	B.3
Quarterly Meeting .	. 26/ 5/1798 - 27/12/1824	B.4
	28/ 3/1825 - 28/12/1857	B.5
	29/ 3/1858 - 1/12/1903	B.6
	10/10/1715 - 4/ 2/1759	

Women's Quarterly Meeting earlier also in E.38	1837 - 1884	B.22
Minutes of Quarterly Meeting and Yearly Meeting	1823 - 1849	B.24
	1849 - 1892	B.25
	1885 - 1895	B.29
	1848 - 1898	B.29a
Minutes of School Committee (Mountmellick)	1784 - 1814	B.10
	1814 - 1834	B.23
	1784 - 1801	B.33
	1907 - 1920	B.39

MEMBERSHIP.

Records of Sufferings	1719 - 1723	B.8
	1706 - 1714	B.9
	1656 - 1701	B.20
Burial Register	1840 - 1848	B.13
Family Lists	17 cent.	B.14
Birth Register	1841 - 1858	B.19
Marriage Certificates	1764 - 1716	B.15
	1716 - 1775	B.16
	1775 - 1807	B.17
Register	1812 - 1848	B.18

FINANCE.

School Subscription Lists	1785 - 1822	B.11
	1831 - 1843	B.12
5 Ledgers relating to Camden St. School	1840 - 1844	
Rough or Duplicate Minutes of Quarterly Meeting and Six-weeks Meeting	29/10/1757 - 4/ 8/1770	B.26
	15/ 9/1770 - 3/ 5/1782	B.27
Women's Quarterly Meeting	1852 - 1879	B.28
School Committee	1809 - 1815	B.35
	1815 - 1820	B.36

EDUCATION.

Rules for Provincial School	B.34
See also books of Mountmellick School.	

MISCELLANEOUS.

Replies from Committee on Discipline	1692 - 1710	B.21

PROPERTY. Nil.

MONTHLY MEETINGS

5. Of the following records of Monthly Meetings the earliest minutes are those of Cork, 1675. The Men's Meetings, which were held at first at varying intervals according to the locality, appear to have grown gradually from a need of fellowship and spiritual companionship, and in response to the advice of George Fox to settle such meetings that all in the Church might share responsibility. As the years went by these meetings assumed the name of Monthly Meetings, and the character of meetings for business. They gradually took over some of the work of Province Meetings, and perusal of the minutes of each such " district " Men's Meeting shows the minute care devoted to every aspect of congregational life.

The function of the Men's (later Monthly) Meeting was relief of the poor and the sick, collection of necessary funds, education of Youth, provision of the necessary watchfulness over marriage procedure, the providing of horses and hospitality for Friends travelling in the Ministry, and of guides for their journeys when moving from one Meeting to another; and the appointment of delegates from one Meeting to another. Care of Meeting houses and burial grounds and of the " writings " or deeds appertaining thereto, and of the records of the community were also part of the duty of the Men's Meeting.

It is to the faithfulness of the unpaid clerks of successive Meetings that we are indebted for the great accumulation of such records now preserved in Ireland. Almost any concern of Friends may be found in these minutes, but little outside the religious society except in so far as events may have impinged on the lives of Friends. The 18th century minutes reflect the changing attitude of youth and the declension in attendance at Meetings, though in the following century one senses a renewed vigour, occasioned by the philanthropic zeal which became so marked a part of the Society.

CARLOW MONTHLY MEETING

6. Formerly known as Newgarden. This was established before the year 1660, probably at the house of Ephraim Heritage, though apparently at times held in other houses. It was moved to Carlow where a meeting house was built in the year 1716. It is not clear whether there was a meeting house at Newgarden, but the old burial ground which dates from about 1665 still remains on private property.

The following meetings were members of Carlow Monthly Meetings—
 Athy
 Kilconner
 Ballitore
 Newtown
 and for a short time Tullow.

CARLOW MONTHLY MEETING RECORDS

MINUTE BOOKS.

Minutes of Newgarden Men's
Meeting . . . 20/ 9/1678 - 13/ 1/1704 C.7
                10/ 2/1700 - 31/ 8/1710 C.15
Carlow .   . 5/ 5/1710 - 25/ 2/1729 C.8
                 8/ 2/1730 - 23/12/1742 C.9
                 2 /9/1743 - 24/12/1766 C.10
                 4/ 2/1767 - 10/ 4/1782 C.11
                22/ 5/1782 - 11/ 3/1796 C.11a
                 8/ 4/1796 - 11/12/1812 C.12
                 8/ 1/1813 - 10/ 6/1825 C.13
                 8/ 7/1825 - 2/ 1/1843 C.14
Minutes Carlow Men's Preparative Meeting . 1842 - 1877 C.32
       Women's Meeting . . 1754 - 1784 C.16
This includes accounts for 1705 - 1783.
Minutes Carlow Women's Meeting . . 1784 - 1810 C.17
                                    1811 - 1841 C.18
                      11/ 5/1841 - 10/ 3/1880 C.27

MEMBERSHIP.

Register of Births and Burials   . . 1649 - 1815 C.21
Records of Marriages   . . 1660 - 1768 C.22
Copies of Marriage Certificates
Indexed men and women separately   . 1769 - 1810 C.23
Marriage Register   . . . 1812 - 1846 C.24
Birth Notes   . . . 1812 - 1911 C.34
Birth Register   . . . 1812 - 1909 C.35
Burial Register   . . . 1812 - 1907 C.36
Marriage Register   . . . 1812 - 1886 C.37
Copies of Certificates of Removal . . 1712 - 1785 C.19
This has accounts 1700 - 1705.
Copies of Certificates of Removal . . 1786 - 1833 C.20
List of Members   1814   C.38

WILLS.

Copies of Wills and Inventories . . 1675 - 1740 C.26
(Abstracts published by Ir. Mss. Commission 1957)

FINANCE.

Accounts for 1700 - 1705 C.19

MISCELLANEOUS.

PROPERTY.

List of Deeds of Monthly Meeting Property C.33

DUBLIN MONTHLY MEETING

7. An early Meeting is noted in Dublin in 1655 (Wight and Rutty *op. cit.*). It took place at the house of George Latham, near Polegate, and followed one in a room lent by Richard Foulkes, also at Polegate. In c.1657 a Meeting place at Bride's Alley was acquired, probably at the rear of William Maine's house—Barons Inns, part of which property in the year 1669 became the National Meeting House, paid for from subscriptions throughout the nation (see a manuscript copy of Wight's History in the Historical Library Collection at Eustace Street). Both these Meeting places were used in addition to one at Wormwood Gate until 1692 when Sycamore Alley Meeting House was completed. This throughout the years merged into the present building in Eustace Street. Another for the use of Province Meetings was built in Meath Street at the rear of Amos Strettle's house in 1684 and subscribed for by the Monthly Meetings of the Province.

The Meeting at Eustace Street is the only remaining one in the city, there being three in the suburbs. The trustees for the property gradually bought adjoining houses and plots, including the old Stamp Office, the Eagle Tavern and part of Coghill's Court—and the present large Meeting Room appears to have been built on the site of the original one of 1692.

The principal component Meetings in the 17th and 18th centuries were Baltiboys, Kilteel and Timahoe (Kildare).

The minutes of Dublin Meeting are very full and, together with deeds and assignments of property, provide a valuable addition to the history of this part of Dublin.

DUBLIN MONTHLY MEETING RECORDS

MINUTE BOOKS.

Minutes of Men's Meeting	5/12/1677 - 12 /6/1684	D.10
	26/ 6/1684 - 1691	D.11
	1691 - 1701	D.12
	5/ 6/1701 - 16/ 3/1710	D.13
	30/ 3/1710 - 31/11/1716	D.14
	5/ 4/1716 - 7/ 5/1724	D.15
	21/ 5/1724 - 5/12/1733	D.16
	5/ 1/1734 - 29/ 4/1742	D.17
	13/ 5/1742 - 16/ 2/1750	D.18
	24/ 2/1750 - 15/10/1754	D.19
	29/10/1754 - 22/11/1757	D.20
	28/ 2/1758 - 1/ 9/1767	D.21
	29/ 9/1767 - 14/ 9/1779	D.22
	28/ 9/1779 - 12/12/1786	D.23
	9/ 1/1787 - 11/11/1795	D.24
	15/12/1795 - 16/12/1806	D.25
	13/ 1/1807 - 15/11/1814	D.26
	13/12/1814 - 16/12/1823	D.27
Monthly Meeting	13/ 1/1824 - 15/10/1833	D.28
	12/11/1833 - 16/ 2/1858	D.29
	1858 - 1877	D.30
Minutes of Women's Meeting	1757 - 1777	D.6
	1777 - 1791	D.7
	1791 - 1813	D.8
	1813 - 1829	D.45
	1829 - 1855	D.44
	1855 - 1884	D.81
Minutes of Committee of Poor	1805 - 1821	D.36
Minutes of Accounts Committee (see also under Finance)	1797 - 1804	D.83
Letters on behalf of Men's Meeting	1750 - 1803	D.9

D.12 contains many minutes concerning the building of the Meeting House at Sycamore Alley, and also on 30/9/1697 102 names of subscribers to the building of a wall round the burial ground at Dolphin's Barn Lane.

Many books have lists of leases and deeds. D.15 ends with a list of leases belonging to Friends of Dublin Men's Meeting and of Leinster Province; also a lease of Lord Conway to Richard Boys at Lisburn. D.18 has at end a list of manuscripts and printed works belonging to the Meeting.

MEMBERSHIP.

Records of Sufferings	1660 - 1780	D.1
	1782 - 1871	D.3
Records of Births, Deaths and Marriages	c.1680	D.56 ⎫
	1701 and 1734	D.57 & 58 ⎭
	1669 - 1774	D.71
Birth Notes and Burial Notes	1773 - 1811	D.79
Birth Notes	1750 - 1811	D.60
1812 - 1829 and 1829 - 1888		D.62 & D.74
Copies of Marriage Certificates	1738 - 1811	D.59
Marriage Registers 1811 - 1848 and 1845 - 1877		D.61 & D.41
List of Marriage Presentations	1679 - 1692	D.72a
For letters concerning Marriages 1748 - 1791 see book D.91		
Burial Notes	1811 - 1823	D.63
Burial and Birth Notes	1823 - 1840	D.79a
Burial Notes	1840 - 1878	D.78
Certificates of Removal	1682 - 1754	D.64
	1754 - 1776	D.64a
	1776 - 1784	D.65
	1784 - 1791	D.66
	1791 - 1804	D.67
	1804 - 1822	D.68
	1822 - 1844	D.69
	1844 - 1864	D.70
Certificates Received	1840 - 1874	D.48
by Women's Meeting	1825 - 1836	D.53
Certificates Removal from Women's Meeting	1825 - 1836	D.54

D.53 does not state the name of places received from.
D.54 gives the names of places to which the certificates were recorded.
These two books are only lists of names and dates.

Testimonies of Denial and Condemnation (copy)	1662 - 1756	D.49
	1756 - 1789	D.50
	1789 - 1820	D.51
	1820 - 1871	D.52
Tithe Lists	1796 - 1859	D.2
Lists of Members	c. 1810 -	D.39
	1821 - 1825	D.46
	1831 - 1840	D.43
of Women's Meeting	1826 -	D.70
Lists of Members	1748 - 1778	D.80

D.80 contains lists of subscriptions to the building of " the Retreat " at Donnybrook.

WILLS.

Wills and Inventories . . . 1683 - 1720 D.4
1721 - 1772 D.5
Cf. Eustace and Goodbody : *Quaker Records, Dublin, Abstracts of Wills* (Ir. Mss. Comm. 1957).
Affairs and Wills . . . . 1816 - 1850 D.47
1851 - 1855 D.42

These books were records of visits paid by Friends appointed by the Monthly Meeting to enquire whether Wills were being made and monetary affairs put into satisfactory order by individual Friends.

FINANCE.

Poor Relief Accounts	1700 - 1721 D.89
	1720 - 1748 D.90
	1820 - 1837 D.73
Women's	1806 - 1842 D.91
Accounts	1843 - 1851 D.92
	1851 - 1863 D.93
This book has Presentations of Marriage for	1748 - 1791 at back
Women's Poor Committee Account	1843 - 1873 D.94
Men's Meeting Cash Book	1759 - 1795 D.55
	1806 - 1836 D.100
	1855 - 1891 D.38
Subscription Lists	1797 - 1816 D.83
This includes Minutes of Accounts Committee	1797 - 1804
Lists of Subscriptions to Men's Meeting	1822 - 1849 D.84
Accounts Ledger	1795 - 1832 D.85
	1833 - 1892 D.86
Accounts of Rents	1857 - 1878 D.88
Ledger	1849 - 1856 D.37

PROPERTY

Schedule of Deeds . . . 1664 - 1774
(The first Quaker Burial Ground in Dublin was where the College of Surgeons is now built. The deeds are in the Library of R.C.S.I.)
Catalogue of Title Deeds 1905.
Four boxes of old deeds, assignments, etc.

EDENDERRY MONTHLY MEETING

8. By a Minute of the Quarterly Meeting for Leinster 6/3/1731 the Monthly Meeting of Mountmellick was divided, Edenderry and Rathangan forming one by themselves. Dates of material prior to this may be found amongst Quarterly Meeting records.

Early Meetings in the neighbourhood took place in surrounding farmhouses, one being that of John, brother to William Edmundson.

EDENDERRY MONTHLY MEETING RECORDS

MINUTE BOOKS.

Minutes of Men's Monthly Meeting	28/ 7/1743 - 20/11/1765	E.1
Contains list of members	25/12/1765 - 31/ 7/1777	E.2
	10/11/1784 - 10/ 6/1795	E.3
	15/10/1795 - 14/ 5/1812	E.4
	18/ 6/1812 - 13/6/1832 and 17/10/1850 - 12/ 4/1855	E.5
	12/ 7/1832 - 17/2/ 1864	E.6
Minutes of Women's Meeting	28/ 2/1731 - 10/ 9/1794	E.11
	16/10/1794 - 15/ 6/1820	E.7
	13/ 7/1820 - 12/ 6/1867	E.14
Minutes Edenderry Quarterly Meeting for women	12/ 5/1788 - 27/ 3/1809	E.38
	1809 - 1829	E.39

These are copies of Leinster Quarterly Meeting Minutes.

MEMBERSHIP.

Records of Sufferings	1764 - 1871	E.20
"Lineage Book" (Family Lists and Burials)	17th and 18th century	E.21
Copies of Marriage Certificates	1731 - 1810	E.23
Birth Notes	1812 - 1871	E.22
Birth Register	1812 - 1879	E.24
Marriage Register	1812 - 1839	E.27
	1857	E.29
Burial Notes	1812 - 1879	E.25
Burial Register	1812 - 1880	E.26
"Record Book" (Certificates, Lists etc.)	1831 - 1875	E.19
Copies of Certificates of Denial	1731 - 1831	E.16
Removal	1732 - 1776	E.17
	1776 - 1831	E.18
Lists of members are included in	1743 - 1765	E.1

WILLS.

Copies of Wills and Inventories . . 1675 - 1740 E.15
(Abstracts published by Ir. Mss. Commission, 1957).

FINANCE.

PROPERTY.

Box of Deeds, Leases etc. (including Rathangan).

MOATE MONTHLY MEETING

9. Established in 1659, at the house of Thomas English, moving later to that of John Clibborn, who, in 1694, built a Meeting House for Friends on his property.

Its constituent Meetings were :—Athlone, Ballymurry, Clara and Tullamore.

MOATE MONTHLY MEETING RECORDS

MINUTE BOOKS.

Minutes of Men's Meeting	4/ 5/1680 - 20/ 8/1731	H.7
This includes some accounts 1660		
Minutes of Men's Meeting	24/ 6/1732 - 28/ 9/1755	H.8
Includes Sufferings 1660 - 1687 and Certificates of Removal 1715 - 1731.		
Minutes of Men's Meeting	10/ 2/1760 - 30/ 5/1792	H.9
Minutes of Monthly Meeting	25/ 7/1792 - 7/ 8/1822	H.10
	8/ 1/1856 - 26/ 3/1913	H.10a
Rough copies of	13/ 3/1840 - 19/ 8/1853	H.21
	18/11/1859 - 15/ 4/1870	H.22
Minutes of Women's Meeting	31/12/1798 - 30/ 4/1819	H.23
	1846 - 1874	H.14

MEMBERSHIP.

Records of Sufferings	1788 - 1859	H.11
Records Births, Marriages and Deaths	1660 - 1782	H.1
Records Births and Burials	1791	H.2
Copies of Marriage Certificates	1745 - 1810	H.3
Certificates of Removal (copies)	1773 - 1832	H.12
	1832 - 1864	H.13
Testimonies of Denial	1685 - (many loose ones)	
	1685 - 1858	H.6
Birth Notes	1812 - 1913	H.16
Register .	1812 - 1913	H.17
Marriage Register	1812 - 1915	H.18
Burial Register	1812 - 1926	H.19
Burial Notes	1812 - 1926	H.20
Lists of Members	1811 -	H.2
	1794 - 1835	see H.11

FINANCE.

Men's Meeting Accounts from	1660	see H.7

PROPERTY.

MOUNTMELLICK MONTHLY MEETING (including Mountrath)

10. Established about 1659 by William Edmundson, Godfrey Cantrill and William Barcroft, whose names appear in the " poll tax " returns for Rosenallis as the tituladoes in that district, (3 miles northwest of Mountmellick). Its minutes only date back to 1749, though a great deal of material dealing with this Meeting is to be found in the Leinster Province Book.

A constituent of Leinster Province, its component Meetings were : Knockballymaher, Ballinakill, Birr, Mountrath, Ballycarrol—for a short period, Kilconimore—discontinued 1792, Edenderry and Rathangan—formed into one separate Monthly Meeting in 1731, Roscrea c 1773 - 1885, Tullamore—short period.

On the discontinuance of Mountmellick Monthly Meeting in 1888, it, with Knockballymaher and Mountrath were joined to Dublin Monthly Meeting ; Birr was attached to Moate.

MOUNTMELLICK MONTHLY MEETING RECORDS

MINUTE BOOKS

Minutes of Men's Meeting	30/ 5/1749 - 30/9 /1758	G.5
	Followed by queries	
	22/10/1758 - 25/2 /1770	G.6
	22/ 4/1770 - 24/4 /1779	G.7
	26/ 9/1779 - 4/8 /1786	G.8
	1/ 9/1779 - 20/2 /1793	G.9
	20/ 3/1793 - 18/1 /1804	G.10
	18/ 7/1804 - 21/10/1818	G.11
	18/11/1818 - 20/ 9/1836	G.12
	21/ 9/1836 - 23/10/1856	G.13
	19/ 2/1857 - 13/ 9/1888	G.14
Rough copy of	21/ 2/1856 - 19/ 4/1876	G.15
Minutes of Preparative Meeting	1823 - 1884	

MEMBERSHIP.

Records of Sufferings	1656 - 1686	G.19
(This partly duplicates G.17)		
Records of Sufferings	1726 - 1735	G.1
	1762 - 1831	G.30

"Book of Mountmellick Meeting from 1667
"Sufferings, Family Lists, Marriage
"Certificates, Testimonies of condemnation
"and about prominent Friends to middle of 18th century"   G.17
Records of Mountrath Births and Burials 17th and 18th century   G.16
Family lists copies from 16 and 17 with additions   G.18

Records of Births and Burials and Certificates of Removal	1799 onwards	
	1827 - 1895	G.2
Marriage Certificates	1733 - 1804	G.20
Birth Register	1811 - 1887	G.21
Birth Notes	1812 - 1847	G.22
	1847	G.23
Marriage Register	1812 - 1841	G.24
	1845 - 1883	G.25
Burial Notes	1812 - 1847	G.26
	1847 - 1888	G.27
Burial Register	1812 - 1888	G.28
Certificates of Removal (includes Wills)	1755 - 1795	G.3
Certificates of Removal	1798 - 1827	G.31
	1865 - 1887	G.32
Testimonies of Disunion etc.	1681 - 1789	G.33
	1795 - 1851	G.4
List of Members	1869	G.29

WILLS. Abstracts published by MSS. Commission
1957   G.3

FINANCE.

WEXFORD MONTHLY MEETING

11. The first Meeting in the county was settled at Edermine, close to Deeps, the home of Francis Randall. Wight and Rutty (*op. cit.*) give the date as 1657. Later Meetings were evidently held at the homes of various Friends, of whom Robert Cuppage of Bregurteen, near Lambstown, and Thomas Holme were the most prominent. A very large settlement of Friends established itself in the county, the greatest number being in the baronies of Bantrie, Forth and Bargie.

The component Meetings were :—

       Ballinclay, Ballinabarney, Ballintore, Cooladine, Enniscorthy, Forrest and Lambstown, Randalls Mills and Ross.

WEXFORD MONTHLY MEETING RECORDS

MINUTE BOOKS.

Minutes of Men's Monthly Meeting	22/10/1777 - 19/12/1786	F.10
	16/ 1/1787 - 6/12/1803	F.11
	3/ 1/1804 - 8/10/1816	F.15
	5/11/1816 - 9/ 6/1835	F.19
	7/ 7/1835 - 8/12/1857	F.21
	5/ 1/1858 - 3/12/1878	F.24
Minutes of Women's Monthly Meeting	3/ 1/1809 - 7/ 8/1832	F.30
Copy National Meeting Minutes	1735 - 1787	F.9
Copy Leinster Quarterly Meeting Minutes and Yearly Meeting Minutes	1822 - 1850	F.22
	1850 - 1874	F.23
Rough Monthly Meeting Minutes	1/ 6/1790 - 3/12/1793	F.12
	7/11/1794 - 5/12/1797	F.13
	6/ 2/1798 - 7/ 8/1804	F.14

MEMBERSHIP.

Register of Births, Deaths and Marriages	1641 - 1720	F.1
	1641 - 1810	F.2
	1722 - 1797	F.8
Marriage Certificates	1671 - 1811	F.3
	1812 - 1849	F.7
Burial Notes	1812 - 1891	F.29
Papers of Condemnation and Disownment	1680 - 1792	F.4
and Applications for Membership	1686 - 1859	F.5
Certificates of Removal	1749 - 1804	F.6
This book also includes records of Wills and Inventories.		
Certificates of Removal	1804 - 1816	F.16
Lists of Members	1814 - 1826	F.18

WILLS.

Wills and Inventories	1680 - 1760	F.6
(Abstracts published by Ir. Mss. Commission 1957).		

PROPERTY.

Schedule of Deeds in Book of Lists .	F.18

WICKLOW MONTHLY MEETING

12. Established 1669. Two Meetings seem to have been settled in the same year in Co. Wicklow, one at the home of the Penrose family at Ballycane, and one at Thomas Trafford's house at Garrymore—he later removing to Wicklow.

The first minute books are those of the Ballycane Meeting.

The other component Meetings were Ballinaclash, Ballymurran, where the old burial ground remains.

WICKLOW MONTHLY MEETING RECORDS

MINUTE BOOKS.

Minutes of Ballykeane Men's Meeting . . . 12/ 4/1767 - 14/10/1800 W.4
    Men's select Meeting   13/ 4/1778 - 23/ 3/1800 W.2
Copies, Minutes and Advices of Yearly and Provincial Meetings   8/ 9/1671 - —/ 3/1723 W.6
Copies, Minutes and Advices of Yearly and Provincial Meetings   8/ 5/1754 - 6/11/1768 W.7

MEMBERSHIP.

Records of Sufferings including lists of Visiting Friends . . . . 1731 - 1796 } W.1
                                             1698 - 1801
Record of Births, Deaths and Marriages . 1677 - 1800 W.5
Burial Notes (Ballymurran) . . 1849 - 1908
(This is a parcel with two sets of Burial forms of which only 21 have been used. There are also records of three earlier deaths, and a note giving approximate location of graves in the burial ground).
Testimonies of Denial and Certificates of Removal . . . . 1768 - 1800 W.3

WILLS.

FINANCE.

MISCELLANEOUS.

PROPERTY.
    One box of Deeds.

MUNSTER PROVINCE MEETING

13. Very early Meetings took place in Cork and in the surrounding country, following the visits of Friends from England who travelled throughout the country, making a very strong impression in the south of Ireland. Minutes date from 1675, those for the city and the provinces being bound together in Cork 1. for the years 1675 to 1694.

These are full Minutes and contain a considerable amount of material not easy to find elsewhere. The isolation of the southern counties of Ireland made Cork Meetings, to a large extent, independent in thought and outlook, and, while their representatives played an important part in the National Meetings, one can read throughout these Minutes a sense of care that in no way should this isolation detract from a very strict adherence to Friends' principles.

The Province embraced the large Monthly Meeting of Tipperary, which in 1692 formed its own six weeks Meeting for the transaction of business between the Province Six Weeks Meeting. Waterford became affiliated to this but the Monthly Meeting for Tipperary was at Knockgraffon, Waterford retaining its own. In 1794 on the discontinuance of Six Weeks Meetings both counties retained their Monthly Meetings as constituents of the Province.

> The constituent Meetings of Munster Province were : — Cork, Limerick, Co. of Tipperary, Waterford, Youghal, Charleville, Bandon and the West, the latter including Skibbereen.

A few smaller Meetings were from time to time set up in the Province which only lasted for short periods, that at Moyallow (Mallow) being dissolved after the Williamite Wars, during which period the minute books give a picture of the distress in the south of Ireland. (See particularly Munster Province Meeting of 21/8/1689).

The Women's Meeting of Munster was an active one and the earliest Irish Province Minutes of such are Munster Six Weeks Women's Meeting (15a) 1680 - 1696. The National Women's Meeting was an outcome of a letter from the Women's Meeting in Cork signed by Elizabeth Hodson and 30 others asking that one should be formed. (National Meeting 8/3/1678).

MUNSTER PROVINCIAL MEETING RECORDS

MINUTES.

Munster Provincial Meeting	1694 - 1706	Cork 7
at back list of Family Visits paid in 1699		
Munster Provincial Meeting	1706 - 1720	8
	1720 - 1739	9
	1739 - 1757	10
	1757 - 1773	11
	1774 - 1798	12
Quarterly Meeting	1798 - 1837	13
	1838 - 1865	14
	1865 - 1894	15
Women's Six Weeks Meeting 30/ 8/1680 -	7/10/1696	15a
Epistles from Quarterly to Half-Yearly Meetings	1746 - 1783	50

(this also includes answers to queries and testimonies to deceased Friends).

Memoranda of Province Meetings	1741	59
Sufferings	1750 - 1811	52
	1812 - 1863	53

MEMBERSHIP.

Register of Births, Marriages and Deaths 17th, 18th and 19th century		Cork 0
Marriage Certificates	1700 - 1770	17
Testimonies deceased Friends (this book also contains Epistles)	1673 - 1724	42

FINANCE.

Munster Province Meeting Accounts	1740 - 1767	16
Female Bounty Fund	1775 - 1833	43

EDUCATION.

Minutes of Munster Provincial School Committee	1796 - 1821	45
	1825 - 1839	46
	1839 - 1855	47

PROPERTY.

Schedule documents re Suir Island School	62

CORK MONTHLY MEETING

14. From the year 1655 Cork had a vigorous Meeting, and a great deal of material is available through Minutes and Deeds of property, and through various family letters and journals preserved in the library.

Its component Meetings were Bandon, including Castlesalem, and Skibbereen, Mallow, including Charleville, Kinsale (had a Meeting house but no regular Men's Meeting), Youghal,—as well as smaller Meetings held from time to time in private houses.

CORK MONTHLY MEETING RECORDS
(including Bandon and Charleville)

MINUTE BOOKS.
Cork Men's Three Weeks Meeting 28/10/1675 - 16/2/1694 Cork 1
(includes Six Weeks Province Minutes)

	30/ 5/1694 - 17/11/1708	2
	7/12/1708 - 13/ 6/1722	3
	3/ 7/1722 - 7/12/1731	4
	18/ 6/1753 - 20/12/1756	5

Lists of Committees appointed and of queries to be read precede the Minutes.

Monthly Meeting .	20/ 3/1787 - 1/12/1806	24
	8/ 1/1807 - 6/ 8/1829	25
	10/ 9/1829 - 8/ 8/1839	26
	5/ 9/1839 - 7/ 2/1861	27
	7/ 3/1861 - 1/ 1/1885	28
Committee of the poor . .	. 1780 - 1799	37
	1799 - 1829	38
	1829 - 1862	39
(Women's) .	. 1786 - 1833	40
Cork Women's Three Weeks Meeting . .	7/ 3/1763 - 17/ 8/1784	6
(This contains Petty Cash a/c at back)		
Memoranda of Men's Meeting .	. 1741	57
Three Weeks .	. 1788 - 1792	58
Minutes Cork City Preparative Meetings .	. 1839 - 1872	41
Minutes Bandon Meeting .	. 1677 - 1700	55
	1680 - 1715	56

Also in above two Family lists, etc.
Minutes Charleville Meeting   .   1689 - 1720 ⎫
and loose Minutes for   .   .   1721 - 1731 ⎬ Cork 54

A few books of the Minutes of Select Meeting for Ministers and Elders from 1760 to 1826 are catalogued but not numbered.

MEMBERSHIP.

There is no book of Sufferings of Cork Monthly Meeting.

Birth Notes	1812 - 1894	30
Marriage Certificates	1812 - 1846	31
Burial Notes	1812 - 1863	29
Copies Certificates of Removal	1739 - 1766	19
	1776 - 1804	20
	1804 - 1839	21
	1839 - 1864	22
Certificates of Removal Women's Meeting	1784 - 1839	23
Testimonies of Disunity	1745 - 1857	51
List of Members	1815	33
	1830	34
Records of Friends Travelling in Ireland	1664 - 1755	60

FINANCE.

Treasurer's Accounts	1740 - 1790	35
	1790 - 1840	36

MISCELLANEOUS.

Historic Narrative of Ministers Visits	1708 - 1877 Cork	44
London Yearly Meeting Advices alphabetically digested		48
Dublin Yearly Meeting Proceedings	1798 - 1839	49
Library Committee Minutes	1842 - 1860	
Summary of Minutes of National Meeting	1669 - 1704	61

PROPERTY.

A large quantity of deeds remain in Cork Meeting House.

LIMERICK MONTHLY MEETING

15. Wight and Rutty's *History of Friends in Ireland*, gives the first date of this Meeting as about 1655. It was a constituent of Munster Province Meeting and its component Meeting was Killaloe, for which there are no minutes, though it appears in the list of Meeting for Munster Province in 1685 (see Tipperary 33).

No 17th century material is available for this Meeting, except for an early family list book and a few letters and copies of journals of Friends.

The Meeting was held at the house of Richard Pearce and his son Thomas for many years (see Wight-Rutty- *History of Friends in Ireland*, and a collection of Pearce family material in the Library).

LIMERICK MONTHLY MEETING RECORDS

Minute Books.

Minutes of Men's Monthly Meeting	6/ 4/1779 - 16/12/1828	L.5
	13/ 1/1829 - 11/ 7/1848	L.6
	14/ 3/1848 - 12/ 8/1870	L.7
Minutes of Ministry and Oversight	13/ 7/1832 - 4/ 4/1853	L.17
Minutes of Women's Meeting	13/ 7/1726 - 14/ 5/1793	L.1

This book includes accounts of Women's Meeting to 1811.

Minutes of Women's Meeting	11/ 6/1793 - 11/10/1842	L.2
	15/11/1842 - 26/ 6/1881	L.4
Copies Munster Quarterly Meeting Minutes	21/ 1/1811 - 28/ 4/1832	L.10
	16/ 1/1843 - 18/ 9/1893	L.12
Yearly Meeting and Munster Quarterly Meeting Minutes	16/ 7/1832 - 9/ 7/1866	L.11
Letters on behalf of Men's Meeting	11/ 6/1777 - 1841	L.13

The back of this book has lists of " Sufferings "

	1785 - 1857	L.13
Library Committee Minutes	1826 - 1842	L.19

Membership.

Family Lists	1653 - 1929	L.8
Certificates of Removals and Denials	1782 - 1864	L.3
Birth Notes	1812 - 1912	L.14
Birth Register	1812 - 1948	L.15
Burial Register	1812 - 1919	L.16
List of Members	1817 -	L.20

Finance.

Accounts of Women's Meeting to 1811	.	L.1

Miscellaneous.

Letters concerning Relief	1847 -	L.21
		L.22
		L.23

TIPPERARY MONTHLY MEETING

16. Six-weekly Meetings for the county took place from 1681, for which records are preserved in a book only found in the present century. This is catalogued now as 70. It throws an interesting, though slight, light on conditions during the Williamite Wars.

This Six-weeks Meeting, held first at Clonmel, varied between that place and Kilcommonbeg after 1685. Between 3/6/1690 and 13/5/1691 no business was transacted though Friends appear to have met. In 1692, by arrangement with the Province and Half-Yearly Meeting, a Monthly Meeting for business was held at Knockgraffon—" to concern Tipperary Friends only," following the 1st Day Meeting for Worship. The Minutes for this Meeting occur in Tipperary 33. At the same time a Six-weeks Meeting (subsidiary to the Province Meeting) was held alternately at Kilcommonbeg, Clonmel and Waterford, the latter joining with Tipperary after 20/12/1692. On 16/9/1709 the two Meetings decided to divide, but an arrangement was made by which there were to be regular inter-visitations between the two Meetings. This continued until 1724.

The component Meetings of Tipperary Monthly Meeting were : Cahir, Clonmel, Cashel, Kilcommonbeg and Knockgraffon (where the Monthly Meetings were held until removed to Cahir in 1702, after which it was held six-weekly), Waterford—until 1710.

COUNTY TIPPERARY MONTHLY MEETING RECORDS

MINUTE BOOKS.

Minutes of Men's Six-weeks Meeting . .	14/ 6/1681 -	Tip.70
Monthly (Knockgraffon)	16/ 9/1694 - 21/ 4/1724	33
Six-weeks . .	2/ 6/1724 - 12/ 4/1760	34
	25/ 1/1761 - 17/ 4/1787	35
Minutes of Men's Monthly Meeting	28/ 5/1787 - 1804	36
	3/ 5/1804 - 26/ 2/1818	37
	2/ 4/1818 - 28/ 6/1849	38
	2/ 8/1849 - 2/ 8/1878	39
Copies of Minutes ot Munster Quarterly Meeting .	16/ 1/1775 - 21/ 4/1800	28
	28/ 4/1800 - 20/ 4/1818	29
	20/ 7/1818 - 19/10/1846	30
	18/ 1/1847 - 14/ 7/1884	31
Minutes of Women's Quarterly Meeting . .	21/ 6/1784 - 12/1/ 1883	59
	11/ 4/1853 - 12/ 6/1896	58
Minutes of Women's Six-weeks Meeting . . (this book includes accounts)	9/ 9/1735 - 18/11/1764	51

Minutes of Women's Monthly Meeting	30/12/1764 - 30/10/1793	Tip. 52
	31/10/1793 - 29/ 5/1817	53
	3/ 7/1817 - 28/11/1839	54
	2/ 1/1840 - 21/12/1871	55
Minutes of Monthly Meeting for Ministers and Elders	1777 - 1787	60
	1788 - 1879	61
(Limerick copy)	1832 - 1853	63

MEMBERSHIP.

Record of Sufferings	1783 - 1798	Tip.16
	1799 - 1868	17
Register Births, Marriages and Deaths	1694 -	3
Registry of families of Friends corrected to	1860	2
Copies of Marriage Certificates of the Province Women's Meeting	1701 - 1730	7
Birth Register	1812 - 1897	4
Birth Notes	1812 - 1861	5
	1860 - 1897	6
Marriage Register	1812 - 1845	8
Burial Register	1812 - 1919	9
Burial Notes	1812 - 1869	10
Copies of certificates of Removal	1692 - 1714	18
	1784 - 1797	19
	1797 - 1825	20
	1825 - 1869	21
Copies of certificates of Disunion also see end of Tipperary 19 and 20.	1825 - 1895	24

FINANCE.

Account Book	1717 - 1800	13
	1800 - 1838	14
	1839 - 1901	15

see also Tipperary 59.

DEEDS.

Old book of lists of Deeds of property belonging to Monthly Meeting.

Another list of Deeds is at front of T.20. This gives the title of a holding in Cashel recited to 1652.

WATERFORD MONTHLY MEETING

17. Waterford Meeting appears to have been established in 1655 (see Wight and Rutty), but 17th century records for the Women's Meeting only survive, except for an early family list book. A Meeting house was built in 1694, but the Six-weeks Meeting of Kilcommonbeg on 10/6/1701 asks Friends of Waterford to draw up the dimensions of their (Waterford) proposed new Meeting House.

The Men's Meeting remained a component part of Tipperary Monthly Meeting until 1710, from which time separate Men's Meeting Minutes follow (12/6/1711).

WATERFORD MONTHLY MEETING RECORDS

MINUTE BOOKS.

Minutes of Men's Meeting	12/ 6/1711 - 16/ 4/1742	Wat.1
	16/ 4/1742 - 18/ 1/1760	2
	29/ 2/1760 - 6/ 6/1777	3
	17/ 7/1777 - 25/ 9/1789	4

Up to 9/7/1778 this was a Six-weeks Meeting, then a Three-weeks up to 25/9/1789.

Minutes of Men's Three-weeks Meeting	16/10/1789 - 2/ 4/1805	5
Changed to Men's Monthly Meeting	31/ 7/1792	
Minutes of Men's Monthly Meeting	30/ 4/1805 - 29/ 6/1819	6
(indexed)	27/ 7/1819 - 21/11/1839	7
Minutes of Monthly Meeting	1839 - 11/ /1869	8
Minutes of Women's Meeting	1676 - 1738	9
	1714 - 1723 - 1743 - 1755	10

These contain some Minutes, epistles, collections and lists, etc.

The Men's books contain lists of queries from 1711 - 1777 and in many are list of " Guides " for travellers.

MEMBERSHIP.

Records of Sufferings	1784 - 1804	11
	1804 - 1834	12
	1834 - 1855	13
Family Lists	1652 - 1862	14
Birth Notes	1804 - 1811	15
Birth Register	1812 - 1858	16
Copies of Marriage Certificates	1787 - 1804	17

Register of Marriages, Waterford .	. 1812 - 1848 Wat.	18
	1848 - 1917	19
of Co. Tipperary	1846 - 1907	20
Intentions of Marriage . .	. 1846 - 1864	21
Burial Notes . . .	. 1812 - 1924	22
Copies of Certificates of Removal .	. 1754 - 1782	23
	1782 - 1796	24
	1796 - 1810	25
	1810 - 1821	26
	1822 - 1846	27
	1846 - 1864	28
Testimonies of Denial . .	. 1787 - 1869	29
Copies of Certificates of Disownment	. 1829 - 1869	30

FINANCE.

Accounts of Property at Barronstrand Street (with Poor Fund Accounts) .	. 1750 - 1795	31
	1796 - 1853	32
Accounts of Waterford Men's Meetings (Ministers' travel items included)	. 1791 - 1810	33

PROPERTY.

Four undated books of Lists of Legacies and Deeds of Waterford and Tipperary Monthly Meetings. . . . .
$\left\{\begin{array}{l}34\\35\\36\\37\end{array}\right.$

PART II

THE documents preserved in the library at 6 Eustace Street are here described with a view to showing what may be found on further search.

The extracts given are only indicative of the type of material contained in the various collections and are in no way meant to be exhaustive.

PART II

DOCUMENTS IN THE HISTORICAL LIBRARY AT 6 EUSTACE STREET, DUBLIN

(Available on request)

FENNELL COLLECTION

Selina Fennell (1833 - 1917) was the wife of Robert Fennell (1822 - 1866) of Banbridge, Co. Down. She was the daughter of Edward and Sarah (Leadbeater) Barrington, her maternal grandparents being William Leadbeater and Mary, author of *The Annals of Ballitore* etc. The collection of letters catalogued under her name in the library consists of about 1,670 items, most of which are letters to and from the members and descendants of the Shackleton family of Ballitore, Co. Kildare, who intermarried with many well known Quaker families.

Box I

a.

132 letters 1775 - 1821.

18. A miscellaneous collection addressed with a few exceptions to Mary (Shackleton) Leadbeater. Not in strict chronological order, and many bearing no date, they are stitched into a post office circular, (date missing) giving foreign letter rates. The first, from Thomas Chandlee senior, writing from Dublin, to Thomas Chandlee his son, in Athy, mentions price of cotton 2/2/1775 as 14d. per bag to 14$\frac{1}{2}d$. which he considers high. Two letters only (2 and 8) of 1798 make brief reference to the state of the country. Many of the earlier letters are written by the Watson family of Co. Carlow, cousins to the Shackletons, and there is a collection of letters of Dr. Paul Johnson, formerly of Ballitore, later of Dublin, whose friendship to the Shackleton family was combined with medical attention until his mental illness of about 1822. Letter 61 is from Richard Shackleton to Paul Johnson in reply to the secession of the latter from the Religious Society of Friends. Among other names mentioned in this section are, Beale, Boake, Boardman, Dawson, Doyle, Duckett, Lecky, Pike, Pim, Rayner, Wright.

b.

33 letters 1781 - 1791.

19. From Anstis Sparkes to Deborah (Shackleton) Chandlee. Anstis Sparkes was of an Exeter family with connections in Ireland where she visited her sister, and made many sojourns with other Quaker families. The letters are entirely composed of gossip and minor anecdotes.

c.

13 letters 1773 - 1777.

20. Anne Jackson, later Gatchell, to Deborah Shackleton. The Jackson family of Kildare were related to most of the big Quaker families. These letters are mainly addressed from Coolegegan and are of minor domestic and family interest. Number 5, 1775, in allusion to the fatigue of travel mentions the use of diaculum as a palliative and asks that a further ¼ lb. should be sent to the writer.

d.

68 letters 1759 - 1780.

21. From Deborah Shackleton (later Chandlee) 1749 to 1824, to her parents Richard and Elizabeth (Carleton) Shackleton. This section is one of two in the Fennell Collection devoted to the early letters of Deborah Shackleton, she being the recipient of practically all the others. She was the eldest of the four children of Richard Shackleton's first wife Elizabeth Fuller, and for the whole of her life corresponded with many people. Her own letters after marriage have not been preserved. The early letters are from Kilconner, Waterford, (where her earliest education took place under the care of an aunt) and from Edenderry where she attended the newly formed boarding school in 1765. Interspersed with later letters from Ballitore, where she took charge of the family in her parents' absence, are letters from Whitehaven and Lancaster where she stayed with relatives (whose names appear throughout the remaining sections of the collection). There are many letters from Clonmel where she paid long visits to her sister Margaret, married to Samuel Grubb, and from Dublin, Waterford and Wicklow (where she drank the waters letter 17). A postscript to letter 30 (1776) says : " Joseph Pike writes to Cousin Morris that he forwarded the letter for William Rathbone by Wight Pike ; the hearth money man has been here affrighting the people." No. 54 has an interpolation by her brother concerning the proposal by Sir Edward Newenham to introduce a motion (in Parliament) re payment of tithes. There is considerable material here relative to Ballitore village.

e.

86 letters 1771 - 1792.

22. An interesting series of letters from Hannah and Sarah Pim, daughters of John Pim of Tottenham to Deborah Shackleton, later Chandlee. John Pim (1718 - 1796) settled his family in Ballitore where they became firm friends of the Shackleton family some being educated by Richard Shackleton. During this time he lived in Dublin until, to his family's dismay, he decided to move to London. The earlier letters written from Dublin, while they lived there temporarily, reflect their feelings on contemplating leaving Ireland, and describe the journeys to England in parties led separately by Hannah and Sarah with different members of the large family. Letter 13 from Hannah Pim is from lodging in London where she finds only one family (Samuel Hoares') wearing the traditional dress of friends, and few who adhere to "the plain language." They attend a plain little meeting called the Peel— 'I suppose the plainest in the city.' Her impression of the English as a race was prejudiced. "They have not the hospitality about them that the Irish have, each person seems to mind the getting money and seems quite indifferent about anything else except to save it" (letter 13). Letter 14 modifies this judgment. Sarah Pim (letter 15) describes the journey of the later portion of the family when all were seasick and the ship held up by reason of a gale which finally made the journey so quick, that the boat had to lay by for several hours for fear of reaching Chester bar too soon. The same letter, written from the new house Tanner's End (Tottenham), states that the Pim family is likely to meet many friends from other meetings, "many citizens have country houses in this neighbourhood whose family in the summer attend Tottenham meeting." Letter 17 is a fuller description of the journey, the wonder of Penmaenmawr and the discomfort of the ferry crossing etc. and letter 18, written on 17/7/1772, describes persons met at Yearly meeting in London—Cousin I. Inman, Richard Chester, James Freeman, John Eliot, Thomas Corban, Rebecca Ransome, John Stephenson, Sarah Morris (an American), James Gough, Lydia Hawkesworth, Elizabeth Robinson, John Fry, Hannah Brown, Isaac Wilson and his sister-in-law married to William Birbeck, father of Morris.

There are items of English and Irish interest all through these letters, and considerable information about members of the Society of Friends. Very occasionally wider interests are touched on as when on 28/3/1775 Sarah writes " the present situation of affairs are so evidently alarming as to authorise even children to lisp disapprobation. Burke seems the admiration of the age . . . We saw the Philadelphia epistle and since that a testimony given out by friends of that place, neither gives us satisfaction, they reflect on their struggling brethren, and flatter their oppressors. The friends in London act a nobler part." (Letter 32).

During the yearly meeting of 1775 (to which came Catherine Phillips of America) a visit was paid to " the Queen's Palace, (formerly Buckingham House)" where they saw the Raphael cartoons of which a description is given in letter 36. In the following year it was hoped that Yearly Meeting time might be, for the future, disassociated from the period of Whitsuntide (the motion having been proposed by Quarterly Meeting (Middlesex).

While these letters became more personal as time goes on, they are worth reading for the interchange of thought and outlook between the two countries, and for the great number of persons and incidents mentioned. A few of the letters between 1780 and 1784 are dated from Norwich where Hannah Pim acted as governess to a Friend's family, others from Keswick and a few from Anner Mills Clonmel, Sarah Pim having married John Grubb of that place in 1784.

f.

88 letters 1769 - 1782

23. These letters from Mary Roberts (1735 - 1807), to Deborah (Shackleton) Chandlee are of minor interest except for the information available concerning the Roberts family of Queen's County. This material has been made use of by the late Mrs. E. J. A. Impey in her book, *A Roberts Family* (Butler and Tanner 1939) where a resumé of the life of Mary Roberts is given. The letters are written from Clonmel, Borris in Ossory, Kyle (the home of this branch of the Roberts family) and Ballinakill, where the sisters Mary and Nellie Roberts set up a shop. They were related to many Queen's County and Tipperary families whose names occur throughout the letters—*viz.* Dudley, Grubb, Clibborn, Malone, Walpole, Pim. The letters are disappointing in trading details, the sole mention of a purchase for the shop being diaper suitable for nightcaps, costing 20 pence or two shillings a yard.

Box II

(a : removed to diary section)
b : 33 documents. (1693 - 1760)
not in strict chronological order.

24. The first document is a devotional exhortation by John Sanders, dated from Coleraine 29th of 4th month 1693. The dying sayings of Ann Humphreys of Exeter who died in Ireland in 1711 were recorded by Robert Hoope, Toby Courteney, William Whitsitt sen., and jun., and James Garrett in document 2.

The next six letters concern the Fuller family of Co. Wexford and Ballitore being mainly from or to Henry Fuller of Ballintore, Co. Wexford, the names include his wife, Deborah, Samuel Hopwood and Jacob Fuller (father of Henry) who sends a prescription for his daughter in law and child which includes manna and sulphur. Henry is concerned by Amos Strettle's debts in 1733 (letter 5) and in 1733 sends his letters from Wexford (where he is drinking the waters by Dr. John Sully's orders) by cousin John Cooper, (letter 8). On January 3rd 1737 - 8, the Kildare County Authorities ordered their treasurer to pay Henry Fuller £16 4s. for making new ditches and levelling the old ones and planting quicksett (hedges) on the turnpike road from Kilcullen to Carlow (7). Most of the remaining letters are of family interest, the names mentioned including Barcroft, Jackson, Pim, Newenham, Boake, Maddock and Watson. In 1756, Samuel Watson of Kilconner married Deborah Fuller, widow of Henry. Letter 33 from John Barcroft to cousin Joshua Clibborn is dated from Arkhill (Edenderry) in 1719 and discusses the tenure of land of [Renoognan] and the attendance of Friends at Quarter Sessions for the purpose of the registration of the meeting houses at Arkhill, Timahoe, Kilteel and Christianstown.

c.

10 letters 1779 - 1781.

25. From Margaret Christy afterwards Pike of Stramore near Moyallen to cousin Deborah Shackleton—all of a domestic nature mentioning family names only.

d.

10 letters 1774 - 1780.

26. All to Deborah Shackleton from her cousins Jane Deborah and Elizabeth Fuller, one (10) from Thomas Fuller in Dublin who sends ½ barrel of port which he hopes will please aunt. The letters are full of family gossip and approaching betrothals dated variously from Cork, Carlisle, and Blackrock. (Merrion Avenue) where the sea was so rough that " the women were hardly able to stand against the waves with us in their arms. Hundreds bathe every day " (letter 5). At Kirby Steven (letter 4) 1800, are reputed to have attended meeting in a booth specially erected near the Meeting House. Among the engagements or courtships mentioned are Hannah Green and a young man Woodcock of Wexford—Joe Garret and Molly Pike, Samuel Neale and Debby Newenham, Isaac Simmons and Betty Pim, Sam Pim and cousin Peggy Penrose, Billy Penrose and R. Nevins.

e.
80 letters 1805 - 1819.

27. All to Deborah Chandlee from her friend D. Fitzgerald, except no. 1 dated 1777 which is a schoolboy letter written at Ballitore by W. Fitzgerald to D. Chandlee, and no. 51 which consists of two poems written by D. Fitzgerald. These letters have little merit being mainly records of trivial happenings, and the minor interests of friends of long standing. No place of origin appears in most letters, except " Mt. Ophaly," one or two only being headed thus. The glove making industry of the Chandlee daughter is mentioned several times.

g.
64 letters, 1806 - 1818.

28. All from Mary (1792 - 1861), third daughter of Thomas and Deborah Chandlee, mainly written from Dublin while she supervised the household of Thomas Fayle, a widower of 63 Thomas Street, and cared for his small daughter. These letters are mainly of domestic nature with news of family and friends. They occasionally reveal items of social value, but have little of historic interest. In about 1813 (letter 3 undated) she paid 15/6 for two pairs shoes, 13/6 for a pair of boots and 50/- for the material to make a pelisse. A year or so later she thinks it worth paying the high price of 10/6 for a pair of cork soled shoes. In 1815 she pays Jos. and Henry Leland hat manufacturers of Meath Street £1 6s. for her father's beaver hat. The bill is receipted, (document 17). Though little diversion beyond visiting is mentioned she does, in the year 1815, attend Botanical lectures three times a week between 8 and 9 a.m.

Letter 19 has attached to it a pattern of dress material resembling alpaca, at 1/8 per yard.

There are many allusions to health including the suggestion of giving Ether to her father to counteract fits, not telling doctor or apothecary (letter 1) " It is cheaper in Dublin than Carlow." Doctor Cretan, attending daily at the Foundling Hospital, is called in to see Margaret Anne Fayle but pays small attention to the child. The hard winter of 1815 is mentioned, (letter 26), and allusion is made to the revival, in that year, of the custom of holding a special Youth Meeting among Dublin Friends. Letter 27 contains an account of the interview between a well known philanthropist, Thomas Clarkson, and the Emperor of Russia who had already met some of the Religious Society of Friends, including William Allen. House robberies are mentioned, and Mary Chandlee interceded vainly with the Lord Lieutenant for the life of one man who had broken into a Friends' house (letter 41). In 1817 contrary winds prevented coal reaching Dublin and the household was miserable without fires (letter 47). Mary's small nephew, Richard Johnson, was taken to be vaccinated by his mother in 1817 and slept through it. (Vaccination was not made compulsory till 1854). She is concerned by the splashing of carts in Skinners Row, though finds a silk cloak not ruined thereby, as Tabinet would have been, but by 1818 she writes " whole Tabinet very rarely made now, only saw it at John Shannon's, and that 10/- per yard." Silk greatly risen in price, (letter 61). West in Skinner Row will give 5/10 per oz. for plate to be melted down, higher for that fit to use (letter 64). (This is Mathew West, alderman, jeweller and goldsmith).

Mary Chandlee later married Joseph Humphrey, the first superintendent, and friend of the founder, Dr. Charles Orpen, of the Claremont Institution for the deaf and dumb. She alludes briefly to him in these letters. He told her (letter 42) that the Prisoner of Chillon was not worth reading.

h.
45 Documents.

29. The first two are poems written by Mary (Shackleton) Leadbeater, one written in 1785 in memory of Jonathan Haughton of Ballitore, who died that year, and the second in memory of Mary Leadbeater's sister, Deborah Chandlee, who died in 1824. The remainder are a miscellaneous collection of letters, all except 2 being written to Deborah Chandlee before and after marriage. The early ones are from her English relatives, the Pembertons, Birbecks, Bradfords, and Halls and are written from Bath, (where M. Pemberton in 1773 found neither the waters nor the people congenial) Kendal, Lancaster, and Tottenham (from the home of the Pim family). A few names well known to the Society of Friends in the 18th century occur : Fell, Dillworth, Gurney, Wilson, Birkett. The letter of M. Bradford (no. 18) 20/10/1781 bears the imprint of a seal with the words " Sans Larcin." Of four letters by Jane Watson (20 - 23) three are written while on a religious visit to England in 1781 - 2, the fourth dated 8th 3rd mo. 1799 from Rathangan asks for assurance that 10 doz. of wine has reached Ballitore and that the family there are well, ugly rumours having reached Rathangan.

The remaining letters are of family interests and concerns, no. 37 dealing with proposed inoculations (for smallpox) to be done by Mary Leadbeater. Letter 45 relates the story of the impression made by Samuel Fothergill on Admiral Tyrrell during the time of the French War, so that he waited in silent prayer before leading his fleet to victory against a superior force.

i.

37 letters 1770 - 1787.

All these from Thomas Chandlee, of Athy to his wife Deborah (Shackleton) Chandlee. Only the first seven are prior to their marriage in 1781. Thomas Chandlee had a linen draper's shop in Athy which he combined with sundry other concerns. Details of prices, of modes of travel, and commissions to be performed in Dublin appear frequently, as well as news of Friends and of Friends Meetings held in Dublin and elsewhere. The minute instructions necessary to synchronise travel arrangements by those who probably only kept one horse are of interest, as is the practical usage of the Grand Canal in its early days. " To be met at Sallins by Larry who is to have 1/- for the Turnpike which he will have to pay at Athy, coming out, and at Kilcullen Bridge " (letter 26) ; or ; " Mare is to be led by Larry who is to borrow his father's or T. Molloy's horse for himself. To give the horses a stone of oats at Dadd's in Naas, and to put them up in Dublin at the Wheatsheaf in Thomas Street, near James's Gate, then to come to 24 Kevin Street. He will need money for the turnpike (half-pence) and about 19 or 20 pence for oats. He could borrow an old sirtout which is hanging in the hall ". Though not approving of travel on 1st day, Chandlee thinks the occasion warrants it. (Letters 30). Letters from him to Deborah in Dublin were usually addressed c/o Thomas Bewley, South Earl Street, and always include commissions to be executed : — " Tell brother John that Grimes Rose wants him to call at Jas. Dexter's for the price of 15 quarts of Water at 10*d*.—12/6—and if he wants any more simple waters to send account of them . . . Buy 2 yards superfine Green cloth " ¼ wide " at Hodson who give wholesale price, some listing from Fieldings and 3 doz. large gilt buttons, plain at middle with carved edges—were 3/3 doz. may be cheaper now." (Letter 31).

In the 11th month, 1784, he writes instructions re the drawing of hay, and is sorry the cow has died, hopes hide and fat have been kept " but what will you do for milk " (letters 28 and 29).

Volunteers are mentioned twice. In 1782 " a great dispute among the Volunteers (in Athy)—Bob Johnston at the head of the malcontents marched off and talks of forming a new company " (letter 19). In 1784 in Dublin, " The volunteers here are raising recruits as if they mean war. Wish both sides may act with prudence." Friends travelling to meetings throughout Ireland are mentioned often and in 5th month, 1784, both Dublin Meeting Houses were to be open for the Public Meeting. Among those mentioned were Jno. Pemberton, Wm. Matthews, the American women Hannah Bevington and Sally Stevenson. The English men Friends, not yet arrived, are travelling via Scotland.

FAMILY COLLECTIONS 61

This small section is worth reading for its many social details, covering matters of interest to Friends and non-Friends. Only a few examples being given. One or two letters are out of chronological order.

k.

28 letters, 1794 - 1816.

From Jane Chandlee (1783 - 1858) to her Mother Deborah Chandlee. These few letters also contain much of sociological interest. Jane Chandlee (1783 - 1858) came up to Dublin to housekeep for the widowed Robert Fayle, and the later letters are mainly of domestic interest and family and other visits. She records among these that of the young William Forster, later the advocate of anti-slavery, and one of the prime movers and most active workers for relief at the time of the Irish Famine. At the time of these visits he was only 30 but a great preacher and liked by all. He visited both Newgate and Kilmainham jails while in Dublin as well as travelling in the west (letters 25 and 22), and other parts getting to know the people among whom he had contacts in 1847.

Among prices prevailing were a bonnet 9/9, (a cheap one), lace 3/9½ per yard. "Henting 16d. per yard, cotton 7/7 per lb., (letters 10 and 11). Aunt wants lavender to make drops to put in her coco, E. Johnson knows a woman who will alter hats, material for a gown costs 3/- a yard in Bride Street—much increased, hears sugar likely to fall (letter 12). No coating as low as 9/- so got a neat English one for 10/- per yard—gown to be ' dyed ' will cost 5/5."

Box III

a.

58 letters, 1772 - 1788.

32. Arranged in folders by names of writers with enclosed list in box. Mary Shackleton (later Leadbeater) to her (half) sister Deborah Shackleton (later Chandlee). All these, written before Mary Shackleton's marriage show the steady development of her power of writing. The early ones are written when she was about 14 years old, and have a lively wit, coupled with the classical taste evinced later in her work of translating Maffeus. Through them too are many anecdotes of her father's pupils. Her sister Deborah had a facial skin trouble and was often away at the sea in search of cure. The later letters are written after her sister's marriage. All have much detail of Ballitore news, though occasionally written while visiting elsewhere.

b.

60 letters, 1772 - 1798.

33. Mostly written by Sarah Hall (later Birbeck) of Skipton in Yorkshire, where Abraham Shackleton senior had held his first teaching post in the school of David Hall, and where was the former home of his wife Margaret Wilkinson, a relation of the Hall family. The recipient of Sarah's letters is " Cousin Debby " Shackleton, and up to 1776 they are signed S. Hall (letter 18) after which she became the wife of Morris Birbeck, from whom are a few letters in this bundle. They give a picture of travel in England, and between England and Ireland, and include many names of interest. The Birbeck family were merchant bankers of Yorkshire and Morris (1734 - 1816) who had an insurance business in London devoted his spare time to Quaker bibliography and to the collection and cataloguing of books c/f. *Journal of the Friends' Historical Society*, viii 9 - 15.

Letter 8 (28/11/1773) from Morris Birbeck to his son (by his first marriage) written from New Garden Settlement, North Carolina, is of particular interest in its minute description of the journey from Philadelphia, and of the wild and botanical life of Carolina. He returned to England in 1774 though the letter conveys his intention of settling in Carolina.

c.

19 letters 1777 - 1782.

34. Jane Boake—later Haughton—written to her cousin Deborah Shackleton later Chandlee. Written from Summerhill, Cork, where Jane Boake was living with her relatives. All of family interest.

d.

17 letters 1778 - 1796.

35. From Mary Gough, later Bewley, to her friend Deborah Shackleton, the first eight are dated from Dublin, where she lived with her father, a schoolmaster, the remainder from Mountmellick after her marriage in 1779 to Mungo Bewley of that town. All of domestic interest.

e.

36 letters, 1774 - 1822.

36. Twenty-eight of these are written by Deborah (Shackleton) Chandlee before and after marriage—all to her sister Sarah Shackleton.

Those up to 1882 are written from Clonmel and Ballitore the later ones all from Athy (" a town dead in every sense of the word, even the prospect of the canal does not enliven us "—letter 18) except 27 and 28 from Ballitore and Claremont (Dublin) respectively.

The remaining 9 letters are from Sarah Shackleton to Deborah Chandlee at long intervals except for a note (36a) from Margaret (Shackleton) Grubb.

All are of family and local matters though one from Minehead in 1798 refers to the Irish troubles of that year.

Box III f.

3 Folders   (1)   1 - 47   1766 - 1770
              (2)   48 - 79   dates vary c. 1769 - 1788
              (3)   80 - 128   1766

38. This collection of letters written by Robert Jackson, of the printing and publishing house of Jackson in Meath Street, Dublin, are almost entirely devoted to a series of astronomical studies between the years 1766 and 1779. They are written when Robert Jackson was ending his apprenticeship to his father, Isaac Jackson, and starting work as a journeyman. The recipient of the letters was Thomas Chandlee junior, apprentice to Robert Fayle, Linendraper, of Bride Street, Dublin. They show a very considerable knowledge of astronomy and are full of detailed observances ; it apparently being the object of Jackson to instruct Chandlee in the knowledge he already possessed himself.

Folder (f1). Most of the letters are undated except for the day and month, but have been endorsed with a full date on the back in another hand. The first 10 letters relate to other subjects including a service (apparently Catholic) in the Court House of the Liberty of Thomas Court and Donore into which some disturbers tried to introduce a bull (8), and an account of a journey to Ballitore crossing the new bridge at Kilcullen below stream from the ruins of the old, returning by Dunlavin, Ballymore Eustace and Blessington. Letter 11 speaks of a house at Crumlin used by the young astronomers for observance, and alluded to several times in this series of letters. After this all the letters refer by astronomical signs to the courses of the stars and planets, and to the comparison made by this group of young men with other work recorded by magazines and almanacs of the day. The approaching Transit of Venus in 1769, an eclipse of the sun by the moon in the same year with

---

Through an error in compilation there is no number 37 either here or in index.

instructions for observing it are mentioned in letters 14, 15 and 24. An offer of a quadrant to observe altitude of fixed stars, the discovery of " Mencar in the Whale's jaw " in 31. A comparison of almanacs for the year 1770 in letter 35 draws attention to errors in those of Laboissiere, Scanlan and Watson, the last, it being stated, having hired a mathematician to write his astronomical notes. Letter 36 is a dissertation on comets in view of one expected in the year of writing, 1770.

In this series there are also letters written on the subjects of the approaching publication of John Gough's large arithmetic (13 and 42), on the wisdom of using marbled paper in book-binding for fear of damaging leather by use of vitriol and copperas (16) on the recognition of watermarks in paper (20) and a discourse on logic (45).

39. Folder (f2). Thirty-one letters and other documents of varying dates, but the majority undated. No. 50 is an old printed account, headed *Speculum Mun* (paper torn), of the eclipse about to take place on the 18th February, 1737. Part of this article belongs, strictly speaking, to the realm of astrology. It is signed by James Nevill who notes that " Laboissere in his Almanac for this present year inserted this Eclipse on the 10th February." The paper is printed by James Hoey of Skinner Row. Documents 50 to 54 are, apparently, exercises from a proposed geography, including astronomical calculations and a definition of the making of a meridian line. Several letters are headed Crumlin House and one (56) gives the distance between this and a place called " Dublin Hygrometer closet," computed to be 1 20/23 miles. It appears from several references that a house at Crumlin was for a time rented by a group of people interested in astronomy. It might have been half of Crumlin House, divided in the mid-eighteenth century, though it seems more likely that the term Crumlinhouse was a generalisation. Letter 72 dated 17/4/1768 mentions preparations being made by the Empress of Russia to observe the eclipse due to take place in 6th month 1769.

40. Folder (f3). Forty-eight documents, many being letters of a similar nature to those above, all of which are undated, but by the contents almost all belong to the year 1768. The remainder consist of diagrams, tables, illustrations etc. of astronomical data. Number 87 is a manuscript table giving the magnitude, longitude and latitude of 38 fixed stars within fourteen Constellations. 88 is a diagram showing appearance of principal stars about 9 or 10 at night at beginning of 5th month. 89 apparently part of a draft for a simple work on astronomy under nine headings. Other papers include discourse on Parallex ; rules when Mercury may be seen ; on signs of the Zodiac ; an explanation of terms used in the solar system and several copies of a paper called

FAMILY COLLECTIONS 65

Starry Intelligence, this apparently being a commentary on current observations. The last two documents are printed, 127 a circular diagram showing signs of the Zodiac, 128 a page from an astronomical almanack of 1766.

g.

26 letters, 1813 - 1817.

41. From Deborah Johnson (formerly Chandlee) to her mother Deborah Chandlee. Letter 1 mentions the high price of wine " making it only fit for medicine." All these are concerned with family matters and children's health etc. The importance of sea bathing for health is mentioned several times and a visit to Dalkey described. Deborah Chandlee, the younger, married Francis Johnson about 1809, of Ballitore and Dublin. They lived in Parliament Street, where they had a shop, and it is apparent that after the birth of the children they owned, or rented, a house on Kingstown Hill, where the children lived with an aunt and servants. The Directory for 1825 shows Francis Johnson, 6 Parliament Street, a watchmaker, and John F. Johnson, 19 Parliament Street, watchmaker and jeweller.

Box IV

Folder **a.**

13 letters, 1777 - 1789

42. William Raynor to his cousin, Deborah (Shackleton) Chandlee. William Raynor was the orphaned nephew of Richard Shackleton, being the son of Richard's sister Elizabeth, by her clandestine marriage to Maurice Rayner, an usher in Shackleton's school. Some are from Ballitore, some from Waterford, to which city William Rayner moved on his failure to succeed as a schoolmaster.

b.

13 letters, 1776 - 1780

42 (contd.). Elizabeth and Ann Shannon to their cousin Deborah Shackleton (later Chandlee). Most of Elizabeth's letters are written from Springmount, Cork, where she lived at this period in the household of Samuel and Sarah Neale. Anne lived at Harold's Cross, Dublin. Mainly of domestic interest, with a few letters descriptive of travel in Ireland.

c.

23 letters, 1773 - 1785

42 (contd.). Elizabeth Gatchell, formerly Strangman, to Deborah Shackleton from Mountmellick before and after her marriage to William Gatchell, a farmer of that town. Domestic letters, interspersed with some levity such as a poem " On returning a borrowed umbrella " (no. 12).

d.

46 letters, 1770 - 1783

43. Hannah Hodgson, later Piper, and her sister Dorothy Hodgson to Deborah Shackleton. Most of the letters are from Whitehaven in Cumberland, between which town and Dublin, Captain Joseph Piper plied a passenger cum cargo ship. The majority of the letters are written by Dorothy, who lived with the Pipers, and occasionally came to Ireland. The names of well known Irish Friends occur frequently, viz. Richard Pike, Peter Cambridge, Samuel Neale, Thomas Wyly, etc. There is a social value apparent in this group of letters. 26a. describes clothes in detail. 31. " a hundred smallpox innoculations in this town (Dublin) of which all but two successful, and they recovering." 37. describes dangers of trading because of American privateers, which have even attempted to land at Whitehaven (19/6/1778) and to set the town on fire.

e.

107 letters, 1771 - 1805

44. Margaret Shackleton, later Grubb, to her sister Deborah. The first twelve letters written before her marriage in 1776 are dated from Carlow, Clonmel, Dublin and Ballitore. The remainder are mainly from her home as wife of Samuel Grubb, a miller, in Clonmel and later in Clogheen. Very human letters of a busy wife and mother, the early ones evincing the lively sense of humour which runs through all the Shackleton family letters, coupled with a sense of duty to others. In Dublin she visits the two Eyre children who had been removed from Ballitore school and sent to work at an early age (letter 6). She is shocked by a public execution close to her windows, fears inoculation (1778) against smallpox, is a keen gardener. There is a short account of the 1798 troubles (letter 102) and a mention of the disunity among Friends in 1800 (103 and 106) when her brother Abraham and others left the Society.

FAMILY COLLECTIONS

g.
26 letters, 1807 - 1814

45. From Thomas Chandlee junior to his mother Deborah Chandlee. The first one is a schoolboy's letter, undated. The remainder are dated from Clogheen, Co. Tipperary, where he had joined his uncle in the milling business. They are mostly filled with family news and evince a tender affection for his mother living in Ballitore with her invalid husband, and for his very many relatives. There are one or two allusions to the French war, to the prosperity of business and to prevailing prices.

h.
34 letters, 1772 - 1796

46. From Sarah Shackleton to her sister Deborah (Shackleton) Chandlee. Beginning when she was 12 years old, these letters show a very lively sense of fun and an endearing freedom from restraint. They give an uninhibited view of this broadminded family, and continue through the years with the same frank, fresh outlook. It is worth while comparing them with those of her elder sister Margaret (IVe). The evident love of the sisters is a pleasing feature.

j.
31 letters, 1772 - 1780 and one of 1814

46 (contd.). A miscellaneous collection of letters from various friends and relations to Deborah Shackleton before her marriage. The writers are the Cambridge family of Dublin and Cork; Aunt Deborah Carleton at Ballitore; and Samuel Carleton to whom, in addition there is a letter from Deborah Shackleton (both of these mention the school in Dublin to which Mary Shackleton was sent to be cured of a stammer); Mary Pike from Harlem, a mill on the road above Old Bawn, Dublin; Abigail Johnson, Mary Haughton, Jos. Williams and Sarah Tuke from York. The letter from William Tuke (21) in 1774 is of interest as he writes relative to a woman who is said to have a cure for scurvy and mentions three cases of treatment known to his apothecary. He gives advice for and against Deborah Shackleton coming to York to try this 'cure.'

(William Tuke (1732 - 1822) was the promoter of the retreat at York for the care of mental illness).

k.
4 letters stitched

46 (contd.). Abigail Thompson while staying at Stramore, the home near Dungannon of the Christy family, to Deborah Shackleton—local news, largely occupied with health.

Box V.

a.

47. A collection of newspaper cuttings pasted into a letter-copying book whose cover is dated 1735. It probably belonged to Thomas Chandlee, merchant, of Athy (1701 - 1776) the letters T. C. appearing on the vellum cover. The pasted-in cuttings almost totally cover the manuscript.

b.

48. A memoir of Sarah (Fawcett) Phillips, (1753 -   ) partly autobiographical, partly a collection of her own letters made by her husband. Included in this book is a long elegiac poem by John Gough to Richard Shackleton commenting on the worldly evils of the 18th century and the reply in the same manner of Richard Shackleton to him.

Sarah Phillips was daughter of Samuel and Sarah (Poole) Fawcett of Waterford.

c.

41 letters, 1769 - 1790, stitched

49. Abraham Shackleton to his sister, Deborah, (later Chandlee) with a few from Lydia Mellor (later Shackleton, by her marriage to Abraham). This is a series of amusing letters well written and with considerable wit. They are the letters of a young man of high spirits to his greatly loved elder sister. There is little or no restraint and they give a delightful picture of the times, though the writer does not part from a sense of religious and family responsibility. His comments on current medicine are enlightening : " Sally got a cold as usual she was to force the whole charge through all her pores, vulgarly called sweating, so was put to bed and the 407,520,000 gates set open to expel the enemy, meanwhile the fort being exhausted becomes considerably weakened and exposed to attacks of an enemy from every quarter " or again " Aunts as usual, one with rheumatic gout the other with gouty rheumatism."

His marriage to Lydia Mellor, daughter of Ebenezer and Margaret of Edenderry took place in 1779 after which the letters show the weight of family cares. Names mentioned in travelling in this period include Duckett, Clibborn, Grubb, Lecky, Routh, Thompson, Ridgeway, Watson etc.

FAMILY COLLECTIONS 69

d.
82 letters 1765 - 1792, stitched

50. From Richard and Elizabeth Shackleton to their daughter Deborah, mainly before her marriage (1781) but a few following it. Most of the letters are from Richard Shackleton and portray his character in their good humour, lively wit, affection and moderation of style. There are the little quips, jests, and turns of phrase so often seen in the familiar correspondence of a closely knit family. They abound too in the reliance on God, in times of adversity, of those whose Faith comes uppermost and easily, throughout life.

Three of the letters (numbers 3, 4, and 5) are to his grandchildren from Abraham Shackleton (1696 - 1771) the founder of Ballitore School. The last of these, written in 1769, is from Dublin where he was apparently attending the National Meeting. Both Richard Shackleton and his wife Elizabeth were at times among those appointed to travel in the Ministry, and many of the letters are written during these visits made to every Meeting in each province, and to many individual friends. Others are of a family nature, often to see their daughter in Clonmel, Margaret Grubb, and, while there, sending home news of the large numbers of friends in Tipperary and Waterford. Elizabeth Shackleton's letters are less frequent than those of her husband, and generally written with some solicitude to absent children, being particularly concerned for Deborah's skin trouble, for which letter 66 recommends a cure of the famous Dr. Fothergill. This is a delightful series, worth reading for its pure prose as much as for its material value.

Box VI
193 documents, 1776 - 1819

51. This bundle, which is wrapped in a sheet of printers waste consisting of four title pages to Byron's works (Murray 1820) and with a Post Office circular relative to the payments made to Chelsea pensioners in Ireland as a backing, is a series of poems and letters written for Mary Shackleton (later Leadbeater) by her friends Dorothy and Abigail Roberts. Dorothy Roberts, of Kyle, Queen's County, died in 1788 and the series should properly be divided here, as a document (40) and poem (41) are written by Mary Shackleton following Dorothy's decease. After this the correspondence and poems between Abigail and Mary resumed in 1809. It closes with a letter acquainting Mary Leadbeater of Abigail's failing eyesight in the year 1819. Abigail Roberts, daughter of George and Dorothy of Kyle, was born in 1748 and died in 1823. This correspondence is mentioned, with a brief account of her life, in *A Roberts Family* (E. J. Impey, Bentley and Tanner, 1939).

Box VII

a.

170 letters, 1777 - 1825

52. All are to Mary (Shackleton) Leadbeater. 87 letters mostly of a domestic nature are from Deborah Chandlee and her husband. After the death of Thomas Chandlee senior in 1816, the majority of the letters come from the children of the family, now scattered, some married. The letters of the sons are those of young men of strength of purpose and responsibility. Little is mentioned of the political affairs of the day, though French developments of 1815 are noted in letter 104. There are several of social interest, e.g. 115 which is " glad to hear of new ways of taking bees without putting to death." 74 is an inventory of fixed fittings in a house in Athy, and 117 gives the price of copper sheeting for flue lining at 3/- per 14 lb. sheet, the price varying by weight.

Letters 122 to 170 in this series are those of Joseph Humphreys, who in 1819 married Mary, daughter of Thomas and Deborah Chandlee. They are of greater interest than others in this collection, covering as they do, the period of the publication of much of Mary Leadbeater's work. They discuss literature of the day—Byron, Cowper, the merits of current books (which appear to have been lent by Humphreys) and topics of general literary interest. They are written from 6 Dawson Street, from Kildare Place and from Claremont, Glasnevin, the Institution for Deaf and Dumb boys and girls, of which Joseph Humphreys was the first superintendent. He was a close friend to Dr. Charles Orpen, the doctor instrumental in founding this Institution, and letter 142 is a vivid description of the great meeting of " not fewer than 1,000 persons " which inaugurated the philanthropy.

b.

120 letters, 1803 - 1829

53. The first 70 letters of this group are to Elizabeth Leadbeater from her cousin Deborah Johnson, (27 letters, 1803 - 1821), and from various members of her family and friends. Cousins Chandlees and Johnson, and Humphreys, sister Grubb in Clogheen and many Ballitore and neighbouring inhabitants are alluded to ; the Doyle sisters, Mary Haughton, Fanny Bewley, Abby Carter, C. Fayle are all mentioned in letter 40 from Jane Chandlee, who is looking after the Johnson children in Kingstown (1824). There are curious little details and prescriptions, only found in intimate family letters. A method of removing superfluous hair might be out of favour now, including as it did the application of hot beeswax and resin spread on leather—" as it hardens a smart pull should be given " (letter 34). 5/- for gout medicine was enclosed in letter 39. Francis Johnson's mother died in 1824 (letter 42) causing a family upset—his son runs away (letter 43) and asks a coachman to take him to Cork for nothing. Letter 47 gives the price (at R. Fayle's shop in Dublin) of full bleached sheeting 1¼ yards wide from 1/9 to 2/6 per yard, 54 to 57 yards in a piece, and number 51 in a comparison of Brussels and Wilton carpets gives their price at 6/6 per yard. Pickle forks are 16/- British.

The Johnsons were not Friends, and a little of Dublin's gossip appears here and there. The widow who married a man called Savage reputed to have a wife and son—an agent to the Cork glass company (letter 60). A letter (56) of August 2nd, 1826 tells of Frank, Jane and John (Johnson) having gone to see the Menai bridge on Saturday evening, home to breakfast on Monday. All very sick at sea. An account of the death in a Castle Street fire of an old Mrs. French, (59).

Letters 71 to 120 are to Elizabeth Leadbeater from 'Father.' As little has been written of William Leadbeater's side of the family, these throw a valuable light on the lives of his sister, Mrs. M. A. Higginson, and his nieces or great-nieces—Sarah and Jane Fitzsimmons and M. A. Montgomery. The correspondents in addition to the above are Dennis Rowe, (102), John Dowling, (93), and Malachi Dowling (103). The Higginson family lived first in Clonmel, then in Carlow. In 1804 Jane Higginson writes that "the coach will stop on the 20th of the month" (January) after which her mother will have several horses to dispose of. An interesting side-light on the relative importance of Ballitore village is given in letter 78 when Aunt Higginson requires 2 lbs. of the best black tea and 2 lbs. of coffee from M. and A. Doyle (in Ballitore) as she cannot get them good in Carlow. She also in 1827 (100) sends listing to Ballitore to have shoes made, and "Rob-Roy" for a cloak and dress at 5/- per yard. (112 and 113).

LETTERS OF RICHARD SHACKLETON OF BALLITORE (1726 - 1792)

23 letters, 1752 - 1784

54. These are copies of letters written to various friends by Richard Shackleton, headmaster and owner, in succession to his father, of Ballitore School. The copies are apparently made by his daughters, one or two appearing to be in his own handwriting. Some of these letters appear in the printed collection of the letters of Richard and Elizabeth Shackleton compiled by Mary Leadbeater, his daughter in 1849.

Most are in a strong religious vein evincing an unusual clarity of outlook, and an ability to express thought without any self righteous approach. Letter b. to Joseph White of Pennsylvania (1761) mentions the reception of Christian teaching by Indians and asks for more information. Letter e. is of particular interest in that it sets out Richard Shackleton's reasons for refusing to become headmaster of the new Provincial School proposed for the education of Friends alone. He is more content with his sphere as master of a school open to all sects, his view being that, while approving of a " select Boarding School for Friends," he feels that his own métier lies in giving a virtuous education, and conscientious care to others, who then become dispersed among those not acquainted with Friends' principles.

Many of the letters are written to those suffering from illness or loss.

The names of the recipients are :

(a) Mary Pim — 1752
(b) Joseph White, Pennsylvania — 1761
(c) Jane Shelley, London — 1762 — re setting up a school, in London.
(d) " E. H." — 1763
(e) " Cousin " John Christy — 1765
(f) John Hancock — 1763
(g) A. Balfour — 1763
(h) T. Greer — 1766 — Death of R. S.'s Mother in law and sister Rayner
(j) John W. — 1766
(k) Cousin Thos. Carleton — 1767 — Annotated by Mary Leadbeater who states that the family have original of this letter.
(l) William Haughton — 1769
(m) Robert Dudley — 1769
(n) John Whitworth — 1771 — Criticising manuscript.
(o) Alexander Shelley, jnr. — 1774
(p) " Cousin " Robert Grubb — 1777
(q) Eliza. Box — 1777 — Reply to her query re religious practice.
(r) Sir Edward Newenham — 1778 — re powers of magistrates in distraining goods etc.
(s) Anne Stephens — 1780
(t) Edith Lovell — 1781
(u) Mary P. Lecky — 1782
(v) Joshua Strangman — 1783
(x) Mary Davis — 1784
(y) Ebenezer Pike — 1784

LEADBEATER—SHACKLETON COLLECTION
In four stitched bundles

I

a.
1-43

55. Written between 1809 and 1812 by Edward Carbutt, tutor to the family of John Barrington of Glendruid, Cabinteely, Co. Dublin.

The first seven are addressed to Elizabeth, daughter of Mary Leadbeater. Following her refusal to marry him, Carbutt continued corresponding with Mary Leadbeater, the author of *Annals of Ballitore*, Poems, Biographies, Essays, etc. During this period Carbutt acted as her agent in Dublin for a second edition of her *Anecdotes taken from real life for the improvement of children* and several letters contain material relative to printing, publishing and binding. The charge of a woodengraver is 10/- for cutting a full page and 4/- for half a page.

Letter 14. A statement of costs in 1810 reads :

Binding 200 anecdotes at 3*d*. each .	£2	10	0
„ M. Trench's poems . .	0	1	10

(Note : see Mrs. Trench's letters in *Annals of Ballitore* II).

½ ream paper		13	6
Blotting paper and gloss ditto . .			2½
A penknife		2	2
A bottle of Indian rubber . .		2	2
Paid Robert Fayle . . .		8	8 (letter 21)

Printers and publishers mentioned in this series are—Carrick, Collis, Dugdale and Keene of Dublin and Johnson of London.

Maria Edgeworth's association with the publication of Mary Leadbeater's *Cottage Dialogues*, for which she wrote a preface, is discussed in letter 34, and the following remarks made : "While such people as the Edgeworths encourage the printing of *Irish* literature out of *Ireland*, why do we wonder after the present state of the *Irish press* ? "

The next letter conveys an impression of Miss Edgeworth, " She is very low, in stature I mean, not thin nor yet very fat, of a yellow complexion with very ordinary features, her nose rather long but not broad, nor yet very sharp ; her eyes I did not particularly observe, her hair I believe is dark ; her voice is not uncommonly pleasing nor yet very disagreeable ; her countenance is grave and heavy—I don't think she smiled once, her manners are not remarkably fascinating, and to conclude she was in mourning up to the chin."

Carbutt had evidently been commissioned by Mary Leadbeater to interview the Edgeworths (father and daughter) on their proposal to print her *Cottage Dialogues* in England.

Edward Carbutt commenced the study of medicine in 1812 and the correspondence ceased.

b.

33 letters

56. 44 - 77 from Sarah Shackleton to her niece, Elizabeth Leadbeater, between 1804 and 1820—all of family and domestic interest, written from houses of various relations in Ireland—Clogheen, Clonmel, Woodmount, Stramore (N.I.), Carlow, Dublin, Griesebank the home of the Shackletons in Ballitore and Mountmellick.

Sally Shackleton went blind and advice was sought from Dr. Maharg (of Mountmellick) who promised to write to Surgeon Peile. There is little reference here to events in Europe.

Three letters to Elizabeth (Leadbeater) Cole from friends subsequent to her Mother's death in 1826.

c.

78 - 120

57. Letters of Joshua Beale of Myrtle Hill, Cork, to Mary (Shackleton) Leadbeater written at varying dates between 1787 and 1826, there being none from 1789 to 1805. 79 is the rough draft of an appeal for a Charitable Institution (Cork Infirmary) sent with a request to Mary Shackleton to write verses for circulation with a pamphlet asking aid for the charity.

Letter 81 (1788) purports to enclose a letter of Henry Sheares— " A good man," but this has not survived. Mary Shackleton's desire to publish as early as 1788 is alluded to in a letter of advice (84). Later letters refer to her other writings but the majority are concerned with local details and comments on passing events. Mention of the publication of Trotter's *Walks through Ireland* and an extract from it are in letters 97 and 98. The later letters are of much interest in describing the formation of an Anti-Slavery Society in Ireland in 1826, detailing the work being done in Cork by a Committe of all denominations and urging the formation of county committees throughout the country. Petitions to the government were to be signed by all influential and all " respectable " persons, though females were ineligible to sign. The vigour with which the cause was pursued is shown in these letters.

Mary Leadbeater died in June 1826 and this correspondence comes to an end.

II

114 Documents

58. The letters of Elizabeth Leadbeater (later Cole) between 1806 and 1826, written to her sister, Deborah. The first twenty are written while Elizabeth was at Anne Shannon's school at Mountmellick, followed by five from Bloomville, the house of Aunt Harper, near Portarlington. Subsequent letters are written from Ballitore, Clogheen and Youghal while Deborah was at Anne Shannon's school, and just before her marriage, at the age of seventeen, to her cousin, Ebenezer Shackleton, of Moone, Co. Kildare. There are a few letters written by Richard Leadbeater to his sisters, from Green Row School near Whitehaven. They describe his journey there and the school activities.

Elizabeth Leadbeater was a fluent writer and the letters give an insight into local customs, though mainly of a gossiping nature. She obviously played the part of a second mother to the younger members of the Leadbeater family, whose confidences are revealed here. The letters to Deborah end in 1826. They are followed by a few to other members of the family, including one to Mary Leadbeater dated 1823.

The bundle contains, at the back, stitched in, a number of tiny notes written on scraps of paper, the contents being such as would to-day be replaced by telephone messages.

III

a.

133 letters

59. Eight letters from Mrs. C. Harper to her brother, William Leadbeater; one from the latter and three from her husband, Ephraim Harper. A memorandum (13) of his own life written by James Doyle of Cooladine, Wexford, 1716 - 1778. Two scraps of paper, 14 and 15, containing lists of household necessities sent to Athy for the Assizes in 1813 (presumably from William Leadbeater's Inn at Ballitore).

b.

16 - 34

60. Eighteen letters from Mary Davis (later Merryweather) to Richard Shackleton of Ballitore between the years 1784 and 1789, written mainly from Minehead and Milverton, Somerset, and two from Ringwood, Hants., her home after marriage. Mostly of a devotional nature, but include some information of West Country Friends. Two letters of Jno. Davis dated from Waterford.

c.

35 - 55

61. Letters of John Conran and of Louisa Strangman, later Conran, to Richard Shackleton between 1772 and 1788, and one to Mary Leadbeater in 1823 from John Conran. Louisa died in 1805.

d.

56 - 133

Nearly all written to Mary Leadbeater by various friends between 1790 and 1826. Her correspondents were Anne Robinson of Moate ; Mary Pim of Mountmellick, John Walker, who writes in French at the request of Mary Shackleton in 1789 and also sends her a long poem in blank verse and an amusing rhyme ; Anne (Gough) Bewley, daughter of James Gough, a schoolmaster of Dublin—see his life—(Friends Library, 1781). Anne married John Bewley, Dublin, and the correspondence continues from 1777 to 1826, the year of Mary Leadbeater's death. Some of the most interesting letters are from Haarlem, a house near Blessington, to which the Bewleys removed, and where for a time they had a printing works. There is a very detailed account of this house and of its situation below Mount Venus, where Lord Ely's house was already in a ruined condition—letter 109. Many of these letters are written from Mountmellick where Anne Bewley's sister, Mary (Gough) Bewley lived, her husband being Mungo Bewley, brother of John, of Irishtown outside that town. There is some mention of Dr. Jacob who attended the many disorders in that district. John Bewley and Anne finally removed to Ropers Rest, a house in the Donore area of Dublin, letter 133 is dated from there, written to Elizabeth Leadbeater after her mother's death.

There are a few letters with social details of the period. Letter 106 describes the work and wage of a servant in a middle class household. Letter 123 in 1816 discusses the cotton trade in which wages average four to five shillings per week for work done at home, whereas a few years previously 12/- per week could be earned by working hard.

FAMILY COLLECTIONS 77

IV

83 Documents (a) 1 - 61 : (b) 1 - 22

62. This bundle contains 61 childhood letters and documents of Mary Shackleton (later Leadbeater) and her sister Sarah. One or two are from schoolboys, written in both verse and prose ; the remainder are from one sister to the other between the years 1768 and 1772, a period during which long intervals were spent by Mary at the home of her Grandmother and Aunt Carleton at Griese-bank, Ballitore. Sarah appears to have been mainly at the school with her parents. Mary addresses her letters to her there " Noisy-House," while Sarah writes to " Greece-bank," Mary saying " Is not that a pretty name." ?

Four documents take the form of a magazine or journal called *The Retreat Journal* (1774) and *The Retreat Isis* (1776), the name coming from the house to which Richard Shackleton and his wife finally retired in Ballitore. These letters are " not to be shown to any grown up, aunt excepted," and when prose fails the writers sometimes make up for the loss by lapsing into verse.

The last 22 items are apparently a collection for a commonplace book, and a list of clothes to be taken by boys and girls to the Provincial School.

Note : See Ms. Annals 1: 235 for fact that the Retreat was untenanted in 1771.

LECKY LETTERS
405 Documents

63. This collection pertains almost entirely to that branch of the Lecky family which settled in Youghal, Co. Cork, in the middle of the 18th century. The main branch (which appears to have its early roots in Scotland) lived in Donegal in the 17th century, but on intermarrying with the Watson family of Co. Carlow settled, before 1700, at Ballykealy and Kilconnor.

Robert Lecky (1736 - 1772) married Margaret Harvey of Youghal in 1763, daughter of a Cork merchant family, and settled there, dying in 1772 when his son, John, eldest of a family of five, was only eight years old. His widow lived until 1835, having after her husband's death, sustained his business of ships' chandler and supplier.

The family letters of the earlier period reflect the closely interwoven lives of the big Quaker families of Southern Ireland—Fennell, Harvey, Jacob, Fisher, Lecky and Grubb are among the names recurring in the correspondence, providing a background to the picture of Margaret Harvey Lecky and her five growing children. Less ordinary letters are interspersed ; one, No. 5 being from William Fennell to the eccentric Major Eiles, the Tipperary scientist. Fennell sends him a quarter of venison as a mark of gratitude for the major's civility to his daughter and nieces.

The letter—No. 20—of David Heas to his brother, a Catholic priest in Spain, on December 30 (1775) seems inexplicable at first sight in such a collection, but the reference at the end to the safety of addressing letters to Thos. Harvey, jun., of Cork may account for its inclusion. It seems worth reproduction.

Rath Cormk.
Dec., 30th, 1775.

Dear William,

I have here by me your last letter to my father which came to hand only last week bearing no date ; what an absurd blunder and is still, as I observed before, owing to the want of a little attention which in a recluse I think ought to cost but little. We are all proud of your promotion and that you have not been *factus minus habens quando appensus in statera es* ; but I fear the Spanish examinations are as lax as their morals, otherwise I do think you would not have been ordained to that tremendous order of the Hierarchy before you knew the obligations and danger of it ; and without observing the Canonical Interstices, you'll tell me there was a dispensation for them *non-fidelis sanc ut ait S. Bernardus sed crudelis dissipatio* : however, my only consolation in this matter is that I hope you had no hand in it, but passive obedience. Wherefore I pray earnestly that the H. G. may grant you *a mensuram plenam, confertam et coagitatam* of his divine grace to fulfil the obligations annexed to your order, and hope as you have much more time than we have here you will never forget to pray for the grace of final preservance for us all, in particular your father who begins to feel the infirmities incident to old age.

Give all our compliments to your Br. Thomas, is it not singular that having said so much about him you did not say whether he was ordained or not. I am sure he must be as capable of it as you were. Tell him I saw his brother Dennis yesterday and his father lately, and they are all well. I had a long chat with his father about the Dear Provincial, who in fact has paid the debt of nature early last summer ; the present Provincial's nephew has succeeded him ; he told him the money the deceased left for you both he had sent off ; it was the same that had miscarried before. Let me know in your next if ye have got it ; it was 9 guineas if not more. Mrs. Walsh means to write to your brother Thomas.

Do not regret my leaving Ballyhooly *dura enim cervice et in circumcisis cordibus Spiritui Sancto resistunt.* Your poor brother Danl. who is here and brought me your letter, lives still in the same place and means to hold it for a second year. Believe me he is a great charge to me : the rest of your friends are all well and desire to be remembered to you. The only news of consequence we have here is that last year there was an Act of Parliament passed enabling Catholicks to testifie the allegiance to the King and Government, which they are, after many debates, taking very fast ; the last paper gives an acct. that the Archbishop of Cashel, and many of the Gentlemn. Clergy and laity have taken it ; we expect great benefits from it ; Mr. Ryan mentions to me he has taken it ; if you can discharge any Masses I think I can procure you some Intentions from him.

The second piece of news I can give you is an Epidemical disorder which is this season universal over all the North of Europe ; it is called Influensa, it has killed many in England and Holland and in Dublin. Thank God it is not much here, your father has got it at present, I got it last Sunday and am scarce rid of it yet, the Common people call it a cold. I thought it wd. have broke my head ... Our dear Mother may be still in Purgatory, wherefore say some Masses for her and our next deceased relations. I hope I have acted my part hitherto pretty well in regard to them all, but perhaps not sufficient for their poor souls. Write to me by hand as soon as possibly you can, it may be the safest way as our post offices are very failable. Adieu believe to be

Your most affectionate Brother,

David Heas.

P.S. You may always address to Thos. Harvey Junr. when you write to your father or me, or to Mr. Jno. Dannahy, Mercht., Mallow Lane, Corke, when you write to me by hand.

Mind your study of Morality much closer than that of Speculation, and as soon as it is no more to your interest to remain in Spain get your General's recommendatory letter to study Morality in some small College in France, but don't come to Bordeaux.

Hitherto my dear William I must own I have kept a close hand to you, partly in good truth on account of the reasons I gave you in my letter, partly also on account of your natural simplicity knowing how easily you may be choused by wanton monks out of what may be absolutely necessary for yr. poor brothers, but now that I hope you have got more sence I tell you if you say you want it I will share to the last penny of my emoluments with you. I do insist on't that you will let me know what share you have got out of the money of Kingsale Convent since you went abroad, without this never write home, for it is loudly spoke of here.

Addressed to

> Al mui Reverendo Presbitero Senor
> don Guliermo ô Heas guarde Dios muchos anos
> Carmelita Calzado en su Collegio
> de Sn. Alberto en la Ciudad
> de Sivilla
> Espania.*

Margaret Lecky's son, John, (1764 - 1839) is the writer or recipient of the majority of the letters, which begin in his childhood spent with his uncle Francis and aunt Abigail Harvey in Cork. Here he was sent to school, prior to a short period at Ballitore school, after which at the age of 14, he was apprenticed to his uncle, a ship's supplier.

Social details of the period are of interest and value. Quotations of prices prevailing, orders to Youghal for goods to be sent by boat to Cork and vice versa. The advisability of insuring ships. Prices 16th 11 mo. 1798 (letter 95) oats about 7½d. per stone ; barley 10d., wheat 18/- to 23/- ; pigs 22/- ; lard 40/- ; rough tallow 8/8 ; butter (r on board?) 79/- to 80/- ; coarse 75/-, ex 7½ (?) ; potatoes 70/- "looking up," ; kelp 7 guin. (The same letter, from John Lecky to his wife, ends "We began to melt tallow yesterday ; hope thee will be able to bear the smell.") Details of the shipping of pork hams etc. in barrels for vessels for abroad. These items can be found by the discerning among the mass of family detail such as the supervision of a schoolboy's pocket-money at 6½d. a week " to be carefully supervised," the wistful letter of a little Quaker at school in Clonmel who despairs of being able to see the " new regiment of foot now near Cashel " or that of the small boy who looks forward to the drum his uncle will bring him from Cork.

The liberal educational ideas of the Quaker community in Ireland reflect themselves in the variety of interests shown by John Lecky in his later years. The name of his school-master is unspecified, but his period at Ballitore must have been under the famous Richard Shackleton, friend and schoolfellow of Edmund Burke. Lecky's opportunity for travel was limited, but letter 74 to his mother gives a detailed and amusing account of his visit to London Yearly Meeting in 1794, when he saw the

---

* I am indebted to Dr. Micheline Walsh of University College, Dublin, for help in deciphering this letter.

Zoo, studied a steam engine, thinks business slack as the Government very unsettled. During this period in Cork he buys, among other commodities, stone and potash from Washington; and his mother writing from Waterford requests supplies of silks, tea, cheese, calico and " sugar if dry." Imports of tea includes " Congo and Hypon."

John Lecky became an astute business man, later known as " Lecky the Banker," but his personal tastes lay in the field of astronomy, an interest shared by his brother-in-law, Richard Jacob. Among some of the correspondents in this collection are Lord Donoughmore (a dinner invitation to John Lecky), Roger Dartnell, Sir William Herschel, the astronomer, and Dr. J. Longfield enclosing precision tables for astronomical work, (some of Longfield's effects were bought at his death by John Lecky and were later deposited in the South Kensington Science Museum).

In 1816 (letter 134) a letter from Richard Sainthill, jnr., in London, employed by the mint, requires an accurate drawing of a shamrock which is to be used as a design for Irish coins (this was made by Susannah, daughter of John Lecky, and sent to the mint but the shamrock was never used on coins).

Letter number 55 is from J. Brinkley of Dunsink Observatory, written on August 14, 1819 and thanking John Lecky for his observations on the Comet of that year, saying that they closely coincide with those made at the observatory and giving a table of comparison, and drawing attention to the observations published in the Dublin Journal of July 14th. This is a long letter and encloses a table of Pole Star and Polaris variations. It concludes with an appreciation of the fact that Lecky's Transit Instrument is in requisition for ascertaining " the (reading) of the chronometre, which must be of great importance to ships putting in at Cove."

By his marriage to Susannah, daughter of Joseph and Hannah Jacob of Waterford, John Lecky cemented the close business connections of the Munster Quaker trading families, and while the majority of the letters between 1771 and 1810 are of family interest only, there are interspersed, many references to costs, to modes of transport, and to the procuring of supplies and materials which add value and interest. The first reference to his banking interest is in 1810, (letter 116) when a letter is addressed : —Newenham and Lecky, Bankers, Cork.

Many letters are to and from his daughter, Hannah, (married to Joseph Pim), whose lively mind shared many of his interests; e.g. a lecture on the Deaf and Dumb, a visit to the College Museum, a journey by stage coach from Holyhead to Liverpool, which includes a " human ferry " at Conway.

As his family grew up, John Lecky expressed anxiety that every opportunity for a broad education should be used to advantage in spite of limited means. The letters passing to and fro between parents and children while his younger daughters were at school at Clonmel, and his son, Robert John, at Ballitore, are of more than casual interest, as are those to Hannah Pim.

As his son grew out of the childish attitude to school, the correspondence between father and son on scientific matters foreshadows the future of the son who became a Marine engineer.

The period covered includes the formation of the Royal Cork Institute, the building of a private observatory in Cork and the importation of telescopes for it, the comet of 1819 and the eclipse of the sun of the following year, all of which are noted and commented on by this intelligent circle. Electricity and electric experiments, the first lighting of the streets of Dublin and Cork by gas, the problems of coach travel when cross country connections were scarce, all provide, with much else of value, material for the domestic historian. Allusions can be found to some of the bank failures of the south of Ireland about 1820, which affected many traders.

Document 217 is a partial copy of a letter from Sir Thomas Brisbane to John Lecky after the appointment of the former to the Governorship of New South Wales. It outlines the many improvements intended by the new Governor, particularly in the better employment of convict labour.

Though this correspondence covers the whole period of the Napoleonic Wars, the growth of the United Irishmen, " the 1798 " and the rise of Daniel O'Connell, there appears throughout little of interest in political activities, or indeed little outside the immediate life of these County Cork Friends.

This is not due to ignorance of events—Robert John Lecky's school letters ask that newspapers may be sent to him " not those taken by other boys "—but rather to the realisation of the fullness of life close at hand.

A letter (222) of 4/3/1822 does indeed describe the lawlessness of the country—fighting in parts, 12 persons hanged, " Worse in Limerick " country parts proclaimed and a 9 a.m. curfew. A shopkeeper had been tried for selling gunpowder, and being " a novel case " had been sent to the Assizes. The same letter speaks of the " Union of Trades " being pretty quiet, and also of a very large American ship being at

FAMILY COLLECTIONS 83

Lecky's Quay where her materials and the ship were sold by auction. Two others having discharged their cargoes of iron and cotton " we are now busy killing and singeing 400 pigs."

Included in the letters is a small sketch by Crofton Croker, who was a friend of the Lecky family and who in 1824 asked John Lecky to help him on the proposed second edition of his History of the South of Ireland. He needed to revise the chapter on Youghal and appended to the letter are Lecky's suggestions. Also included is a small sketch book of water colours done by Susannah Lecky, daughter to John.

GRUBB COLLECTION

This Collection, which is the largest in the Library, consisting of several thousands of documents of a varying nature was collected and kept by the family in Clonmel until the death of Susanna Grubb youngest daughter of Joseph Grubb (Benjamin) in 1911. She left them to her nephew Joseph Ernest Grubb whose son and daughter presented them to the Friend's Historical Library in 1947. The careful arrangement of the papers was made by Isabel Grubb prior to the gift to the library and the full catalogue which now accompanies the papers was made by Muriel Hicks in 1959.

The Grubb family removed to Ireland from England as planters in the 17th century. Settling for a short time in Kilkenny county they then removed to Tipperary. Most of the following records pertain to that branch of the family which settled in Clonmel.

Box I

S.C.I NOS. I - 7

64. A bundle of miscellaneous documents relating to Clonmel Charities, etc.

Clonmel Famine Relief Committee Book, 1846 -7. A record of the day to day visits paid, by rotation, by the members of the local Famine Relief Committee with their comments on the work done. It begins on the 11th of 9th month 1846, and the last entry is that of 12th April, 1847. On the end page is the recipe for making porridge from Indian meal and oatmeal, which was the fare for Fridays instead of the usual meat soup. The highest amount of soup distributed is shown in the entry for 6th of 3rd month 1847, when 940 gallons had been given out before the close of the day. The signature of the women visiting are given— among the names being Strangman, Grubb, Greer, Murray, Davis, Bell, Sargint, Strene, Jacob, Murphy, Moore, Malcomson, Boyd, Worrall, Wilkinson, Phelan and Lane.

S.C.2

64 (contd.). Minute Book of a Committee set up in Carrick-on-Suir in 1885, to administer a fund for the Relief of unemployed men, who, on making application to the Board of Guardians for assistance, refused the only relief in the power of the Board—viz. admission to the workhouse. The scheme ended in 1886 for lack of funds. A letter from J. Ernest Grubb to his sisters, Anna and Lydia Grubb, is enclosed.

S.C.3

65. Proceedings of the Annual Meetings of the subscribers to the Clonmel Lying-In Institution. Minutes from 5th of 1st month 1854 to 8th of 1st month 1874, and two Committee Meeting Minutes of 1857, when a new matron was appointed, the previous one not being willing to remain at a salary of £6 per annum.

The Treasurer's accounts are included for each year, and there are also printed balance sheets for the years 1849 and 1874, which include the names of subscribers.

S.C.4

66. Minutes of the Committee Meetings of Clonmel Charitable School for the years 31/12/1861 to 23/7/1863, when it closed for lack of pupils, and for the year 1883 when the Committee met twice for the purpose of winding up the affairs of the school, the remaining funds being devoted to the support of a night school at the Literary Institute.

The Committee which met in 1863 were Martha Riall, Anna M. Baker, Lydia Grubb, and Susa Grubb. Two of these members, Anna Maria Baker and Susa Grubb, were on the 1883 Committee when it was stated that Lydia Grubb, the treasurer, had died in 1881. Rules for conducting the school, printed in 1790, are included in this section, together with reports (printed) for the years 1809, 1836, 1858, 1859 and 1862.

S.C.5

67. The original Minutes of the Meeting called to establish a Sunday and Day Charitable School in Clonmel, dated 3rd Dec. 1789, and giving a list of annual subscribers numbering 156.

The Minutes of six Committee Meetings held in 1790 follow, with the names of those willing to act as visitors. There is a statement of accounts for 1862 with a list of subscribers, (fallen to 46), and a letter of acknowledgment from the Literary Institute of Clonmel for £63. A statement signed J.E.G. (J. Ernest Grubb) dated 19/XII/(19)05 follows giving a brief resume of the affairs of the school, quoting the will of Robert Grubb of Suir Island who demised premises and money for the education of poor children in 1797.

s.c.6

68. " The House Book of Sarah Grubb of Anner Mills 1779." In 1778 Sarah Pim of Tottenham, London, married John Grubb, of Anner Mills, near Clonmel, Ireland, and this appears to be her first housekeeping account book, which she classified by pages labelled, Butchers meat, Fish, Poultry, (two fowls 1/1, 4 couple chickens 3/8*d*.), Bread, Beer, Cyder, Wine, Spirits, (a gallon of rum from William Boddy 6/-), Groceries, Garden etc., etc. She only kept it thus for a year, and the remainder of the book is dated subsequent to her husband's death in 1784, and is erratic and involved, though obviously her future son-in-law, John Barclay Clibborn, who came as clerk to the mill in 1786, did his best to sort out her affairs, as evinced by his appended dockets re servants' wages.

s.c.7

69. Account book of Rebecca Grubb of Carrick-on-Suir, apparently in account with Benjamin Grubb as her Trustee 1844 - 1875.

s.g.a. (4 Folders)

70. A collection of documents and letters of the 17th and 18th centuries relating to the Grubb family.

Thirty-seven documents, many being copies—all of considerable interest.

Folder 1

A copy of the demand made by King Charles I in 1642 on John Grubb, then in England, for £200 in money or plate for the King's support— to be repaid with interest (doc. 1).

Folder 2

71. Copies of the marriage certificate, with a family list, of John Grubb (- 1731) and Ann Willan (1688 - 1765), (doc. 2). Copies of the Wills of William, 1705, and of Mary Willan of Forrest, Co.

Wexford (c/f *Quaker Wills, Eustace* & *Goodbody*), with a full inventory, (doc. 3). Original certificates from Wexford Monthly Meeting to Tipperary Monthly Meeting for John (and by implication Ann) Willan on the 27th of 5th month, 1719.

Folder 3.
9 documents. 4a to 12

72. All relating to the removal of John Grubb to America, where he was hired to build a boat for Francis Annesley, a Bristol Friend. His certificate, 1727, Kilconnor (4a), his letters to his sons from Rancocas (5), list of goods taken with him and his losses by tythes (6). Original returning certificate from Burlington to Kilconnor (7) 1731, signed by 19 Friends. Original Testimonial of Freeholders and Officers of the County of Burlington, America, to John Grubb testifying to his honesty and good repute, 1730, (doc. 8).

Copy of letter to Francis Annesley signed by eleven Friends of New Jersey, 1730 (9).

Letter of Amelia Gummere to Isabel Grubb with detail of research done into the affairs of John Grubb, and the ship he built, 1730 (doc.10).

Original testimonial to John Grubb signed by 17 Friends of New Jersey (doc. 11).

Letter of John Grubb to his son Joseph, dated from Rathronan, 173(8) (doc. 12). The date on this is indecipherable. It is probably a letter of John Grubb who died in 1731 (birth date unknown). It is addressed to son, Joseph, in Waterford giving advice as to keeping Jonny (or Tommy) in his present situation.

Folder 4
24 documents, 1755 - 1799. 13 - 37

73. Letters with a few other documents such as a statement of accounts of the estate of T. Wiley in 1782, to which a long list of names is attached (doc. 27). There are letters to Benjamin Grubb from Joseph Hatton, Eliza Tomey, Robert Dudley, Susannah Lightfoot, Samuel Neale (travelling in England) and an acknowledgment of promissory notes due to George Newsom of Cork, together with sundry other letters to members of the Grubb family. Also the original notice, which was pasted on to the door of Benjamin Grubb's house during the rebellion of 1798, giving the names of persons resident in the house.

S.G.B./I

4 Folders. Letters 1 - 62

Letters, etc., pertaining to the Grubb family of Anner Mills, near Clonmel.

74. Anner Mills, standing about 3 miles from Clonmel, were built by Joseph Grubb, son of John and Ann (Willan) in 1765, and the adjoining house was, until lately, the property of descendants of the family.

Folder 1

Letters 1 - 14, 1771 - 1779 and one of 1754

The first letter from Dublin to " Dear Cousin " in America signed " Elizabeth Pike," in 1754, mentions recipient's uncle, Samuel Peisley. Records and accounts by James Pim of state of Meetings in the North of Ireland (where " things seem dull ") and in Leinster and Munster, where a large visitation is extended to the youth. Many by name, including " Uncle Judd," send love.

Most of the remaining letters in this section are between the Shackleton family of Ballitore, and their friends, Sarah and Elizabeth Pim, who, with their parents and large family of brothers and sisters, had removed to London. Of this Pim family the eldest, Sarah, married in 1778 John Grubb, by then the owner of Anner Mills, and thereafter lived in Ireland, becoming, after her husband's death in 1784, one of the most prosperous millers of Southern Ireland. Two letters are from Catherine Phillips, well known as a Minister in the Religious Society of Friends.

Folder 2

Letters 15 - 31. 1779 - 1798

75. All these are of interest in varied fashion. No. 16 has a note of John Gough's projected History of Friends, an account of Philadelphia Yearly Meeting of 1784, and a subsequent journey towards Carolina. The prospect of opening a boarding school for girls in Clonmel is mooted in letter 18.

Letter 21, written in 1788, gives an account of the successful efforts made by the Comte de Vergennes to procure recognition for French Protestants. Thomas Lightfoot, writing from Pikeland (date obliterated), letter 25, refers to the Lots at Port Royal, regarding which he had been sued by Charles Hurst—action abandoned and Hurst paid rents accruing to 1790, Lightfoot's securities being Neale, Baker and Abel. Richard Frampton of Bristol, applying through Robert Dudley, to have shares in Lots.

In 1798 David Sands of America was in Ireland (letter 28). In that year Quarterly Meeting was held as usual in Enniscorthy on the day after the battle of Vinegar Hill, and letter 29 describes the conditions. The following two letters set forth reasons why Friends should not accept public relief, the difficulties of business, the shortage of coin and the formation of a Quaker fund for public assistance, from which upwards of 2,200 were helped.

Folder 3
Letters 32 - 50, 1798 - 1809

76. All but four are to Sarah Grubb whose hospitality at Anner Mills made her the recipient of many letters conveying thanks and giving particulars of travelling Friends. Among the writers were David Sands, Sarah Stephenson, (making a family visit in Ireland), Samuel Smith, Frederick Smith, who is concerned by the appeal of " H(annah) B(arnard) in the case of proceedings against her at Devonshire House, the Meeting there not approving of her Deistic views, and Richard Jordan who had a perilous voyage from America, and writes from Falmouth. The next letter (41) describes his return journey and gives his address as c/o Robert Browne, Pearl Street, New York, or Thomas Stewardson, Auk Street, Philadelphia.

A long letter from Lindley Murray, Holdgate, near York, to Abigail Pim in Dublin defends his use, in his writings, of fictitious, romantic and martial passages, though of the last he does not understand to what she has alluded (letter 43). Thomas Scattergood of America, in writing to thank Sarah Grubb, wishes to be rememberd to " the little captive maid, S.L.", this allusion being to Sarah Lynes of England who later married John Grubb (1766 - 1841), and became an eminent woman preacher. Thomas Shillitoe wrote from Cork and Lurgan, in both of which places he was concerned in family visits, (45 and 46). In Cork alone he paid above 100 visits.

Folder 4
Letters 51 - 62, 1811 - 1854

77. There are among these, several allusions of the Gurney family of Earlham (of whom Elizabeth Fry was one). Hannah Pim writing to her niece, Elizabeth Clibborn, in 1810, alludes to the adoption of the " plain dress " by Priscilla Gurney (57). Letters 56 and 58 are from Priscilla Gurney at Milford and at Earlham (the Gurney home), to Elizabeth Clibborn at Anner Mills.

The cholera outbreak of 1832 is noted (60), and a long account of the death, by fire, in America of A. A. Jenkins and her daughter (60a).

The visit of Joseph Sturge, Robert Charlton and Henry Pease to Petersburg on a deputation to the Czar in 1854 was well received (61) by the Russian Prime Minister, who was to introduce them, with their message condemning all war, in two or three days time.

Box II
S.G.B./2
Documents 1 - 90 in four folders, pertaining to the Grubb family of Anner Mills

Folder 1
16 Documents (1-16), 1766 - 1788

78. Varied letters of family interest, fragments of diaries and an account in a small notebook of the visit in 1766 to London Yearly Meeting by John Grubb of Anner Mills, giving names of accompanying Friends and of those by whom they were given hospitality. The second part of the book contains a number of business entries, many being orders for wool, yarn, etc., to be fulfilled on return to Ireland. The letters include those of Sarah Grubb and other relatives.

Letter 12 is labelled original, but seems more likely to be a copy, kept by Sarah Grubb, of that written to her brother soon after the death of her husband, John Grubb. It is a remarkable exposition by a woman who, whilst still young realised to the full, the implications of continuing the administration of her late husband's business without the entanglements of partnership, and yet with the knowledge that only by the aid of competent clerks could she achieve success. Subsequent justification of her decision appears throughout the later letters of this collection.

Folder 2
Letters 17 - 37, 1789 - 1808

79. Of these, ten are letters dated from Anner Mills, written between Sarah Grubb and her family and close acquaintances, Number 27 is an extract from the early part of the journal of Elizabeth, eldest daughter of Sarah Grubb. It records the engagement, while visiting London, of Sarah Lynes, who married John Grubb (1766 - 1841), son of Benjamin. She was a noted Minister in the Religious Society of Friends, especially after her removal with her husband to Suffolk in 1818.

Letter 32 records the gift by Sarah Grubb of £100 each to her nephew, Richard, and three nieces, Ann, Sarah and Margaret, on their decision to carry on business at Clogheen, thereby revoking a codicil to her Will.

Documents 35, 36 and 37 are respectively an appreciation of David Barclay, d. 1809 (grandson of Robert Barclay, the Quaker apologist), and two letters from him to his cousin, John Barclay Clibborn.

Folder 3
38 - 60, 1811 - 1832

80. Testimonies to Sarah (Pim) Grubb, 1832, to John Pim of Belfast, 1811, and to Elizabeth, daughter of John Barclay and Elizabeth Clibborn, 1829, occupy eight of these documents. Two (nos. 41 and 42) are intimations of gifts made by Sarah Grubb to reduce the debt on Newtown School, the first sent to Joseph Strangman, 4th 8th month 1818, for deposit in Newports Bank, (Waterford); the second to Samuel Alexander on 19th of 9th mo. 1818. Amongst these papers is a finely wrought silhouette of Rebecca, d. of John and Sarah Grubb of Anner Mills.

Folder 4
61 - 90, 1837 - 1886

81. This folder consists entirely of personal recollections, letters, appreciations, and genealogical details of the families of Grubb and Clibborn, in whose possession Anner Mills House remained for 200 years. In many cases the documents are duplicated elsewhere, as Elizabeth Clibborn (born Grubb) left copious accounts of the family to each surviving member of her family before she died in 1861. Her descendants include members of the Grubb, Pim, Goodbody, Newsom, Richardson, Clibborn, Greer, Pike, Haughton and Malcomson families.

S.G.C.

One Folder—47 documents (not in chronological order) ,1787 - 1842.

82. A miscellaneous collection of letters and documents, mostly relating to Joseph Grubb (1768 - 1844) and his family. Letter No. 2 is an extract of a letter from Münster, Germany, giving particulars of the itinerary, the Meetings held and the persons met by Sarah (Tuke) Grubb, written to her husband, Robert, on 9th of 11th month 1790. His letter to " Uncle Richard Shackleton " accompanies it.

The question of buying sugar, gained by slave labour, occupied the thoughts of many Friends at this time, and document 3 is a printed slip saying that John and Joseph Grubb " respectfully inform their customers that they will discontinue the sale of West India sugar when present stocks are exhausted." Other allusions to this appear through the letters.

Statements of accounts for the meal fund administered for necessitous poor in 1800, and prices paid, appear in documents 4 and 5.

In 1825 Col. Bagwell proposed to erect a building for the Clonmel Savings Bank (letter 25). This letter also contains part of a correspondence arising out of the question of the pre-payment of Government duty on sugar, there being no redress when the ship containing it foundered.

A proposed private Society for collecting and diffusing information relative to the conditions of argicultural labourers in Ireland is contained in a letter written to Joseph Grubb from William Allen in Stoke Newington in 1827. The analogous Society proposes to correspond with a Committee in Dublin. Letters had been received from the Dukes of Bedford and Wellington, the latter having asked William Allen to call on him (letters 26 and 27).

Letter 39 is a strong criticism by Joseph Grubb of the publication of memoirs, lives, journals, etc., of Friends, by John Barclay, which Grubb apprehends have not been submitted to the Morning Meeting of the Society as was customary. Letter 40 is a full reply by John Barclay from Stoke Newington.

The plans of Roland Hill for new postage are criticised in letter 41, it being thought that such a decrease in the revenue will occasion the imposition of a new tax.

The collection contains many letters relative to visits to Yearly Meetings, and ends with a full account of the reception given to the deputation of the Religious Society of Friends at Dublin Castle on the occasion of the presentation of addresses to King George IV by Church bodies in 1821.

S.J.
JACOB - LECKY LETTERS
335 Documents. 1722 - 1855

83. The family of Jacob originated in Somerset, migrating to Ireland about 1764, and settling first in Cork, then in Waterford, intermarrying with many of the well known Irish Quaker families of Munster. Most of the following series of letters passed between the family of Thomas Strangman Jacob of Waterford and that of John Lecky of Cork, whose wife was a sister to Thomas S. Jacob.

S.J.
JACOB FAMILY LETTERS

Folders (1) 1675 - 1722 (25 letters 1 - 25)
       (2) 1772 - 1778 (25 letters 26—50)
       (3) 1785 - 1790 (25 letters 51—75)

84. These are of family interest but contain some items of social value, a few giving prices of commodities viz : letter 50. Bullocks 5½ cwt. 17/6d.; letter 58, prices of commodities from America, going through customs at Waterford. Letter 1 contains the testimony of Waterford Meeting to Joseph Jacob 1675 - 1722, and No. 2 is an account of Elizabeth Head, later Jacob.

Among the names in this series are, besides the Strangman, Jacob and Lecky families, Susanna Hatton, Anne Fothergill, R. Gurney, Sarah Broadbent, John Petters, William Weldon, James Gough. Many letters are from Thomas Jacob (son of Joseph) to his brother-in-law, John Lecky of Cork. Letter 57 is a description of a journey to Youghal riding via Wexford, Waterford and Clonmel. 66 speaks of danger, by storm, to ships returning from Newfoundland. Subscriptions have been raised to send a succour ship. This had been gone a week with provisions. A premium of five guineas was to be paid for every ship aided with over 50 passengers, and one guinea for those with a lesser number. Letter 70 is from Thomas Lecky, apprenticed to the Grubbs of Anner Mills, Clonmel. Hopes to understand all milling on leaving there. Corn prices quoted—a tendency to fall.

Folders   (4)   1790 - 1796 (25 letters 76—100)
             (5)   1796 - 1797 (25 letters 101—125)
             (6)   1798 Jan. to June (25 letters 126—150)
             (7)   1798 - 1799 (25 letters 151—175)

85. Many references to trading and prices occur in the earlier letters. Thomas Harvey writes to John Lecky in 1793 ' Pork to be sold 62/- to 64/- per barrel ' (85). Potash prices and the French embargo on goods (88).

In 1795 cargoes of Newfoundland oil were shipped from Galway on the sloop " Friendship " (96). In 1796 the price paid for kelp was £4. During that year a British landing was made in the Bay of Bulls, Newfoundland, but ships and stores lost (115). Many failures occurred in Southern Ireland and allusions are made to losses by French ships of war. Prices in November 1796 - Pigs 32/- to 33/-, wheat 26/- to 27/-, oats 7/7d. to 8/8d., barley 16/- to 18/- (118). Mould candles were shipped to the West Indies.

Newtown School was started in 1798 with seven girls and eight boys. There are several allusions to the school in the series. Many prices quoted : kelp, potash, soap, salt, pork, etc. Ether was used to relieve T. Jacob's gout (126).

Letter 137 is a transcript of one written from Carlow (in May 1798) where the effects of the rebellion were serious. Subsequent letters allude to subscriptions raised to help distress and hardship, particularly in the town of Ross. Thomas Jacob in Waterford being disturbed at night to let in soldiers, had now fixed two rooms so that he could 'lodge all without being in the house.'

Arrangements were made to hold the Quarterly Meeting at Enniscorthy in spite of war, and disturbance throughout the country, (letters 148 and 149).

The ship "John and Susan," captain James Tuckett sailed for Newfoundland from Waterford in August 1798, taking pork from Thomas Jacob. In November he awaited shipping to despatch 3,000 barrels of oats. In February 1799 prices in Waterford were soap 54/- wholesale, 56/- housekeeper's; dipt candles 8/-, molds 9/6 to 10/-; rough lard 40/-, best rendered white 50/- to 52/-; potash 70/- to 73/-. "Kelp scarce, I believe as would sell for 68/-, would it be safe to ship tallow and lard with the cotton? I thought it seemed very damp and perhaps danger of heating." (157, 161, 164). The latter letter has a pattern of drab linen attached and asks for similar material to be bought. A subsequent letter speaks of the use of kilns for drying the cotton.

S.J.

(8) 1799 - 1805 (25 letters 176—200)
(9) 1805 - 1817 (25 letters 201—225)
(10) 1817 - 1822 (25 letters 226—250)

86. Most of these letters are between the Jacob family of Waterford and Clonmel and John and Susannah Lecky of Youghal. Many give valuable social detail and mention prevailing prices. Letter 177 is addressed to John Lecky "Bank," Cork and 179 asks for the name of the person in London who engraved wood plates for Lecky's banknotes. Isaac Jacob writes from Clonmel in 1802 (182) wanting 300 flour bags as soon as possible. This is endorsed 5th of 1st mo. 'Harvey Lecky, 140 bags at 2/2d.; J. B. Haughton 160 at ditto.' Richard Jacob writing in 1803 asks for advice on the question of having dealings with "Le Mesurier" or "Mesuriam House, London." The connection between John Lecky, of Lecky and Mark, and George Newenham's Bank, Cork is noted (187).

Trade in potash, kelp, grease and tallow, as well as butter and Newfoundland oil is mentioned, and ham, cotton and deerskins arrived in 1806 from America on the vessel 'Active'—Captain McKeown.

A letter from Joseph Jackson to John Lecky asks for help in obtaining the release of an apprentice from the Tipperary Militia. A law suit involving Newtown School is mentioned in 199.

There is a two year gap in the letters here, the next one (203) giving prices in 12th month 1808—butter 110/- and 7/7d. Pigs, scalded 41/- to 43/-, singed 44/-,—rough lard about 80/-.

John Lecky's new house (Laurel Lodge) in Cork is described in rhyme (204—206). Letters from Cirencester are dated from David Dent's Seminary and transactions in antiquarian coins found locally are alluded to.

Only one mention of European affairs occurs. " What wonderful news came yesterday about Buonaparte " (216). Letter 223 contains observations on the eclipse of the sun 7th of 9th mo. (1817) and 223a consists of two cartoons of which a note on the back says " Believed to be H. Jacob's copy of two of Mr. MacClise's grotesque pack of cards, in the possession of R. Sainthill." Four letters (226—229) are written by W. W. Phelps in 1817 from Corpus Christie College, Oxford, and from ' Wilton.' They are deeply religious. One compares the merits of Oxford University with Trinity College, Dublin, stating that the advantages of the former do not outweigh the difficulty of entry.

In 1819 Butter was 110/-, bacon hogs 52/-, scalded 45/6d. In the same year the creditors of Isaac and Samuel Jacob met and appointed as trustees, Chas. Riall, David Malcomson and Josh Grubb (Benj.). Later (December) in the same year prices are again quoted; butter 83/-, pork 38/- to 44/-, singed 42/- to 44/-; wheat 31/6d., oats 12/-, barley 14/- to 17/-.

Letter 247 is from Marmaduke Trattle to " Friend Jacob " dated March 5th, 1821 from Rectory House, London Wall, making enquiries about purchasing a collection of ancient coins.

(11) 1822 - 1825 (25 letters 251—275)
(12) 1825 - 1830 (25 letters 276—300)
(13) 1831 - 1852 (35 letters 301—335)

87. Most of the letters 251 to 300 are addressed to Susanna Lecky by her brothers, Thomas Strangman, Jacob and Isaac Jacob, and a few by her nephews, Isaac and Thomas. The business of Thomas S. Jacob declined from 1822 to 1825 when he became bankrupt. Letters 277 and 278 give a full description of his appearance before the Commissioners in bankruptcy, written to his brother-in-law, John Lecky. 261 is from Hannah Kilham to the girls of Suir Island School, dated from

Dublin, June 3rd 1823, asking them to visit and help to clothe "the sickly and feeble infants who lie in their mothers' laps in the spinning room of the Mendicity Institute in Clonmel." 266 raises the interesting problem of the insertion of a second Christian name to that given in registration in infancy. Mountmellick Meeting had raised the query in connection with Susanna Eustace who added the name Fennell while at school. Isaac Jacob, writer of the letter, writes for advice. He has added the name Thomas after Isaac, and now is about to apply for a certificate of clearness to marry. 270 states ' John is going to England, the income from his profession in Dublin being very small.' Several of his drawings of the dissection of the eye have been published in the Medico-Chirurgical journal.' Letters 309 to 316 are out of place, being dated 1847 - 1855. They include death of Thomas Jacob (son of Thomas S.) while doing famine relief work. Costs for a patient at the Retreat (Donnybrook) are in letter 322—shoes 7/-, repairs to shoes 1/3d. and 2/-, cloth for trousers 4/6d., trimmings 7½d., making 2/6d. ; taylor for sundry repairs 3/6d.; snuff ½ oz. weekly for 52 weeks at 3d.—13/-.

Letter 334 is an extract, undated, describing the welcome home to Boston of Sybil Narcissus Jacob, daughter of Eli and Sybil Jones.

Box VII

GRUBB-LECKY LETTERS

1 Folder

22 Documents, 1764 - 1884

88. The first letter written in 1764 is concerned with the opening of the new boarding school for girls at Edenderry. No suitable master having yet been found for the boys' side of the school, the opening of this is deferred.

The following two sheets are proceedings of the school Committee. Prices of flour in 1790 are quoted in letter 2. Letter 3 is a description of London Yearly Meeting in 1794. The remainder of the letters are at widely spaced intervals between 1803 and 1884, giving some prices, etc. Letter 12 consists of an extract from a letter of 1823 written by Sir John Brisbane to John Lecky dated from Government House, Paranatta, New South Wales. Observations are made on experiments conducted to ascertain the affects of climatic conditions on sheep. Also notes on the growth of tobacco and cotton in the Colony, and various astronomical notes.

Adam Calvert of Thomas Street, Dublin, is to employ Joseph Samuel Grubb at £40 per annum (14).

Letter 17 describes the discovery of a vein of amethyst in Blackrock, Cork, with other mineralogical detail. The same letter notes Daniel O'Connell's strong speech at the annual anti-slavery Meeting in Cork City, 1830. Tonnage and price of two sailing ships at Cork in 1845 in letter 21.

Robert J. Lecky recalls in letter 22, dated 1884, his arrival at Ballitore School in 1821, " the year in which King William III statue in College Green was draped in orange and blue for the last time."

S.L.

GRUBB-LYNES LETTERS

1 Folder

1—58. 1773 - 1842

89. Letters of Sarah Lynes before her marriage to John Grubb of Clonmel. She was the daughter of a sail and spar maker of Wapping. At the age of 14 years she came to Ireland to care for the five children of the lately widowed Sarah (Pim) Grubb of Anner Mills, Clonmel. The earlier letters describe her care of the children, being written in the absence from home of their mother. Gradually she acquired the gift of preaching, for which she became later famous, and later letters are written while at Meetings in Cork, Waterford and in London, and other parts of England.

S.N.

NEWSOM FAMILY LETTERS

1 Folder

1—129. 1820 - 1850

90. All family personal letters to various members of the Newsom family of Mount Wilson, Edenderry, and to the branches of the family in Cork and Limerick. They are all written between 1820 and 1850.

Two correspondents outside the immediate family are Thomas Chandlee of Fermoy, and Sarah Pim, aged 83, then of Ballitore. The letters of the latter are mostly dated 1850 and discuss the problem of her income, most of which came from rents, seldom paid, owing to the state of the country.

S.P.
STRANGMAN-PIM LETTERS

1—35

91. A miscellaneous collection between the Strangman family of Waterford and that of James Pim of Grange Lodge, Mountmellick, mainly between the years 1800 and 1860.

The first, however, is dated 12th of 4th mo. 1780, from Mary Strangman to her sons, Joseph and Samuel, at Jacob Cras, Waginigen, Guelderland—abjures them to write once a week, is glad Providence has preserved them in the dangers of the voyage.

The last letter, dated April 12, 1860, is an account of a journey in South America, written by James Pim Strangman.

S.S.
SHACKLETON-PIM LETTERS

S.S. 1—60

92. Letters of Richard Shackleton of Ballitore between the years 1770 and 1792, except No. 1 which is dated 1757 and addressed to Catherine Payton shortly after the death of Mary (Peisley) Neale. Most are to Elizabeth, daughter of John Pim of Tanner's End, London, with whom he kept a lively correpondence from the time of the departure of the Pim family who had lived in Ballitore. Many letters were written to Anner Mills, Clonmel, where Elizabeth Pim made her home with her married sister, Sarah Grubb.

Document 17 contains copies of three letters to John Pim from Joseph Grubb, Richard Shackleton and John Grubb prior to the proposal of the latter for the hand of Sarah Pim in 1776. A letter (47) of Elizabeth Pim to Richard Shackleton mentions James and Richard Abell, David Malcomson, Richard Gurney, ' Aunt Pike,' R. and Mary Dudley, J. and M. Eliot and one to Addy Bellamy which (in 1788) encloses a copy of a letter of E. Marcillac concerning the method of bestowing civil rank, in France, on Protestants, in which the Society of Friends were to participate, and outlining the broad principles envisaged. 51 and 52 allude to William Leadbeater and to his forthcoming marriage (1791) to Mary Shackleton, daughter of Richard.

S.Y.

93. An account written by Benjamin Grubb, son of Joseph, of his visit to London Yearly Meeting in May, 1830, including the journeys to and fro.

z.

94. Four commonplace books containing copies of letters, testimonies, extracts, etc., apparently kept by Benjamin Grubb (1805 - 1858). Many are of 17th century origin. These have now been indexed, and Books 1 and 2 fully catalogued. Two further books of a similar nature, unindexed. A bound collection of essays, mainly scientific, written by boys of Newtown school, c.1855. (Similar books are preserved at Newtown School).

Four bound testimonies, Thomas Godfrey Power, Margaret Grubb, Jane Jacob, all of Clonmel, and John Grubb of Bury. Recollections of Eliza Clibborn of Clonmel, two diaries of Lydia Grubb for 1846 and 1847 containing soup kitchen accounts and records. Two volumes of miscellaneous letters. Extracts from memoranda of Anne Grubb. Brief account of the establishment of Suir Island School. Names of Friends from England and America who visited Ireland 1756 to 1861. The mathematics book of Mary Jacob at Suir Island School c.1821. A volume of poetry and poetical extracts.

s.

95. 208 miscellaneous documents relating to the Society of Friends between 1668 and 1869. Of much interest are 17th century marriage certificates (some with original signatures); an account written by Ann Wright (—— 1670) of her visit to King Charles II 1670—(appears to be original); an address to King James II, 1687 from the Society of Friends in the handwriting of Thomas Ellwood (1639 - 1713); a list of times of Meetings for the Province of Munster, 1695; a direction for the aid to be given to James Russell by the purchase of cows, of which he is to have the produce; a statement of the times of Munster Meetings 1694 - 1775 and a list of Meeting Houses and private houses registered for Meetings in Tipperary in 1719 (doc. 52); nineteen papers relating to education 1680 - 1904 include quotations from George Fox on the care of youth, 1680. Document 171 notes the connection between the Yearly Meeting of Ireland and that of London.

An extract from the will of Joseph Grubb (Benj.) mentions property in Clonmel, Ballyvaden and Cloneheen (Tipperary), College Green (Dublin), Ballybrumhill (Carlow), lands of Boythenrath (called Belleview Park) and Cashel. Also testimonies, Epistles, advice and letters.

Catalogued in the Grubb index.

FAMILY COLLECTIONS 99

PART OF BOX II, BOXES III AND IV, PART OF V

S.G.D.

LETTERS OF JOHN GRUBB (1766 - 1841)

96. This collection of 695 letters is contained in boxes, divided by folders. John, son of Benjamin Grubb was a partner with his brother Joseph (1768 - 1844) in the grocery and general merchant trade in Main street, Clonmel. All the letters are written from England to Joseph between the years 1789 and 1841, and many of them contain allusions to prices and the state of trade between Ireland and England, as well as a great deal of information concerning the Religious Society of Friends, family matters, and political controversy, particularly, that of the Slave Trade. John Grubb married, in 1803, Sarah Lynes an Englishwoman who for some years in her early youth was governess to the family of Sarah Grubb of Anner Mills. She became one of the most noted women preachers in the Society of Friends, and because of her concern for this work she and her husband left Ireland for England in 1818 with three children, living first at Bury St. Edmunds, then Chelmsford and Stoke Newington, until in about 1838 they retired to Sudbury in Suffolk. The partnership between the brothers continued until 1825 Joseph managing his brothers affairs in Clonmel, Ireland. As was usual in many parts of Ireland where different branches of one family lived in one neighbourhood the Christian name of the father was bracketed after a son—thus we get John Grubb (Benjamin) to distinguish from other John Grubbs in Clonmel.

S.G.D.a

Folder 1   (1789 to 1803)   25 letters

96 (contd.). These are written during periods when John Grubb (Benjamin) was travelling on business or occasionally acting as escort to his aunt Mary Dudley, whilst she made religious visits to Friends and Friend's Meetings in England. Four letters (9 to 12) give an account of the rigours of such travel, including the, then, dangerous passage of the Irish Sea. The names of English Friends visited are given. The Welsh places visited are of some interest because few of the large numbers who attended Meetings in Wales were Friends. Meeting Houses in many localities, which had been built before the great emigration to America of the 18th century, were opened specially for the use of itinerant preachers where they were not in regular use. The letters record two visits to the great iron works at Coalbrookdale. He writes, whimsically, on one such tour with his aunt that he " knows not what the next move will be." Other companions with whom he travelled are

William Crotch, William Penrose, John and L. Conran, J. Abell, " Cos." Sally and daughter, Abraham Neale, Alex. Wilson, Fran. Penrose. Letter 15 gives an account of seeing Dr. Herschell's big telescope at Slough.

S.G.D.a.

Folder 2 (1803 - 1816) 36 letters, 26 to 61

97. From John to Joseph Grubb, after the marriage of the former and while he and his wife still lived in Clonmel. The early ones include letters written at the time of his marriage to Sarah Lynes which took place at Isleworth on the 9th of 9th month 1803. During the following year visits of a religious nature were paid to Ross, Worcester, London, Colchester, and Isleworth (where some time was spent owing to the illness of Mrs. Lynes, mother to Sarah Grubb, and to the necessity of finding a partner in the work of her daughter's school.

There are no letters for the following three years. In 1807 a prolonged visit was paid to Scotland where Meetings were crowded, so that Perth Guildhall proved too small and a large Dissenting Meeting House was used, but " as many people were turned away as would have filled a average church." (letter 38). The ancient Meeting House of Old Meldrum and Kinmuck were visited, and hospitality received from the Wigham family (letter 39).

Letter 42 discusses the restrictions made, voluntarily by Friends on the use of sugar imported from the West Indies, owing to the traffic from Africa of slaves destined for the West Indies.

The next letters occur in 1814, in which year parts of England and Wales were visited and journeys minutely described. Details concerning the butter trade and the price of sugar occur as well as many particulars of travel in England and Ireland. The price of corn engaged attention in 1816 (61) as did the proposed bounty on sugar destined for Ireland through England (59).

S.G.D.a

Folder 3 (1818 - 1819). 14 letters 62 to 75

98. There are no letters for 1817. From other sources it is evident that considerable opposition was met with in Ireland to the proposal of John and Sarah (Lynes) Grubb to remove to England with their three children, in order to engage in religious work there. These letters are filled with details of the journey following the departure from Waterford on the 10th of 9th month 1818 and travelling by Milford, Newport, Swansea, Burford, to London, and from there to Bury St.

FAMILY COLLECTIONS 101

Edmunds where they bought a house (described minutely in letter 68) at South Gate Green. Mrs. Lynes senior who had joined them died on the 4th of 11th month 1819 and letter 73 conveys some interesting comments on the difference prevailing in the funeral customs of England and Ireland.

S.G.D.a

Folder 4   1820 - 1821 (24 letters 76—99)
        5   1821 - 1822 (26 letters 100—125)
        6   1822 -   (25 letters 126 - 150)

99. Most of these letters are written from the Grubb's house at South Gate Green, Bury, in the intervals of travelling from place to place in the Eastern Counties of England on religious visits. News of relations and friends in Ireland, accounts of meetings, including some in London, details of home affairs and comparisons of ways of living, of prices, customs, etc., in England and in Ireland occupy most of the contents. While at Aldborough (Aldeburgh) Suffolk (letter 83) he wrote " in Bury fresh butter is sold by the lb., here by the pint, in Cambridge by the yard." A series of religious visits were made by John and Sarah Grubb at the end of 1823, and letters between the 19th of 10th month and the 28th of 12th month are from London, Dover, Wellingham near Lewes, Shaftesbury, Austell (Cornwall), Newbury and Clapham. Many other places were visited and Meetings for Worship held, as well as attendance at Meetings for Discipline (letters 87 to 93). Letter 97 contains a list of the names of those with whom they stayed during this journey viz : Sudbury, John King ; Chelmsford, Mary Marriage ; London, Thos. Christy; Rochester, Wm. Rickman ; Margate, Thos. Newby ; Dover, Thos. Beck ; Folkstone, Joseph Marsh ; Ashford, Thos. Nickalls ; Maidstone, Edw. Wheeler ; Wellington, John Rickman ; Lewes, John Godlee ; Brighton, John Glaysier ; Chichester, James Hack ; Southampton, Joseph Evans ; Pool, John Merryweather ; Shaftesbury, John Shipley ; Marnhull, Wm. Boyd.

Repeated queries by John Grubb as to the state of his rents and monetary affairs in Clonmel point to Irish difficulties of the period. Letter 94 states " John Pim, (of London) told me that they bought £10,000 worth of gold at the Bank, sent it to the Mint and had it coined into sovereigns for Jo. Pike (of Cork) (letter 94). The series is filled with anecdotes, recollections, price comparisons, and occasional Meetings with men whose names became well known. Lindley Murray (letter 118) and William Tuke, Fowell Buxton, Sir James McIntosh speaking on prison reform (108) etc. In 1822 a long visit was paid to northern counties, staying at Spalding, Stockton, Kendal, Liverpool, York (from each of which a letter is dated), Durham, Shields, Sunderland, Darlington, Brough, Yealand and Crook.

S.G.D.a

Folder 7   1822 - 1823 (25 letters 151—175)
        8   1823 - 1824 (25 letters 176—200)
        9   1824 - 1825 (25 letters 201—225)

100. Letters are written from Bury up to 1823 when the family moved to an old house in Chelmsford rented from Joseph Marriage. Few journeys are recounted in 1822 owing to Sarah Grubb's serious illness. Two letters are written from Dover where a holiday was spent. Bank failures in Southern Ireland are commented on during the earlier letters. John Grubb attended a big anti-slavery meeting addressed by William Wilberforce at a London Freemason's hall on the 17th of 5th month 1823. (letter 172). Elizabeth Fry drew crowds at a Chelmsford meeting in 10th month 1823. Letter 175 alludes to the possibility of rebellion in Ireland—14th of 7th month 1823.

There are many references to costs of commodites, and comparison of English money with Irish is made in letter 181. Irish butter had a big market in England, Limerick butter costing 10$d.$ per lb., but Clonmel appeared to be losing business owing to the superiority of Strangman's of Waterford. Beef cost 6½$d.$ per lb., (letter 181 to 183), mutton 7$d.$, a pair of sole 2/- and a good plaice 6$d.$, (letter 190).

John Grubb, hoping to visit Ireland expects to hear that steampackets will be introduced on the Waterford route before he does so. This did not occur and the subsequent journey to Holyhead is minutely recounted, with mileages. On the return journey a new method of slinging their horse aboard at Howth is described. The 400 miles from Holyhead to Chelmsford was accomplished in twelve days. By August 1824 three steamboats were plying on the cross channel route, and letter 198 gives a graphic comparison between conditions of travel then and in the last decade of the 18th century. Letters 200 and 201 mention the new British weekly newspaper the Colonial and British Register.

201 to 225 are very largely concerned with the loss sustained by the Grubb brothers when the ship "Hibernia," conveying sugar, sank. The long correspondence is an interesting comment on business methods, the sugar having been bought, duty paid, by the broker of Pim's discount house, with which the Grubbs dealt, though it should have travelled in Bond. The Grubbs disputed the matter hotly with the Pim firm. All the letters contain family news, a great deal about health and medical detail, and accounts of meetings attended and visits paid in the Ministry. Such visits were made with a minute of the Monthly Meeting, acting as a letter of introduction. In this period Essex Meetings were visited, there being 17 particular Meetings attached to that Quarterly Meeting.

FAMILY COLLECTIONS 103

Folders 10   1825 - 1826   (25 letters 226—250)
         11   1826 - 1827   (25 letters 251—275)

101. With the exception of three these letters are dated from Chelmsford, and are mainly concerned with domestic matters and with health, the latter including a discussion of treatment by a surgeon-apothecary, only calling in a physician in serious cases (267—268), Dr. Abernethy's use of mustard seed is noted (236). Money affairs; Ireland's change to English currency (235—6), fees at Tottenham Friends' School; different prices of provisions—turkeys " never less than half a guinea, five times the Irish price," rump beef $7\frac{1}{2}d.$ per lb. etc., occupy several letters. The certificate given to Elizabeth Fry when about to visit Ireland is noted (271), and Sarah Grubb's visits to families in the Chelmsford area, in addition to those to meetings in London. These visits were performed in their own " chair " drawn by a mare, now showing her age. John and Sarah Grubb's son Jonathan drove occasionally and John's journey to London by coach is described in letter 271. During this period the two Grubb brothers ended their partnership and their financial affairs as well as the precarious state of England's finances are of interest.

S.G.D.a.

Folders 12   1827 - 1828   (25 letters 276—300)
         13   1828 -   (25 letters 301 - 325)
         14   1828 - 1829   (25 letters 326—350)

102. All the earlier letters are from Chelmsford. In spite of constant poor health Sally Grubb preached and visited meetings and persons, regularly, during this period. Places mentioned are Malden, Helveden, Coggleshall, Bardfield, Colchester, Layer Breton, Thaxted, Stanstead, Stortford, Dunmow. At the end of 1828 John and Sally Grubb went to live in London (while the children lived at Hastings) and visits were paid to most of the Middlesex and London Meetings.

There is a great deal of interest in the letters of this period, the Anti-Slavery agitation was at its height; the Society of Friends in America was split by a secession movement, steam boats had become a reality and steam coaches were mooted. Commerce was expanding and one Friend made a good living by the export of rabbit and hare skins from Liverpool to America. Hats made by Christy cost 35/-; a fashionable dentist earned £7,000 per year, whilst the wage of a groom-cum-gardener was 11/- a week. In 18 years the London Truss Society helped 48,904 persons suffering from hernia. Guinness's porter was sold " in vast quantities " in England. Irish affairs were difficult and the disfranchisement of 40/- freeholders was debated. John Grubb had conversations *in Irish* with workmen at Kensington and with two women whom he overheard speaking it in London.

S.G.D.b

Folder 1 — Jan. 1830 to Sept. 1830 (25 letters 1—25)
       2 — Oct. 1830 to July 1831 (25 letters 26—50)
       3   June 1832 (25 letters 51—75)

103. The move from Chelmsford to Stoke Newington (by a 7 horsed wagon) occupies earlier letters, and comparisons of food prices in each place are made. London University, which was raising funds by the issue of £100 shares, offered one share to Grace Church Street Meeting—this was declined (letters 5 and 9). Records of petitions against the death penalty recur through the series. The earlier letters describe social details such as preparation for a wedding; hire of a room to facilitate comfort between sessions of Yearly Meeting; a deputation with an address to the King, coach fares, etc.

There is more international and political detail in these letters than heretofore. Arrival of King Charles X of France in England, election news, Catholic Emancipation, the Liverpool steam coach, the rise of Daniel O'Connell appear. The vast agitation for the abolition of slavery became prominent, as did the Reform question. Sir Robert Peel's resignation is discussed in letter 30, *et alia*. Lord Brougham undertook to read the petition of Friends on anti-slavery in the House (32). There are many beggars—in spite of soup establishments and coal funds. John Grubb wonders where the legal poor rates go (33). The disturbed state of Ireland is discussed. All the letters are interspersed with details of news of Irish Friends, local (Clonmel) gossip, Friends visiting Ireland. (Elizabeth Fry stayed at Ushers Island in Dublin). Letter 32 asks whether the Clonmel Meeting House is to be heated by warm air.

A Temperance Meeting in Exeter Hall lasted 5 hours.

The American Hicksite movement causes concern and Irish Friends are warned of the visit of Isaac Hopper.

Church rates not to be paid by Friends and it "should be clear that Tythes are considered anti-Christian."

Foreign mission work is mentioned among Friends for the first time.

In July 1831 the doctor described an illness of Sarah Grubb as "the outskirts" of the Cholera which had raged on the Continent. In later letters the ravages of the disease in England are described, daily reports appearing in the papers. Letter 71 tells of the fast and intercessions taking place and of the jocularity with which the disease is treated in songs and ballads and on the stage.

The later letters contain constant allusion to the water-mill bought for Jonathan at Lexden near Colchester and of his removal to live there, his sister housekeeping.

There is a gap between the 4th and 6th month 1832, apparently due to an accident to John Grubb. Among prominent names mentioned in the series are William Allen, John Wilbur (from America), John Pease, Josiah Forster, Thomas Shillito, Stephen Grellett and James Backhouse. The latter having been refused a permit to travel on a convict ship elected to make the journey to New South Wales with a large number of mutinous steerage passengers, amongst whom he helped to restore order.

S.G.D.b.

Folder 4 June 1832 (25 letters 76—100)
        5 June 1833 Dec. 1833 (25 letters 101—125)
        6 Feb. 1834 Nov. 1834 (22 letters 126—147)

104. Political affairs, Irish and English, the slavery question, the divided thought in the Society of Friends, occupy many of these letters. In 76 the Tory party's aversion to the Abolition of Slavery and to Capital Punishment provokes the comment that this attitude may prevent Christians from sympathy.

The journeys of Daniel Wheeler, a well known Friend, whose memoirs were later published, and who lived for some time in Russia, are mentioned. In 1834 he travelled to the South Seas in a one hundred ton vessel, the Freeburg, reaching the Equator in 19 days.

At home, Stoke Newington is so built up that it appears to be becoming part of London; postal services are much speeded; flour sells badly everywhere and Jonathan's mills have heavy losses. The Quaker Member of Parliament, J. Pease, disputes with Daniel O'Connell (125); three M.P.s are attenders at Westminster Meeting. The King has asked for presentation copies of Sewell's " History of Friends " (1st pub. 1722, sixth edition 1834, letter 134) and of the new " Book of Extracts." The cost of lodging for three with room for an extra person and a sitting-room for the two weeks of Yearly Meeting in London is eight guineas. A 5lb. salmon, packed in inch thick ice was bought for 2/6d. Sugar very low at 8½d. per lb.

The state of Irish Charter Schools is mentioned in letter 117.

Detailed descriptions of losses and expected improvements in Jonathan Grubb's mills in Lexden occur (118). Loads despatched may increase from three to ten per week. A journey to London now only takes 5¼ hours.

Cholera deaths in London average 100 per day. A snake is sent to Clonmel and survives the journey.

Folder 7   Dec. 1834 — Nov. 1835 (27 letters 148—175)
       8   Feb. 1835 — Nov. 1836 (23 letters 176—199)
       9   Dec. 1836 — Oct. 1837 (25 letters 200—225)

105. These letters are written from Lexden to which John and Sarah Grubb removed to be near their son. Mention of the separations in the Society of Friends and the publication of pamphlets thereto are frequent. John and Sarah Grubb were strongly adverse to the doctrines set forth by Isaac Crewdson, a Friend of Manchester, who, in 1835 produced a small book *A Beacon to the Society of Friends*. In writing to his brother in Ireland John Grubb describes, in this series, the course of the dispute. He also mentions the Hicksite separation in America, and a travelling Hicksite, Elisha Dawson, then in England. (See particularly letter 155). He is surprised brother has not read *The Beacon* which raises many important points in England and may still do so in Ireland.

Twenty guineas asked in London for accommodation during Yearly Meeting—3 bedrooms, a sitting-room, but no provisions or attendance. Finally found one in Houndsditch for 12 guineas with one extra room.

Money affairs include rents in Clonmel; postal charges; cost of Jonathan's steam engine (189—190), etc. Letter 168 describes course of a journey from Scarborough including a visit to the famous C. Waterton (*Charles Waterton* 1782 - 1865).

After November 1835 letters are dated from Sudbury, Suffolk. Letter 181 has postscript written by William King which discusses the differences in (William) Bewick's descriptions of birds and those of (James) Wilson, attributing the apparent deficiency of the former to the fact that his studies were from preserved, or at best dead, specimens; those of Wilson being from the forest and mountainside. The former made for accuracy in plumage, etc., the latter in habits.

Several letters mention conditions in Ireland, some peaceable, some disturbing. New Irish roads are in progress. Letter 185 alludes to the blowing up of the statue of King William III in College Green. Low prices prevailed at a great auction of tea by Samuel Bewley in Dublin in 1836 (188). In the same year John Grubb wishes Ireland could be declared an independent Yearly Meeting. Decline of the linen trade in the North of Ireland and the woollen in the South (193) and of the recession of the butter trade from Clonmel (194).

Continued resignations from the Society include many Irish ones. Sarah Grubb is by some considered a prophetess; during this period she has held 15 public meetings, 900 persons attending one at Coggleshall. The baptism of Elisha Bates, formerly a member of the Religious Society of Friends, provokes comments on his writings. There is hesitation as to the wisdom of allowing a certificate to Joseph John Gurney, a Friend of evangelical ideas, to visit America. Ireland Yearly Meeting refuses his offer to lecture in Dublin. John Grubb's nephew, Benjamin, considers that " American Friends are unlikely to be influenced by J. Gurney's wealth or greatness."

Extracts from Daniel Wheeler's letters from Tasmania are quoted. The well known Friend, William Allen, is said to be a sort of guardian to young Queen Victoria owing to his friendship with the Duke and Duchess of Kent.

S.G.D.b.

Folder 10—1837 - 1838(25 letters b/226 - 250)

16—1838 - 1839 (25 letters b/251 - 275)

12—1839 - 1840 (25 letters b/276 - 300)

106. All through this series notes on Clonmel news are mixed among the more serious comments on the separation in the Religious Society. Messrs. Darton, the publishers, visiting John Grubb said that publication of Thomas Shillitoe's journal was held up by the pressure of work sent by John Barclay, a strong Conservative Friend. (Footnote : Thomas Shillitoe 1754 - 1830. John Barclay editor Letters of Early Friends *et alia*). c.1838).

A severe illness of Hannah Grubb caused the summoning of a doctor and a physician—the former understood the case better. A man was employed to sit up all night to run for the doctor if necessary. Letter 231 discusses the " legal title " of doctor and physician.

Slavery in the West Indies continues, or increases, since the grant for its abolition (230). Several comments are made on the activities of Joseph John Gurney in America. Mention is made of the state of the Society in Ireland, but John Grubb wishes his brother would tell him more of this (250). Comments also occur on political affairs in Ireland —" Who would have supposed even 20 years ago that a papist should be appointed Attorney General, or that a Popish priest should propose this same person to represent the Borough of Clonmel, and the election carried without opposition" (letter 252, 30th July, 1838). Dungarvan is mentioned as a public watering place and a conveyance carrying 24 persons plies there. Speed of travel everywhere is noted : as also the voyage of Daniel Wheeler to Russia in " Sirius " the first steam vessel to go there. (" Sirius " built at Malcomson's shipyard, Waterford).

The journeys of John Bell to Van Diemens land, Elizabeth Fry to France, Josiah Forster to America, and that of J. Backhouse and C. Wakefield in the interior of Africa where 14 oxen are used for transport, are alluded to.

By the installation of steam Jonathan Grubb was enabled to supply other millers, working water wheels, with flour in a dry period.

Hannah Grubb occupies herself in relieving the poor, amongst whom there is much distress in spite of the new Poor Laws. One woman came to her to know what to do as she understood a law had been passed limiting families to two children and it would be a great hardship to destroy seven of her family of nine!

Sarah Grubb having made up her mind to visit Dublin Yearly Meeting (1839) travelled with Hannah via Clapham, Uxbridge, High Wycombe, Charlebury, Worcester, Coalbrookdale and so to Holyhead Hotel.

In Ireland they met with the followers of Joshua Jacob (the White Quaker leader) though he himself did not meet her. Throughout these letters White Quakers are referred to as " Ranters."

As John Grubb grew older he developed increasingly bad sight, and the later letters require time to decipher. He also became feeble and suffered from the effects of many falls causing minor injuries. His wife was often from home, occasionally for several weeks. His interest in Irish affairs increases and he evinces considerable curiosity about the state of the Society and secessions therefrom. His nephew, John, of Ireland, visited him, travelling by boat and train. "What an extraordinary (speedy) journey " (280) " it might as well be supposed we could fly across."

Jacob Green sailed on the vessel "British Queen" for America. "The largest steamship ever sailed from London; more than 300 including crew on board, and a cargo valued at a million and a half pounds sterling " (280) and arrived in 14 days (284).

In October 1839 John Grubb comments on the extraordinary effect Father Matthew is having in promoting Temperance in Ireland.

Mention is made of many well known Friends, among whom are Joseph Pease, M.P., Daniel Wheeler, Elizabeth Robson, John Chandler (likely to sail to Jamaica), George Alexander and Stephen Grellett.

Sarah Grubb went to see the celebrated " aurist " (not named), but later decided not to repeat her visits to him. Letter 295 alludes to the visit of Elizabeth Fry to Queen Victoria.

s.g.d.b.

Folder 13 — April to Nov. 1840 (25 letters 301 - 325)
Folder 14 — Dec. 1840 - April 1841 (20 letters 326 - 345)

107. These last letters in the series show the increasing feebleness and blindness of John Grubb and the failing powers, too, of his wife. Their steady interest in all matters pertaining to the Religious Society remains as does their knowledge of all happenings in Clonmel.

John Grubb evinces gratefulness to his nephew, Benjamin, for undertaking to look after the business of rent collecting, etc., for him. In spite of great pain in her feet Sarah Grubb continued her religious visits and in April 1840 went by rail to Birmingham, 111 miles, in $4\frac{1}{2}$ hours, " and exactly as if they were sitting in armchairs." He himself has never seen a rail-road.

The first letter in the collection, sent by the new penny post, is that of 23rd June, 1840. A carriage called " a Fly " is mentioned in letter 313.

The Quaker " colony " at Congénies is alluded to in 315, (for this isolated group of Friends descended from Huguenots see "*Later Period Quakerism*—Rufus Jones, 1921—II, 239).

There is constant enquiry for health of sister Lydia (Joseph Grubb's wife) who is an invalid and attended by Dr. Hemphill of Clonmel.

Joseph John Gurney's return from America with 6 certificates from Friends' Meetings there is mentioned in letter 318, and his book on the West Indies in 323.

In January 1842 the thermometer measured 24 degrees of frost, which is duly recorded by John Grubb whose increasing ill health does not decrease his faculties. He comments in letter 331 on the establishment of a Meeting in Wexford town, and recalls incidents of the older Meeting of Forest in that County. His letters get gradually more brief and allude to the illness of the whole family, but even in May, 1841 he got to Meeting and his last letter evinces interest in the forthcoming visit of Samuel Capper to Ireland, who proposes bringing with him a tent in which to hold Meetings.

John Grubb died: 16/5/1841.
Sarah, his wife, died 16/3/1842.

FOURTEEN MISCELLANEOUS COLLECTIONS

Letters of varying importance. These are noted briefly here as to content. All are fully catalogued in the general card index.

NEWSOM LETTERS
1—137

108. A collection of family letters of the 19th century, mostly written by or to the Newsom family of Edenderry, and the Phelps family, merchants of Limerick.

These families were inter-related by marriage.

Other names occurring in the series are Fennell, Strangman, Lecky, Ridgeway, Forbes, Wilson and Adams. Also a testimony of Cork Monthly Meeting to James Abell—copy with 62 signatures.

Three 18th century letters, Hester Smith to Thomas Wilson, 1722, discussing cure for Dropsy dispensed by Mary Rose of Harwich Green, Harwell (120). Thomas Wilson, 1721, to John Barcroft before starting a journey from Bristol or Falmouth to Ireland; from Thomas Wilson while travelling (n.d. c.1721). A paper printed by R. Jackson, Dublin, 1775, subsequent to the printing of T. Wilson's Journal, from manuscript in Thomas Wilson's handwriting.

Many of these letters are on purely family matters, others concern the farm and cattle trade conducted by the Newsom family at Mount Wilson, Edenderry; see particularly 21, 42 and 82; the last describing plans for the erection of a new type of cowshed (1852).

Shipping details and the importation of steel bundles and iron in rod form are described in the letters of William Newsom (writing variously from Limerick and from Cork), and those of Joseph P. Newsom of Limerick.

Prices of deal, oats, shovels, coal are discussed in letter 23 which also proposes letting house in Limerick to Major Maxwell of 1st King's Dragoon Guards just arrived in the city (1830). Coal in the same year was 18/- to 20/- per ton (letter 33).

There is some material relating to coastal trading vessels in these letters. A list is with the collection which is not in strict chronological order.

FAMILY COLLECTIONS III

GOFF LETTERS
Photostat Copies 1759 - 1815

109. This collection is in private ownership. The National Library of Ireland and the Public Record Office in Belfast own photostat copies. There is also a printed account of the letters in the *Journal of the Friends' Historical Society*, XV. London, Friends' House.

Jacob Goff of Horetown, Co. Wexford married (1759) Elizabeth Wilson of Mount Wilson, Edenderry. These letters are family correspondence with considerable social interest, arranged in groups relating to the various members of the family before and after marriage.

Jacob and Elizabeth Goff had twenty-two children of whom fourteen grew up. These married into the following families : Deaves, Edmundson, Forbes, Fennell, Lamphier, Morgan, Penrose, Pike, Sparrow and Wakefield.

There are only five letters written during the period of the 1798 rising, probably owing to the severity of the fighting round Horetown, which became a target for each side. The story of this period is told in the account written by Dinah Goff, the youngest daughter : (*Divine Protection*, London, W. and F. G. Cash, 1857).

PIM LETTERS

110. Eight folders of miscellaneous matter, letters, etc., relating to various branches of the Pim family, and of those families with which they intermarried, particularly the Harveys of Youghal and Cork.

(a) 61 family letters 1792 - 1841, dated variously from Mountmellick, Cork, Youghal, Carlow, Dublin, Moate, from the following persons with most of whom the Pim family was connected by marriage— Harvey, Abell, Goodbody, Grubb, Lecky, etc.

(aa) 25 letters concerning the Pim family of Mountmellick 1795 - 1918, include two letters of Amelia Opie of Norwich (1769 - 1853), a memoir of Thomas Cope of Philadelphia and a list of marriages of the Harvey family of Youghal.

(b) 3 letters relating to the Central Relief Committee of the Society of Friends during the Irish famine 1847 - 9.

(c) 23 letters relating to the property owned by Jonathan Pim (1806 - 1885) at Rossbarnagh, near Newport, Co. Mayo.

(d) 5 letters between Jonathan Pim and R. Vesey Stoney relative to a proposed railway from Newport to Achill Sound 1883.

(e) 13 letters re fisheries and oyster beds in Ireland between Jonathan Pim and the Department of Fisheries and others 1865 - 67 ; also printed schedule of Board of Works re Oyster Fisheries 1865.

(f) 51 letters relating to the American Civil War and to the Negro question 1861 - 1864. (There are no letters for 1863).

(g) 5 miscellaneous documents :—Mr. Burke Sadlier's account of the origin of Newport, Co. Mayo. Letter to Mary White of Ballitore from Naples 1836. Two French passports for William H. Pim 1844 and 1845. Letter of Thomas Pim about a Convent Building Fund, 1885.

(h) 8 letters concerning the state of Ireland in 1848, including a copy of the memorial sent to Lord Clarendon in April of that year.

(i) 53 personal letters to Jonathan Pim, of which 18 acknowledge receipt of his book *Conditions and Prospects of Ireland*, 1848. Among the writers of the remaining letters are :— The Duke of Wellington, (1830), Lord Hatherton, 1847. Sir Charles Trevelyan enclosing note and cheque for relief work 1848 ; William Todhunter concerning value of rentals on Clare Island, Co. Mayo. John Bright, three letters commenting on his own efforts for Ireland in Parliament, on Rate in Aid, and Ulster as part of Ireland and on Corn Laws. Dr. Salmon Provost of Trinity College, Dublin, commenting on Pim's pamphlet " Marriage with Two Sisters," including Salmon's opinions on Slavery and Incest. Dr. R. C. Trench (later Archbishop of Dublin) acknowledging Pim's pamphlet on Marriage, and several others from prominent personalities.

Jonathan Pim was Member of Parliament for Dublin from 1865 to 1874.

HEATHER PAPERS

with notes by J. R. H. Greeves, 1960

111. Genealogy of the Heather family of Kinnego, near Dungannon, Co. Tyrone, beginning with William Heather, who married Mary Gilmore in 1746.

Four Legal Documents : Will, Power of Attorney, Statements of Duties or Assets.

Four Bundles of Bills, Receipts and Accounts.

52 letters, 1833 - 1851 : Correspondence between Thomas Greeves and the descendants of James Heather, who died in 1827, re : legacies. The announcement in 1833 that the money lost by James Heather through the failure of Hannyngton's Bank would be repaid aroused the frenzied interest of Heather's sons, James and William, in their respective inheritances. They had emigrated to Canada and the U.S., and were not doing well financially. The letters include many details on the duties and taxes related to inheritance claims, and those of James Heather, jnr., comment on business and domestic difficulties, and aspects of life in Quebec and New York, 1834 - 1844. The letters of Thomas Greeves, Dungannon, pertain to his actions as attorney for James Heather, snr.

HEAZELTON PAPERS
with notes by J. H. R. Greeves, 1960

112. Genealogy of the Heazelton - Douglass family beginning with James Morton, who married Sarah, daughter of John and Ruth Whitsitt, in 1724.

32 items : 8 family and legal letters, Bonds, Accounts, Power of Attorney, Wills, Memoranda, Receipts for rent paid, and William Heazelton's Rent Book, 1802 - 1816.

The letters concern William Heazelton's financial affairs in Ireland and America. They include reports from John Greeves and Joseph Williams, who, having received Power of Attorney over the estate of William Heazelton when the latter emigrated to America in 1809, administrated Heazelton's lands and collected rents from his farms at Cohannan and Culnagnew. The letters from William Heazelton contain interesting accounts of his dry-goods and grocery business in Pittsburgh, comments on the War of 1812 - 1814, and notes on social distinctions in America. The final letters in the collection concern family quarrels over legacies from the estate of William Heazelton.

RICHARDSON PAPERS

113. 15 items : Notes on the Richardson family tree, and letters.

The majority of the letters are from Anna Richardson ; to her daughters Sarah and Ruth at school, Suir Island, 1822 - 1823, with greetings from family and friends, a promise to send " skipping ropes and shuttlecock," etc., and to her mother, Sarah Grubb, and sisters, 1817 - 1823, with comments on her husband's visits to London, and on her children. Other letters are from Sarah Richardson to her mother, from Suir Island ; 2 with notes from Anne Jacob re : Sarah's health ; from Margaret Grubb, Anne Jacob and Margaret Lecky ; to Sarah Richardson.

Includes short pedigree of the Richardson family.

GOODBODY LETTERS

114. 160 documents, mostly letters, relating to the families of Goodbody, Pim, Harvey, Phelps, Grubb, Pike, Hands, Clibborn and Watson, 1680 to 1913. All the above were connected by marriage with the Goodbody family of Leix and Offaly. 17th century documents include a copy of Friends' Declaration of Faith, 1680, statement relevant to the Co. Kildare estate of James and Charles Moore, 1682 ; biographical note on Elizabeth Hands (1688 - 1762), wife of Thomas Pim. A small notebook descriptive of the life of Elizabeth Goodbody (1753 - 1834), and extracts of letters to her son, Robert, (1781 - 1860).

Correspondents through the 18th century include James Abell, Mary Dudley, Richard Shackleton, Sarah Grubb of Anner Mills, Elizabeth Tuke, Deborah Darby, and many members of the Goodbody and Pim families.

Two letters from George Jubee, a condemned prisoner in 1844. Extracts from the diary of Mary Leadbeater, a list of ministering Friends who visited Ireland, 1784 - 1850.

NICHOLSON LETTERS

115. 37 original papers concerning the appeal against his disownment by the Religious Society of Friends, made by Peter Nicholson. The correspondence lasted from 1753 - 1771. Part of this has been printed.

List with documents.

This appeal is the last one to be made by a member of Ireland Yearly Meeting to London Yearly Meeting.

HODGKIN CORRESPONDENCE (1847 - 1851)

116. 625 documents concerning the attempted establishment of a fishing industry at the Claddagh, Galway Bay. John Hodgkin (1800 - 1875) under whose name this collection is classified was a member of the Society of Friends in England. He was the animating spirit in the effort to introduce improved fishing methods to the Claddagh at the time of the Famine, and to try to alleviate the distress throughout the country. The series of letters is dated 1847 to 1851, and includes a small amount of contemporary printed material ; applications for relief, fishery reports, instructions, etc. The main correspondence with

FAMILY COLLECTIONS 115

John Hodgkin are John Abell, Joseph Bewley, James Hack Tuke, Joseph Thompson, J. W. Strangman, R. Barclay Fox, William Todhunter, the Rev. John Darcy (Church of Ireland, Galway), Arthur Chard, M. Butcher & Sons, Gt. Yarmouth, Henry Christy.

This collection is not catalogued but there is a full list of names and dates in correspondence, in a separate temporary card index.

THOMAS WILSON COLLECTION

117. Twelve letters to Thomas Wilson (1655 - 1725), written by George Rooke, James Dickenson, Samuel Waldenfield, Thomas Mogridge, John Saul, Samuel Hopwood, Benjamin Holmes and Isaac Pickover, between the years 1695 and 1724. Five papers relative to Thomas Wilson, including a certificate signed by 13 Friends of Exeter Meeting. Wilson was a native of Cumberland who travelled extensively in England, Ireland, America and the West Indies. He settled in Edenderry in Ireland after his marriage in 1695 to Mary Bewley of Woodhall, Cumberland.

WRIGHT LETTERS
Bundle — 10 stitched books — 1829 - 1862

118. The Wright family of Waterford and Dublin, merchants and linen drapers were related to the Gatchells of Waterford, and a considerable number of letters concern the winding up of the firm of Gatchell-Walpole, Glass manufacturers of that city, 1835 - 1836.

(1) Miscellaneous papers and letters concerning the Gatchell estate. Query to Counsel concerning will of " M.W." - (alpole), which involved Henry Armstrong, Jonathan Gatchell, Joseph Walpole and various charities. Also description of Skinner Row, Dublin, with list of residents in 1795.

(2) Eight (copies) letters of Jonathan Gatchell, 1800 - 1825.

(3) Sixteen letters of Jonathan Wright, Waterford, to his father and brother, Nehemiah and Nathan Wright of Skinner Row, Dublin, 1829 - 1830. Includes business prices and detail.

(4) The same 1830 - 1831—21 letters.

(5) The same 1833 - 1835, with detail of the failure of the firm of Gatchell and Walpole—33 letters.

(6) 40 letters to Jonathan and Nehemiah Wright, Christ Church Place, formerly Skinner Row, from various correspondents, mainly Knott, Hewson and Gatchell, and one from Anthony Stratford asking for family news on behalf of William Wright of Grahamstown, South Africa.

(7) A scrappy diary kept between 1832 and 1835, possibly by the wife of Jonathan Wright. Ends 31/7/35 " Left the Glass Shop."

(8) 6 letters of John and Jonathan Wright, 1861 - 1862.

(9) 30 letters from Thomas and Elizabeth (Walpole) Knott of Exeter, 1831 - 1837. Most refer to the winding-up of the Gatchell-Walpole Glass works, Waterford. Also letters of Abigail Knott of Rathangan, 1844, and of Jonathan and John Wright, 1862.

(10) 27 letters written from Santiago de Cuba and two from Ohio, 1833 - 1845, by James S. Wright to his aunt, Martha Wright, in Dublin, and to his cousin, Jonathan Wright, also of Dublin.

James Wright was a prosperous merchant and for a time British Vice Consul in Cuba. There are comments on American, Spanish and Cuban affairs, with some details of business and of the troubles of 1836 - 7, and of agriculture. The Anglo-Chinese war is mentioned, as is anti-slavery agitation.

By 1841 Cuba was tranquil, commerce in a healthy state and copper exports large. Letter 34 mentions use of staff signal telegraph system.

29 letters, 1801 - 1807, from Joshua and John Wright to Nehemiah Wright of Ballinclay, Co. Wexford, after arrival in Baltimore, descriptive of hard life there and in North West Province, etc.

Some later letters from New York and Ohio.

PEARCE LETTERS, ETC.
1671 - 1765

119. Documents relating to the family of Pearce of Limerick. These papers have been described by Dr. Edward Maclysaght in *Analecta Hibernica*, 15, pp. 86 - 91.

They include letters, records of sufferings, papers relating to property, religious documents, copies of the wills of Richard Pearce (1681) and of Thomas Pearce (1664). These are précised in the Wills section.

POOLE LETTERS, ETC.

120. 36 documents relating to the Poole family of Co. Wexford, including an early account of the family from 1661. Several letters are to Jacob Poole (1774 - 1827), compiler of the Glossary of the Forth-Bargy dialect of Co. Wexford, names of correspondents being Crane, Diggin, Martin, Sparrow, Walpole, Mary Leadbeater. Among other documents is a receipt for 5/10*d.* dues for a ship passing the Eddystone lighthouse in 1739.

Document 21 is a marriage settlement between Jacob Poole of Growtown and Mary Sparrow on the 12th of May, 1813, the signatories being Deborah Sparrow, Mary Sparrow and Jacob Poole ; Trustee James Webb ; witnesses John Sparrow and Richard Poole. Property involved the lands of Little Killiane and Ballykelly, Co. Wexford, containing 255 acres in the Barony of Forth.

Several wills have been removed from this collection to Wills section q.v.

WATSON LETTERS
Port.3.B. 40.

121. A stitched bundle of 42 letters mainly on religious subjects, written between the years 1723 and 1752 to Abigail Watson, born Craven and first married to John Boles of Woodhouse, Tipperary. She married Samuel Watson (1686 - 1762) of Kilconnor, Co. Carlow, as his second wife in 1735.

Most of the letters are written from Leeds, Yorkshire, by Tabitha Horner. Two (nos. 2 and 3) are written by Abigail Boles, one to Barnaby Rallins, Ballitore, and one to her son John Boles, jun., c/o John Dobbs, Doctor in Youghal.

No. 4 is a letter of John Fothergill, the well-known physician, to Samuel Watson dated 1725.

MANUSCRIPT DRAFTS
MANUSCRIPT OF THE HISTORY OF FRIENDS IN IRELAND

122. In 1682 Thomas Wight (1640 - 1724), the recording clerk of Cork Meeting for many years, asked that particulars of events happening among Friends should be sent to him. From this data he compiled, at the request of the National Meeting, the first part of a book finished by Dr. John Rutty (1669 - 1775) and published in 1751 under the title *The History of the Rise and Progress of the People called Quakers in Ireland.*

In 1707 Wight's book, which ended at the year 1700, was read by the Men's Meeting in Dublin and, having been sent to the Provinces for revision, a decision was made to publish it (Dublin Men's Meeting 13/11/1707). This, however, appears not to have been done. Dr. Rutty undertook to complete the work and did so up to the year 1751, when it was published by I. Jackson, Meath Street, Dublin. In 1733 the National Meeting considered there were defects in the work and it was advised copies formerly sent for correction were to be used as examples for further correction.

The following are manuscripts of the work preserved in the Library :

A. Quarto, bound, MS. volume, evidently that used by Thomas Wight, but interleaved with amendments made by John Rutty. This contains in the front, the names of those appointed by Dublin Men's Meeting to view the work in 1733. John Pim of Belfast owned this book and in a letter to Ethel Crawshaw, former librarian of Friends' House London, he wrote that he believed he had Wight's own copy.

B. A quarto bound volume similar to above but without Rutty's notes and differing slightly in text. The handwriting is probably that of Thomas Wight. Has a pasted slip with names of those appointed by Mountmellick Meeting to view the work. A note under this says : Transcribed by M. P. up to p.91 I expect it to be sent back from the Monthly Meeting. (This is wrapped in a torn parchment deed relating to property in Kilbarry, Cork, and Haywards Hill, alias Ballyhernon, conveyed by (or to) Franklin and Heyward St. Leger.)

C. Bound volume, cloth covered, a very regular 'print' writing throughout. Dates from 1651 to 1705. Text differs slightly from printed version.

D. Large foolscap paper-covered, copiously annotated by Rutty, labelled 'An Account of the further Progress of Truth 1706, 3rd month to 1741 and now brought to 1748.'

E. } Two volumes lacking covers, appearing to be rough drafts of the
F. } work from 1681 to 1693 and from 1694 to 1699, paginated, numbered respectively 5 and 6.

G.⎱ Two small volumes numbered 1st part and 2nd part. Copies
H.⎰ of part of the work, including the preface. Obviously, from the
text, made after the death of William Edmundson in 1712. Differ much from printed version. May be those used to circulate among members. The first one has several handwritings.

(Trinity College Dublin has one small book similar to C. dated 1700 - 1717 (MS. Q.2, 15, 3178). This ends "Total of Friends Sufferings this year taken for Tythes, Priests' maintenance etc., 1699 - 12 - 6."

SHARP MANUSCRIPTS

123. A large collection of letters and other documents relative to Anthony Sharp (1642 - 1707), wool merchant of Dublin.

Thirteen stitched bundles of varying sizes, being copies made between 1707 and 1720 by John Crabbe, brother-in-law to Anthony Sharp, and one MS. book written in Sharp's hand. These were sold by Crabb to the Dublin Monthly Meeting in 1720 but not, however, printed. The originals were not located.

The contents can briefly be described as follows :

A. Personal letters, including correspondence relative to Sharp's first residence in Dublin in 1669, the death of his wife, Hester, his proposal made to Thomas Crabbe of Marlborough, England, that any daughter of the latter might marry him. Letters to various Friends in England and elsewhere, including one from William Penn, 1678, and one from William Edmundson writing from Cork in 1683 while waiting to sail to America, and giving instructions concerning money lent to Friends by him at 8% interest. Several letters ask for Sharp's help in one concern or another.

B. Letters concerning the business and affairs of the Society of Friends in Ireland and elsewhere. Written between 1671 and 1690 these touch on a wide diversity of Quaker history.

C. Letters concerning public affairs. These include letters written between the years 1687 and 1690, referring to conditions under which people were living, e.g., one from William Edmundson asks for Anthony Sharp's intercession with the Lord Deputy for the removal of soldiers quartered on Rosenallis, who ought to be at Mountmellick. Conditions prior to the battle of the Boyne are described.

D. Letters relating to the taking up of land in Pennsylvania, West Jersey and East Jersey. Names of writers include Gavin Lawry, Andrew Thompson, Matthias Forster, William Gibson (this discusses the voting power of proprietors in E. Jersey), Robert Turner, who travelled on 100 ton ship *Trial of Pennsylvania*, and William Penn, now returning to Pennsylvania, 1690.

E. Miscellaneous papers, one of which (S.14) is a manuscript copy of *The Quakers Dublin Weekly Oracle*, 1721. This has been described and annotated by Russell Mortimer, of Leeds University Library in the Journal of the Friends' Historical Society Vol. XLIX, pp.244 - 5.

Books of this collection are numbered S.1 to S.14.

There is a partial index and it is hoped to make a fuller one shortly.

THE FORTH-BARGY DIALECT

124. The original manuscript of the Glossary of the Forth-Bargy (Wexford) dialect was presented to the Library by the family of Jacob Poole (1774 - 1827) its compiler. It differs in some respects from the printed version (William Barmes, 1867), being fuller.

ANNALS OF BALLITORE

125. A contemporary Ms. copy of Mary Leadbeater's *Annals of Ballitore* slightly differing from the printed version and having Mary Leadbeater's original description of Ballitore village (replaced by a descriptive poem in the latter). In four volumes.

MARY LEADBEATER'S DIARY (abridged)

126. Typescript prepared for publication by Isabel Grubb, but never published.

The original is in the National Library of Ireland, Ms. 9292 - 9346.

LETTERS OF WILLIAM LEADBEATER

127. Précis made by Olive C. Goodbody. Original in the National Library of Ireland, Ms. 8671.

SCHOOL RECORDS

LEINSTER PROVINCIAL SCHOOLS

A. **128.** Edenderry : Minute of proposed mixed boarding school (1764). Plan for a general boarding school c.1759 with some relevant queries. Letter and minutes concerning opening of same, Ebenezer Mellor being headmaster 1764. Catalogued in General Index.

B. Mountmellick 1784 - 1921 : Mixed till 1855 then girls only. Eighty books concerning the school from 1796 - 1921. Minutes, Accounts, Admissions, bequests, dividends and rent particulars ; journals, ledgers, petty cash, ' waste ', etc. References listed and catalogued in card index in general manuscript collection; also Grubb collection index.

C. **129.** Munster Provincial School—Newtown School, Waterford, (founded 1798). Four books of the Provincial School Committee, minutes 1796 - 1855, at which date the admission of girls ceased, being gradually resumed in the 20th century, the first girl, Margaret Stokes, entering in 1906. One book of accounts (1796 - 1831), and one of rules.

Many other references in card index and Grubb Collection index. Manuscripts in safe at Newtown School : Two Minute and Proceedings books 1796 - 1847. Registry of scholars with particulars of each, including date of leaving : 1798 - 1855. Proceedings of Joint Committee appointed to arrange details of proposed union between the two Provinces for educational purposes 1855. Superintendent's Reports 1866 - 1871, Robert J. Greer ; 1871 - 1884, Edward Garnet ; 1883 - 1894, Edward Garnet, senior. In 1892 Edward Garnet, junior, signs for some months. General Meeting Minutes 1884 - 1920. Visitors book for Centenary gathering 1898. Some, as yet uncatalogued documents remain at the school.

D. **130.** Suir Island School, Clonmel. See Grubb index for prospectus, 1801, plans and subscriptions, rules, letters, etc., and the general manuscript index under " Clonmel " for isolated items. This school was started by Sarah (Tuke) Grubb in 1787 and carried on by members of the Jacob-Taylor family, and later became Prior Park School.

E. **131.** Camden Street School, Dublin : (1839 - 1844). Ten miscellaneous books between 1839 and 1845, Minutes, accounts, ledgers, letter book and a Library catalogue of 1844.

F. **132.** Ballitore School : This school was not under the jurisdiction of the Society of Friends though conducted as a Friends' School, open to all denominations. It was started in 1726 by Abraham Shackleton of Yorkshire, who came to Ireland as tutor to the children of the Duckett family. On his retirement he was followed by his son, Richard, a friend of Edmund Burke, who was educated at the school. Richard's son, Abraham, became headmaster for a short time but opposed the liberal traditions of the school and eventually closed it in 1803. It was re-opened in 1806 by James White, son-in-law to Richard Shackleton. The library possesses no official records of the school but the general card index and the Grubb index should be searched for a comprehensive list of references, including a list of scholars, letters from and to pupils, subjects taught, Mss. copies of a magazine produced by the boys, an early stenography book of 1786, school activities etc.

Brookfield School. One large folio volume containing names and particulars of admissions 1836 - 1921.

This was an agricultural school for the children of those who attended Meetings for Worship but were not members of the Society. (c/f Isabel Grubb Quakers in Ireland, 1927).

The school was situated in Moira, Co. Down.

DIARIES

133. The following diaries, journals and reminiscences in the keeping of the Religious Society of Friends in Ireland, and housed at 6 Eustace Street, Dublin, are now kept in the New Strong Room there. They cover the years 1697 to 1864, and are to some extent illustrative of the life of Irish Friends during that period, though they may vary very much in detail and circumstance.

In the main they are entirely personal records, and it is only by reading parallel testimonies, minute books and letters that we can appreciate fully the background and course of the respective writers' lives. Unless indicated otherwise, it is the original manuscript which is preserved.

1 1697 - 1724   Journal of Joseph Gill (1674 - 1741).
2 1713 - 1740   Account by herself of the early part of the life of Elizabeth Ashbridge (1713 - 1755) (copy ; printed).

3	1752 - 1756	Diary of Joshua Wight (1678 - 1758).
4	1781 - 1784	Diary of James Abell (1751 - 1818).
5	1785 - 1790	Diary of George Newsom (1745 - 1790).
6	1786	Journal of the visit of Richard Abell (1750 - 1801) to London Yearly Meeting.
7	1781 - 1855	Life of Robert Goodbody (1781 - 1860) by himself original and typescript.
8	1794	Journal of the visit of John Lecky (1764 - 1839) to London yearly Meeting, 1794.
9	1807 - 1818	Journal of Elizabeth (Grubb) Clibborn (1780 - 1861) (original and typescript copy).
10	1772 - 1826	Diary of Mary (Shackleton) Leadbeater (1758 - 1826) (typescript partial copy).
11	1809 - 1812	Journal of Margaret (Boyle) Harvey (1786 - 1832) (manuscript and typescript copies).
12	1813	Journal of Joshua Newsom (1789 - 1833).
13	1824 - 1852	Extracts from private memoranda of Jane Abell (1787 - 1852).
14	1833 - 1836	Diary of William Raynor (*c.* 1758 - ?).
15	1836	Journal of a visit to France, Switzerland and Italy, by " A member of the Pim family."
16	1837 - 1905	Reminiscences of childhood, and other memorials, prose and verse. Compiled by Deborah Webb (1837 - 1921).
17	1847	Sketch of the visit of Richard Davis Webb (1805 - 1872) to Erris, Co. Mayo.
18	1847 - 1868	Diary of James Hill of Limerick (1818 - 1871).
19	1834 - 1851	Diary of Phebe Newsom (1797 - 1851) (copy).
20	1852	Journal of a three months' tour in Italy with W. Harvey Pim (1811 - 1855). (By Thomas Pim).
21	1853 - 1854	Journal of John Abell (1791 - 1861) (copy).
22	1855 - 1899	Recollections of my life for my grandchildren, by John Lecky (1845 - 1929) (typescript).
23	1868	Diary of Edith Webb (1854 - 1924).
24	1864	Journal of a visit to America, by Frederic W. Pim (1839 - 1924).

134. 1697-1724. Journal of Joseph Gill (1674-1741). Folio manuscript bound in boards (original).

Joseph Gill was the son of William Gill of Skelton, Cumberland, a builder. His childhood was spent under the very strict surveillance of his parents, who were Friends, William Gill having been " convinced at the first coming down of George Fox into the County." In the 20th year of his age George Bewley, of Edenderry, persuaded his parents to allow Joseph to return to Ireland with him, with a capital of £50 to start in business. Finding he did not like life in the country at Edenderry he was, with the help of George Rooke of Dublin, introduced to Benjamin Crawley, a builder of that city. He " wrought with his hands " for a time, but his integrity was the means of promotion and he became overseer to work in Wexford and in Carlow. In the latter place Alderman Burton, on the building of whose large house he was engaged, entrusted him with the laying out of further buildings, finding local materials for the same. Following this he engaged himself in the building and furnishing of barracks. This work was uncongenial and caused him embarrassment, and he returned to Dublin as clerk in Crawley's dealyard.

In 1702, he married Isabel Clarke of Carlisle. The " big new Meeting House " of that city was crowded for the occasion. Delay by reason of contrary winds enabled the couple to visit many Friends in the North of England. On returning to Dublin they started a grocer's shop, but finding such work too confining, he took ground for a timber yard. Having prospered, resisting many temptations, and suffering imprisonment at the time of Thomas Rudd's visit to Ireland (1706), he became increasingly interested in the work of preaching and visiting, and the Journal from 1710 to 1724 gives yearly accounts of visits in Ireland, England, Scotland and the Isle of Man. He notes the mileage travelled in 1716 (excluding Ireland) as 781 miles in 71 days, visiting 73 meetings. His wife died in 1713, and he married again in 1716 Anne Durrance, of Carlisle.

135. 1713-1740. Account by herself of the early part of the life of Elizabeth Ashbridge (1713-1755). Three copies, two in large exercise books, one indexed, and one in small leather notebook ; all probably made in the 18th century. One copy contains at the back " A Brief and True Relation of Ann Wright " (*d.* 1670. See also Mary Leadbeater's *Biographical Notices of . . . Friends*).

This extraordinary story belongs to English rather than to Irish biography. Elizabeth Ashbridge, died at the house of Robert Lecky in the county of Carlow, having returned from America to the British Isles on a visit of service. The account of her life has been printed more than once, the first edition appearing in 1755 (see Smith's *Catalogue of Friends' Books*). She was the daughter of Dr. Thomas and Mary Sampson and was born in Cheshire. After making a clandestine marriage when very young and being widowed after five months, she crossed to Ireland where she had Quaker relatives (though her parents were Episcopalians). Finding herself swayed by religious doubts and unhappy, she hired herself as an indentured servant (not realizing the implications of such a position) and travelled to America where she suffered much of an ignominious nature. Three years later she married a man for whom she had no real regard, and who made a precarious living as a schoolmaster. As he never stayed for long in one place, the subsequent story of her hard life is one of constant journeyings through America, beset always by religious doubts. She became a teacher herself and a convinced Friend. Her husband scoffed at her religion, but presently attended Meetings with her. Temptation becoming strong he relapsed into drinking habits with bad company, left her, and joined the Army. Confronted with the need to fight he said he could not, and so severe was his punishment that he was sent back to

DIARIES   125

the Chelsea Hospital, where he died. His wife heard of his death three years later and subsequently married Aaron Ashbridge, with whom peace at last came to her.

136. 1752-1756. Diary of Joshua Wight (1678-1758). Two small leather bound books (original).

Joshua Wight was the son of Thomas and Deborah Wight of Cork. Thomas Wight was for 49 years clerk to Cork Men's Meeting and compiled the History of Quakers in Ireland, later added to and edited by John Rutty. Joshua married in 1708 Deborah, daughter of Richard and Mary Abell. He was a land surveyor (for a time acting for the Penn family) and partner in the drapery shop of Wight and Pike in Cork. Whilst keeping this diary he was surveying the Estate of Esq. Hamilton of Newcastle, Co. Limerick.

At first sight the books seem to consist only of a weather diary, but closer reading reveals far more. He keeps meticulous day-to-day records of weather, but interspersed are shrewd comments on home and European affairs, on social conditions and on current prices of various commodities. He also comments on Meetings visited, with names of Irish and visiting Friends, and mention is made of persons connected with his work or local happenings. The first volume includes " at the request of several physicians " a relation of the story of the natural cure of a great swelling around his eye whereby he had lost the sight of the eye for some years. Six pages have been inserted into the diary at 3.ix.1753. These are written in another hand of which Joshua Wight disclaims all knowledge in his next entry.

A paper read to the Dublin Friends' Institute in 1917 by his great-great-great-grand-daughter Mary Pike on the material to be found in the diary is kept with it.

137. 1781-1784. Diary of James Abell (1751-1818). Two quarto volumes (original). One bound in boards covered with vellum, the other in calf. These are numbered Vols. 3 and 4. There is no record of Vols. 1 and 2.

James Abell was a merchant of Cork who in his later years became a much valued Friend as evinced by the long testimony to him at his death, signed by 62 Cork Friends, and by the appreciation of his life which appeared in a Cork paper at the same time. This news cutting is pasted to the back of a colour wash of him which has lately been presented to the Library. It depicts him as a tall, lean, angular man, with a large umbrella held handle downwards (presumably to let the drops run off after a shower) striding along, with a calm earnest face, possibly bent on one of his numerous charitable visits.

The four years of early manhood covered by the diary were apparently a period of ill health and great emotional strain. The writing is introspective, and conveys a sense of his labouring under a feeling of his own inadequacy. He was an assiduous attender of all meetings and records his impressions of those for Worship and Discipline, Monthly, Quarterly and National. There are records of the preaching and counsel of Friends, both local and visiting, whose names are in many cases known to the student of Quaker History. Marginal sidenotes record a number of marriages and burials. In first month 1782 he records the first time men and women overseers met together in Cork, " in order to assist each other in the exercise of this weighty office."

138. 1785-1790. Diary of George Newsom (1745-1790). Small copy book (original) in worn brown paper binding.

George Newsom was the son of John and Catherine (Lucas) Newsom of Cork. He married Lydia, daughter of Thomas and Mary (Unthank) Wilson and had 15 children, of whom the last was posthumous. He began the diary on the day he moved to a country place at Glenville, Co. Cork, and the title-page styles it " A memorandum of occurrences at Glenville." Though three of his children were born there he mentions none of them. Nor does he mention a grave mishap to a ship owned by him at this period (see Grubb collection, S.195, Eustace St). He appears to have been a very keen gardener and cultivator of his property as evinced by the lists of plants, etc., sown, and accounts of improvements made on the land. The diary, which is very irregularly kept, ends with the entry 20/5/1790 " the red cow bought of O. Murphy calved." He died on the 29th of 12th mo. the same year.

139. 1786. Journal of the visit of Richard Abell (1750-1801) to London Yearly Meeting, 1786. Small leather-covered notebook, closely written (original).

Richard Abell was the son of Abraham and Elizabeth (Morris) Abell of Cork.

This is a full, detailed account of the journey, in company with four others, to London, and of each session of London Yearly Meeting. They sailed from Dublin on the 11th of 5th month, having come straight from the National Meeting there. They landed at Whitehaven after a 36 hour passage and visited several Friends there. Failing to hire horses, they started in a chaise, a method of travel which soon palled. At Workington, where they were welcomed by Jonathan Ellwood, they hired horses and set out on the long journey to London, which they reached on the first of 6th month, having travelled 437 miles. The journal sets forth, in tabular form, the mileage between each stop, showing the route taken through Cumberland, Westmorland, Yorkshire, Nottinghamshire, Leicester, Bedford, Hertford and into London by way of Tottenham. It is a lively, entertaining narrative, the names of those with whom they stayed, or whom they met providing valuable data. They were wont to start each day's journey very early and the diarist records that at one point they had told their hostess not to bestir herself, nevertheless when they arose they found her with a hot breakfast ready. " As I pushed in my chair after the meal the clock struck five o'clock hearken ye wives and learn." In London he attended Meeting for Ministers and Elders by invitation, as well as other sessions and comments on all he saw and heard. He found the Meeting House very hot. The Journal provides an interesting commentary, not only on Yearly Meeting, but on personalities among Friends of that period.

140. 1781-1855. Account of his life by Robert Goodbody (1781-1860) (original).

Robert Goodbody, ancestor to nearly all the family of that name in Ireland, was the second son of Mark and Elizabeth (Pim) Goodbody of Mountmellick. He married (first) Margaret, daughter of Jonathan and Sarah (Robinson) Pim, by whom he had six sons; (2nd) Jane daughter of James and Deborah (Bewley) Pim (no issue). In the 74th year of his age he wrote a full retrospective account of his life. The early part contains much of local interest, of marriages into, and visits between other Friends' families, and details of life of the period. There is a full and vivid account of the Rebellion of 1798, with many details of happenings in Rathangan, Mountmellick and Wexford. Mention is made of the precautions taken and help given by Friends in the very wet summer of 1799, when the timely purchase of potato and other seed, resold at a reasonable price, averted distress.

Robert Goodbody did not follow his father's trade of a tanner, but became a flour miller and baker. Following the death of his wife, he moved in 1826 to Clara, in King's Co., having bought a partnership in the Brusna Flour Mills.

Amongst visiting Friends noted in this life are Job Scott, Thomas Scattergood, William Crotch and Hannah Barnard whose preaching, in 1800, was the cause of closing Sycamore Alley Meeting House for a period. The visit of John Wesley to Mountmellick, about 1789, is also noted.

141. 1794. Journal of the visit of John Lecky (1764-1839). to London Yearly Meeting, 1794. A very small, worn notebook (original).

John Lecky was the son of Robert and Margaret (Harvey) Lecky of Youghal. He was often known as "John Lecky the Banker."
This little journal contains much of value to the social and Quaker historian, giving as it does details of prices prevailing at the period, and mentioning names of persons and places. It was published in *Jnl. F.H.S.*, xv (1918) with detailed notes by J. Ernest Grubb.

142. 1807-1818. Journal of Elizabeth (Grubb) Clibborn (1780-1861) (original and typescript copy). Original in stitched sheets of quarto paper on the first of which is written in the handwriting, probably of one of her daughters. " Elizabeth Clibborn's Journal, this the earliest found, begins 1807." The typescript has at some recent period been annotated, giving matter relative to the names which occur throughout the Journal.

Elizabeth Clibborn was the daughter of John (1737-1784) and Sarah (Pim) Grubb. Her mother who, at her husband's death, had been left with five small girls, continued to live (against her family's advice) at Anner Mills, Clonmel, and to run the mill there. In 1791 John Clibborn of Moate came to assist Sarah and, in 1800, married her daughter Elizabeth. John Barclay Clibborn and Elizabeth continued to reside at Anner Mills, which was left to them at Sarah Grubb's death in 1832. They had 15 children, three of whom died young.

This Journal is one of the most interesting in the Library. It is probable that she kept a diary for much longer periods, as one exists, still in private keeping, for the years 1846- and for 1850; this will eventually come to the Library and it is hoped other fragments may be found. (Sheets of quarto paper, some white coarse and some blue smooth, written in a close, neat, angular hand, should be looked for.) They were possibly divided amongst her children or grandchildren when she died.

Meetings, accounts of visits (and most visiting Friends, including Elizabeth Fry, came to Anner Mills), records of national happenings, fluctuations in trade and in prices, all occur here. But family occurrences occupy the greater part of the Journal, and this is not surprising as the Grubbs and Clibborns were related to very nearly every Friends' family in Ireland. A partly suppressed note of anxiety and worry runs through much of it, as baby after baby was born and she and her husband and family occupied only a bed chamber and nursery (with a little closet off for a maid) and had nowhere to sit or entertain their own friends. This was partly remedied later, but we know that Mother Sarah Grubb was a capable domineering woman, who became known as " The Queen of the South."

143. 1772-1826. Diary of Mary (Shackleton) Leadbeater (1758-1826) (abstract).

Mary Shackleton was the daughter of Richard, master of Ballitore school, and grand-daughter of Abraham Shackleton, its founder. In 1792 she married William Leadbeater, an usher at her father's school, who died less than a year after her own death. Mary Leadbeater is best known as the compiler of *The Annals of Ballitore* (the little Kildare village where her life was spent) more usually called *The Leadbeater Papers*. Her diary, kept day by day, was begun when she was 14 and kept to within a few days of her death. It is a most valuable contribution to the sociological history of Ireland. The original is at present deposited for safe keeping in the National Library of Ireland, but a typescript, with few omissions, was made by our Friend Isabel Grubb, formerly curator of the Historical Library at Eustace Street, and is owned by the latter. It is the diary of a keen alert mind, not narrowed by village life or by difficult financial circumstance, but enriched and cultivated by the intercourse and broadmindedness of her father and grandfather. Her friendships included among many others, that of Edmund Burke, a past pupil of her father, George Crabbe, the poet, Melesina St. George, mother, by a later marriage, of Archbishop Chenevix Trench; and through the Shackleton family she was related to most of the prominent Friends' families in Ireland. The diary covers the period of the French Revolution (made vivid by the imprisonment of Mrs. St. George in Paris), of the Irish affairs of the 1790's culminating in the terrible insurrection of 1798, during which the sufferings of Friends and others in Ballitore are minutely told. Visits to Meetings in many parts of Ireland, inter-visiting with Friends' families, an account of the secessions of 1800-1803, when her brother Abraham Shackleton was among the first to leave the Society, are all narrated with the freshness of reality.

She was the author of a book of poems, of a series of essays known as *Cottage Dialogues* and *Cottage Biographies*, of a translation of Maffeus's Continuation of the Aeneid and of a volume of Biographies of Irish Friends but her diary is the true record of an unassuming and selfless mind.

144. 1809-1812. Journal of Margaret (Boyle) Harvey (1786-1832) of a trip to, and sojourn in, Ireland. Two ms. copies, one in small leather notebook copied by Elizabeth H. Theobald in 1906, the other stitched foolscap made by H. L. Harvey from a copy made from the original by Margaret Boyle Harvey II, grand-daughter of the writer of the original. This journal was printed in America in 1915, and extracts from it appeared in *jnl. F.H.S.*, xxiv (1927) p. 3. The American edition contains a family genealogy, and the extracts printed in the *Journal* are well annotated.

Margaret B. Harvey was the daughter of James and Martha (Williams) Boyle of Pennsylvania. In 1808 she married Edward (1783-1858), son of William and Margaret (Stephens) Harvey of Cork, who had gone to America to further the trade of his uncle Stephens, a maker of beaver hats. In 1809 the couple came back to Ireland, where they lived for three years, and where two sons were born, the first dying at birth.

Cork Friends of the period were a distinct surprise to the young bride and her journal, written purely for the eyes of her sister, expresses her astonishment at the elegance, style and formal etiquette encountered. Constant entertainments tired her out, both in Cork and Dublin, though she was able to appreciate the beautiful scenery of the former and the well-laid-out streets and handsome appointments of the houses in the latter. She had had a simple upbringing, but made the best of all she encountered, though the richness of food rather upset her—" the Banquet, for so I must call it . . . I have read of such but never expected to see anything like it . . . there were about eight courses. The first green Turtle with plenty of soup, which I partook of and talked of, for I was asked a number of questions about our Turtles. I answered with as much Sang Froid as if I had been used to Turtle Feasts all my life."

Many well-known Irish Friends appear throughout the pages of this journal, mostly relatives of the Harvey family, which had a very big connection. She received unstinted kindness from everyone, but was very glad, when the time came, to return home " to our loved ones," when her son Richard was three months old. The journal ends when they had been seven weeks at sea, having a rough passage, but the supplement, added by Margaret Harvey's grand-daughter, completes the account (in the printed edition) with further information concerning the family.

145. 1813. Journal of a trip to England for business purposes and to attend London Yearly Meeting, 1813, by Joshua Newsom (1789-1833) (original). Paper sheets stitched.

Joshua Newsom was the son of George and Lydia (Wilson) Newsom of Edenderry. He was attached to a grocery business in Waterford. His marriage to Isabel Hill, daughter of James and Hannah (Strangman) Hill of that city, points to the supposition that he may have been connected with the extensive grocery business of the Strangmans. This is a journal of a trip to try to further the butter trade of Waterford with the merchants and traders of the Southern parts of England. It is a record of great importance, as he not only gives the names of all towns and cities visited, but also of the persons whom he visited in each one. He ended up in London and gives an account of Yearly Meeting of that year, as well as of the business acquaintances visited in the City. As the butter trade of Waterford had been a very important part of Ireland's economy in the previous century (*cf.* " The overseas trade of Waterford " ; by Louis M. Cullen, in *The Journal of the Royal Society of Antiquaries of Ireland*, Vol. 88, part 2, 1958) this provides a valuable link with later years.

146. 1824-1852. Extracts from the private memoranda of Jane Abell (1787-1852). Copy made by her sister Sarah in 1853.

Jane Abell was the daughter of Richard and Elizabeth (Beale) Abell of Cork. The memoranda consist entirely of a Spiritual Diary, not noting anything but that which had refreshed or helped her on life's way. The third volume speaks of beginning her 9th little book, so that these must be only part of a series. The first shows signs of partial burning, and there is a note expressing a wish that nothing she wrote should ever be published.

147. 1833-1836. Diary of William Raynor (*c.* 1758 - ?). Small paper book (original).

William Raynor was the son of Maurice and Elizabeth (Shackleton) Raynor. His mother was the daughter of Abraham Shackleton of Ballitore School. She made a clandestine marriage (see *Annals of Ballitore*, vol. I, p.27) and, dying in early life, left the child William to be brought up by his grandparents. Ballitore school list gives the entry of Maurice Raynor as 1744. He became an usher. The son William is entered on 13/10/1766.

The diary is a disconnected and sad record of a few incidents in late life, when he was in apparent poverty. Twice there are touching references to the death of his Mother, 68 years previously. From the time of his strict upbringing at Ballitore to the appearance of this unexpected diary, we have no record of his life save thirteen letters written when he was living in Waterford between 1778 and 1789 to his aunt Deborah (Shackleton) Chandlee. Through her he kept in touch with his Ballitore friends.

148. 1836. Journal of a visit to France, Italy and Switzerland, by " A member of the Pim family " (original). Leather exercise book.

A well written, instructive and entertaining account of a conventional European tour, travelling largely by Diligence, sometimes post. There are many such journals of this period, but this has a freshness of outlook, an accuracy of observation and a vividness of description which have appeal. Cities, buildings, cathedrals, scenery, river travel, persons encountered, Friends and others, all give a sense of reality. It was written by a woman, possibly one of the daughters of James and Anne (Greenwood) Pim travelling with her brother, Henry, this latter name being the sole clue to identity in the Journal. Henry (1803-1881) is the only Pim of that name to fit the date.

149. 1837-1905. Reminiscences of childhood, by DEBORAH WEBB (1837-1921). With this is a collection of Prose and Verse collected by the author. Among these is a copy of " Recollections " by Lizzie Poole Addey (1818-1886), who was a cousin of the Webb family and who had been Elizabeth Poole, of Growtown, Co. Wexford.

Deborah Webb was the elder daughter of Richard Webb and Hannah (Waring) Webb of Dublin. Her elder brother was Alfred Webb, the compiler of " A Compendium of Irish Biography." The book (a thick quarto notebook, professionally bound in leather) should properly be styled Memorials, collected by Alfred Webb. The reminiscences, however, kept by Deborah, occupy the first 88 pages, and those of Lizzie Addey the following 57 pages. The next 15 consist of an appreciation of Richard Davies Webb, copied from a Boston periodical of about 1872, and these are followed by copies of two letters written to Alfred Webb, at the time of the illness and death of his father.

Deborah Webb's reminiscences are an important and rewarding aid to the study of the life of Irish Friends of the last century. Brought up in a houshold neither wordly, nor yet too strict, she and her brothers had the advantage of meeting their father's friends in different walks of life, and she recalls her surprise at being, as a small child, kissed by a priest, who later turned out to be Father Matthew, the great Temperance Pioneer.

The reminiscences of Elizabeth (Poole) Addey form a valuable contribution to the history of Friends in Co. Wexford, and her traditional account of the Rebellion of 1798 should be compared with that of Dinah Goff, printed in " Six Generations in Ireland," by J. M. R. (Richardson) (London, *Hicks*, 1893).

150. 1847. Sketch of the visit of R. D. WEBB (1805-1872) to Erris in Co. Mayo (original), paper, stitched.

This essay is marked, at the top of the first title page, " Appendix lv," its full title being " Sketch of R. D. Webb's visit to the Counties of Mayo and Galway by desire of the Central Relief Committee of Friends." It appears to be one of the notebooks kept while undertaking the work of visiting areas struck most hardly by Famine, and making reports on such for the Committee. It is a vivid but factual account of the horror of the period, giving instances of the scenes witnessed in this (one of the most hardly-stricken) area of the country. It was from such reports that the published account of the work of The Central Committee for Famine Relief was later compiled.

Richard Davis Webb was the son of James and Deborah (Davis) Webb of Dublin, and was a well-known printer and publisher. He was a friend of Father Matthew, the Temperance Pioneer, and was active in Temperance work, in the Anti-Slavery cause and in Peace work. A note on his life appeared in *Jnl. F.H.S.*, xiv (1917) 95.

151. 1847-1868. Diary of James Hill of Limerick (1818-1871). One folio volume ; cardboard cover (original).

James Hill was the son of James and Elizabeth (Alexander) Hill and married Margaret, daughter of Thomas and Mary (Unthank) Newsom of Cork. He appears to have grown up a Friend, though his father had been disowned in 1821 for debt. He himself resigned his membership in 1853, and his wife in 1855. The diary begins in 1847, just after the death of his father; his mother died the following year. The first 48 pages have been removed, but the verso of the cover shows the rough copy of an application made by him in 1848 for the post of traveller to the Clonmel firm of Thomas Grubb, and an account of his experiences while travelling. The diary is of very minor interest. It gives day by day accounts of the weather and detailed records of visits paid to London and elsewhere, mainly in search of work (which when obtained he never held any length of time). He visited relatives in America, who tried to employ him, but he came home again. He went to a concert in aid of Irish distress, but never seems to have been aware of the real suffering in the country, only lamenting the high price of potatoes. This diary is worth reading for its picture of a section of Irish people unable to grasp the opportunities of helping the needs of the rest.

152. 1834-1851. Extracts from the diary of Phebe Newsom (1797-1851). Small book bound in thick cardboard (copy).

Phebe Newsom was the daughter of Henry and Elizabeth Ridgway of Waterford. In 1824 she married William Newsom of Limerick. This is a deeply spiritual diary, revealing the religious doubts and uncertainties felt by the writer as to her fitness to contribute vocally and actively in Meeting, and her pleasure as she found that way opened for her to do so. The record is not continuous, there being a gap of three years from 1834, the year in which she became a recorded minister. Following after the end of her memoranda is a long Testimony to her.

153. 1852. Journal of a three months' tour in Italy with W. Harvey Pim (1811-1885). Quarto notebook covered in cardboard (original).

On the top corner of the first page is pasted a scrap of paper ¾ by 1¼ inches with the words " Dear Thos., I shall be very glad of thy company to London, etc., ' on Velvet ' after the books for 2nd month are balanced, thy affec. W. H. Pim."

The recipient of the note and writer of the Journal was Thomas, son of Jonathan and Susanna (Todhunter) Pim, and the invitation was from his uncle. They were both members of the firm of Pim Bros. and Co., wholesale and retail Drapers, Manufacturers and Warehousemen of Dublin.

The Journal begins on the 3rd of 3rd month 1852. It is a complete record, day by day, of the trip, describing, with the fresh vividness of youth routes taken, people encountered, buildings and places of interest visited, and commenting on each with clarity and with the advantage of a well-equipped, well-read mind.

154. 1835-1854. Journal of John Abell (1791-1861) (copy). Small notebook, of which the verso of cover and first page are Richardson and Sons' Almanac for the year 1856. On the third page is written "Extracts from John Abell's Memoranda, copied as a Birthday present for Jane Abell by her affectionate Aunt Sarah Abell, 2nd month, 1st 1863."

John Abell was the 8th child of Richard and Margaret (Beale) Abell. At the time this Journal was kept, his brother Joshua was lately deceased, and John, with his wife, had undertaken the oversight of Joshua's two children, though their mother was still living. It is a slight, irregularly-kept journal, consisting almost entirely of prayers for the welfare of the two children. It jumps from the year 1857 to 1859 and then back to the year 1847 when he records the weight felt by his being made an overseer. He records apprenticing his nephew to Thomas Thompson of Enniscorthy, and the departure of his niece to Penketh School in 1859.

155. 1855-1899. Recollections of my life for my grandchildren; by John Lecky (1845-1929). Typescript, bound in stiff paper, small. (Possibly the original made by John Lecky). Mentions on cover that a copy with appendix was sent to W. J. Lecky, Montreal, August, 1928.

John Lecky was a son of Robert John and Mary (Newsom) Lecky of Youghal. In his tenth year his father, who had been a shipbuilder in Cork, took over the management of a slate quarry on Valentia Island. The journal begins with an account of the journey there, travelling on one of the famous Bianconi cars, and for the first time seeing turf burnt. It describes life on the island, the garden, where Arum lilies grew in profusion as well as much else, sailing and other simple pleasures, the designing and building of a boat for himself by his father, and all the pleasures of a simply happy life. In 1856 the first cable to America was laid from Valentia, and much space is given to that momentous event. Many came to watch and listen for the first transmitted message, among them a little Russian gentleman, who later turned out to be the once famous Dr. Hamel, employed by Russia to find out all the scientific information he could. As is known, this earliest attempt to lay a submarine cable was a failure and this eye-witness account is of the greatest interest.

His schooldays and entry into the tea business follow, with a note of the welcome given him by Dublin Friends. The journal ends on the suggestion to his grandchildren that his success in life has all been due to hard work.

156. 1868. Diary of Edith Webb (1854-1924). Small leather jotter (original).

Edith Webb was the daughter of James and Susanna Webb. This diary was kept by Edith Webb in her fourteenth year. After a retrospective account of some previous weeks, it became a day-to-day account of the happenings in the lives of her and her sisters. It contains an entertaining account of the visit to Dublin of the Prince of Wales and Princess Alexandra. Seen through the eyes of a child, who confesses herself more childish than others of her age, this makes lively reading. Later in the year she and her sister, Gertrude, went to Mountmellick school, and here we find the inward reflections, both on the journey and on arrival, which while common in autobiography, are seldom written at the time. This very small diary could be much appreciated by those who knew Edith Webb in later years, when she took up teaching as a profession, and was for some time Record clerk in Dublin.

The book in which the diary is written was a present to the writer from H. Webb and E. W. Banks on her twelfth birthday (8 February, 1866). The first entry begins; " Note. These first few no‘es are things that I would like to have written down and that happened last year." It is followed by sixteen small pages devoted to events in 1867, before opening the diary of 1868 proper.

157. 1864. Journal of a visit to America, by Frederic W. Pim (1839-1924) (original). Two leather-covered note books. At the end of the second one there is transcribed " The Transit of Venus," this being evidently a lecture given by Frederic Pim to the Dublin Friends' Institute, in 1876. This of course was a scientific lecture, descriptive of the transit of Venus across the face of the sun, a phenomenon which had occurred two years earlier, on the 9th December, 1874.

Frederic William Pim was the sixth child of Jonathan and Susanna (Todhunter) Pim and was a partner in the firm of Pim Bros. and Co., of Dublin, and at the time of this visit to America was representing the Greenmount Linen spinning company, connected with that business. He gives a full account of the journey and modes of travel and people met with. Though based on New York he made his way through New Jersey, by Philadelphia (where he remarked on the neglect of the memorial to William Penn), by Baltimore and Pittsburgh to the Great Lakes. He visited Montreal and Quebec, travelling sometimes by boat, sometimes by train, observing and noting all he saw. He had a grasp of the troop movements of both Northern and Southern armies and was occasionally asked for credentials. His comments on the economic situation in the United States are of much interest, it being a time when the fluctuations in the price of gold and the endeavours of business firms to obtain credit or furnish themselves with the new paper money, were causing embarrassment and acute difficulty to many.

158. 1841-1886. Diary of Lydia (Clibborn) Goodbody (1809-1886).

Lydia Goodbody was the daugther of Elizabeth and John Barclay Clibborn of Anner Mills, Clonmel. In 1842 she married Jonathan, son of Robert and Margaret (Pim) Goodbody and came to reside in Clara, Offaly. A few months prior to her marriage she commenced keeping a diary in small leather bound notebooks, one for each year. This she continued without a break until a few days before her death. Jonathan Goodbody, who was one of those actively engaged in relief work at the period of the great famine, was one of a large family, and the diary contains detail of both Goodbody and Clibborn activities.

It covers the period of and gives detail of the building of the present Clashawaun Jute works which was founded by Jonathan and Lewis F. Goodbody.

The diary is mainly domestic in its character, but conveys a good deal of current events. Each year is followed by a summary of notable events which have taken place, domestic and general.

GENEALOGICAL MATERIAL

JONES INDEX

159. The library possesses a valuable aid to research into Irish Quaker genealogy in a table made a few years ago by our friend, Isabel Jones. This lists every surname occurring in the registers of the Society of Friends in Ireland, showing the Monthly Meeting in which each name appears, thus minimising search time.

Registers have been listed in the archives section; many go back to the 17th century. Those in use are abstracts made in the last century.

PEDIGREES

The Thomas Henry Webb pedigrees are so called from the name of their compiler. They are detailed family pedigrees for 232 Irish Quaker families.

FITZGERALD PEDIGREES

A small collection of family genealogies made by Dr. Fitzgerald in recent years.

ISOLATED PEDIGREES

Shown in general manuscript index.

RESEARCH WORK

In the last ten years all genealogical research work has been filed and is accessible under the name of the family into which research has been done and under the name of the enquirer. Any earlier work, when found, has also been catalogued. This minimises duplication of work.

Lists of names of those who from one cause or another left the Religious Society have been alphabetically arranged with dates; as are Testimonies to deceased persons. These provide a valuable aid to searchers, though they do not provide conclusive material, nor can they be regarded as complete lists.

A small notebook, alphabetically arranged by the late John M. Douglas gives many names of Friends who by marrying members of other religious bodies forfeited membership of the Society in the past. These are mainly taken from the Province Minutes for Ulster.

Names of testators and beneficiaries and witnesses to loose will in the Library are all indexed; as are the names of parties contracting marriages, but not the names of witnesses to marriage certificates. In addition to the books of certificates mentioned in the Archive Section, there are many loose ones in the library. For wills already printed see *Quaker Wills*, Eustace and Goodbody, 1957.

WILL ABSTRACTS

160. ABELL, JOHN, of Riverview, in Borough of Limerick.

To sister Sarah Abell, £15 per annum to be paid either out of asset property or from interest of Corporation Debentures, as may suit her best. To Richard and Jane Abell, both minors, children of late brother Joshua Abell, interest in freehold estate of Riverview at Corbally in Borough of Limerick as tenants in common after decease of Elizabeth Ridgeway Abell, wife of testator, with reversion to George Samuel of Belfast (late of Cork) and to his children and sisters " my nieces Eliza Bewley and Sarah Dixon and their children." Residue of every kind to wife aforesaid.

Advising wife to make will as soon as may be after testators decease making provision to repay money lent by Dublin Monthly Meeting for the education of testator's nephew and niece Richard and Jane Abell, such money having been left in trust to his executors for his wife's benefit.

Executors: Thomas White Jacob, of Waterford, Benjamin Haughton of Cork, and Humphreys Manders Goulding of Cork (my two brothers-in-law).

Dated 17th 9th month 1858.

Witnesses: John Scarr, John Niall.

Proved Limerick, 7th September, 1861.

161. ALLEN, REBECCA, of Waterford.

Money bequests to the following: Brothers Nathan and Samuel Gatchell; niece Elizabeth Walpole, Mary Wood; George Gatchell, Francis Gatchell, Isabella Gatchell, children of late brother Jonathan Gatchell; Jonathan Joshua Gatchell, Mary Ann Gatchell and Henry Gatchell children of late nephew Joshua Gatchell; Elizabeth Gatchell, Rebecca Gatchell and Mary Gatchell, children of brother Nathan, the last named nine being under 21 years. Residue to brother James Gatchell, sole executor.

Dated 20th 9th month 1824.

Witnesses: Abraham Henderson, George Saunders.

162. ALMENT, JOHN, Leaghmore, suburb of Cork, Farmer.

The two-thirds of Leaghmore possessed by testator to go to wife Elizabeth and son John Alment, the latter under 21. Son James Doyle to remain as heretofore in possession of the one-third part of Leaghmore.

To wife, and children John, Sarah, Mark, Joseph and William Alment (all under age) division of effects with provision for James Doyle. Three sons to be apprenticed to trades agreeable to them.

Executors : John Garratt, Richard Chamberlain.

Dated " this day of " 6th month called June, 1752.

Witnesses : James Dreaper, Sam Dreaper, Thomas Wily.

Signature : John Alment.

Inventory dated " this day of the 7th month called July, 1752 " signed by Elizabeth, Sarah and John Alment for selves and other minors. Includes sundry furniture, pewter trenchers and earthen plates and dishes. A gun worth 2/1. Cheese making materials, cattle and horses, a hog worth 8/- a bull worth £1 crops including rye, barley, oats. Debts due from John and Thomas Alment, Jonathan Ash, Geo. Randall, John Smith.

163. BENNIS, WILLIAM, of City of Limerick (copy).

All property in concerns in William Street (Limerick), interest in the house and also books and furniture of every kind. " The Annuity to be paid by Clonmel Annuity Society Interest in Taylor Street (after paying W. W. Harvey of Cork one hundred pounds which he kindly lent on it), any other property.

" Children to be reared up in ancient principles of the Society as laid down by Fox, Barclay, Dewsbury and Penn."

Executors : Samuel Evans and James Fisher.

Dated 29th of 4th month, 1842.

Witnesses : George Horoe, Charles Fitzgerald.

164. BEWLEY, THOMAS, City of Cork, Tanner.

To wife Mary Bewley (sole executrix) and daughters Sarah and Ann Bewley, all estate of whatsoever kind to be equally divided with reversion to survivors or survivor.

Dated 13th of 4th month, 1763.

Father-in-law John Garratt and Ebenezer Pike to see will perfected.

165. BOLES, JOHN, of Woodhouse.

To friend and son-in-law, Solomon Watson of Clonbrogan and heirs rights, etc., in graveyard (unspecified) where son, John Boles, is buried, for use of Quakers of Co. Tipperary (Woodhouse Burial Ground).

Will dated 14th September, 1731.

166. BOLES, JOHN, Woodhouse, Tipperary.

Inventory made by Ann Boles, daughter, and Samuel Watson, executor.

Debts due from Daniel White, Oliver Simmons and R. Sparrow, John Jacobs, John Carney and Mother, H. Blackmore and P. Butler. Jonas Chamberlain, Henry Hillary, William Hughes, John Letham, Charles Howell and Thos. Rigg, Ann Boles, John Godfrey. Cash in John Bagwell's hands in Clonmel. Cash and Cash Notes in house.

Cattle : 9 cows at £1 17s. each. One bull calf and two yearling calves, horses, mares, filly and blind mule, valuation of corn, hay and pigs. Rents due by Thomas Godwin, William Winslow, John Godfrey, Sol. Watson.

John Boles died in 1731, as did his son another John.

167. CARLETON, SAMUEL, Ballitore, Co. Kildare.

To Sarah, wife of Samuel Haughton, of Carlow, £80, and to Elizabeth, wife of John Mark of Dublin, £20 provided that each shall renounce any other claim to the effects of testator or of his late son, Thomas.

My brothers, John and Jonathan Carleton; cousins Thomas and John Chandlee, both of the town of Athy. Children (not named) of Benjamin Greenwood, deceased, of Portarlington. Elizabeth Thompson daughter of John Thompson of Ballinakill, Queen's County. To the Men's Meeting of Dublin £5 for relief of the Poor. To Elizabeth Widdows two guineas and to Mary Nowlan one guinea, servants to Richard Shackleton of Ballitore. Wearing apparel, whether of linen or wool, to brother Jonathan to divide between himself, brother John and Thomas Thompson, son of the late John Thompson. Table linen and second best sheets to Elizabeth, widow of John Haughton; remainder of house linen to Jonathan Haughton of Ballitore; to said Jonathan's daughter, Hannah " my new clothes press which hath a chest of drawers thereto belonging and adjoining." My gun to John, son of Jonathan Haughton. To my cousin Mary, daughter of Richard Shackleton, my mahogany nest of drawers and silver can, to cousin Thomas Chandlee my large Bible, to cousin Elizabeth, wife of Richard Shackleton my two watches and appurtenances thereto. To Sarah and to Deborah Shackleton a silver can and silver cream ewer respectively. Various silver items to cousin Margaret, daughter of Deborah Christy of Stramore, Co. Down; cousin Abigail Thompson of Athy; cousin Thomas Chandlee; Hannah, Deborah and Sarah, daughters of Jonathan Haughton.

Executors Thomas Chandlee and Richard Shackleton.

Dated 16th November, 1779.

Witnesses: Peter Cambridge, Jos. Webster, Amos May.

168. CHAMBERLAIN, ELIJAH, City of Dublin, Merchant.

Cousins John and Benjamin Burder of London, Tailor and Baker, respectively. Cousin Henry Burder of Lambeth, Baker, cousin Boston at the Sign of the Swan and Two Necks in Shoe Lane, London, Grocer. Eldest child of brother-in-law Thos. Cox, of July Street, Southwark, London, Grocer. Brother-in-law Henry Harris in Deptford. To the Men's Meeting of Quakers in Dublin £100 in trust to be used to purchase land on which the interest paid is to be applied to the support of the poor of Quakers at Dublin belonging to their Poorhouse. To John Barclay and Jacob Goff of Dublin, merchants, executors and trustees; to Joseph Maddocks of Meath Street, Dublin; widow Bates's children; Benjamin Holmes of England; the widow of Thomas Russell; Thomas Russell, son of latter; Paul Johnson and Thomas Strangman, all monetary bequests. To the Blew Coat Hospital, Dublin, to the Incorporated Society in Dublin for promoting English Protestant Schools in Ireland. To Ann Russell, daughter of Francis Russell.

Dated 1st March, 1743.

Witnesses: Henry Stearnes, Will Sumner (not. pub.).

See abstract 47 Quaker Wills, of the same testator, drawn up 1755.

169. CONRAN, HENRY, Dublin.

To my wife, Elizabeth Conran, my concerns in Francis Street and Patrick Street, City of Dublin, to be paid out of them subject to head landlords rent, £100 per annum, failing which said money to be paid from concerns in Newmarket and Skinners Alley, Liberties of Co.

Dublin. Reversion to eldest son, James, and to his son, Robert, and his issue in tail male, failing such issue to John Conran, second son of said James and to his issue in tail male, failing which to the other sons of son James Conran, the eldest and his issue being always preferred. Lands in Knocklane, Co. Louth, concerns in Smithfield in Oxmantown (Dublin), Blessington in Fingal, Dolphins Barn Lane. Daughters Elizabeth, Magdalen, Mary, Sophia £500 each, provided they marry with consent of my brother, James Conran. My father James Conran (deceased), my daughter Marriott Conran, ors. Macanalley one shilling.

Executors : wife and brother James.

Dated 16th July, 1767.

Witnesses : Ri. Fenner, Saml. Kathrens, Josh Hamilton.

170. COOPER, DAVID, (contemporary copy).

A long preamble which includes thanks to God for " the little worldly substance committed to my care from His providential hand and my industry."

To Master Saml. Pike twenty five pounds "which is as much as will make up the deficiency of his cash, which I now have the keeping of."

To Saml. Beal, son of Benjamin and Rachel Beal forty pounds. To brother John Cooper £25. To each of own sisters (not named) £15 and to each half sister £5. To Grace Hetherington three guineas. Residue to brother John Cooper. Saml. Beal son of Benjamin to distribute and pay all and see justice to each person.

Dated 28th June, 1753.

Witness : Reuben Harvey.

171. CULLIMORE, DANIEL.

This copy of will is substantially the same as that included in *Quaker Records, Dublin, Abstracts of Wills*, No. 55, as taken from Book F.6.55. (Wexford) but includes two nieces Elizabeth and Ruth and one nephew Isaac all children of brother John Cullimore " of Ross".

The copy attested by John Vallenling. 11th April, 1760.

172. CULLIMORE, GEORGE, Ballykenegan, Co. Wexford, Farmer.

To my natural son, Peter Cullimore of Enniscorthy, cordwainer, £100 and to my natural daughter, Mary Caul, wife of Edward Caul of Growtown, cordwainer, £60. Servants, Mary Coleman and Honor Brien.

Fifty pounds to be paid on trust for the school maintained by the Province of Leinster, or, should it discontinue, to the poor among Quakers of the Monthly Meeting of Co. Wexford. To my nephew, Thomas Vallintine, £70; my nieces, Elizabeth Dalton and Experience Cooper, £20 each; my nieces Mary Murphy and Hannah Vallintine, £5 each. To Elizabeth Hallyer, Mary Clampite and Sarah Barton (daughters of my niece, Sarah White, late of City of Waterford, deceased) £60 to be equally divided. To my nieces, Elizabeth and Ruth Cullimore of Ross, £66 to be divided. All houshold goods, clothes, beds, bedding, kitchen furniture, cattle, crop, farming utensils to Peter Cullimore and Mary Caul aforesaid. Executors: grand-nephew John Cullimore and Joseph Poole.

Dated 1st December, 1785.

Witnesses: William Sparrow, Robert Woodcock, John Furlong, (autographs).

173. WILLIAM EDMUNDSON.

(Copy from typescript presented by Mrs. Doreen (Edmundson) Foley).

To wife, Mary, all household goods, wool, lining, (?linen) brass, pewter plate, money in and about the house, together with two cows, one horse or mare and £100 sterling in money forever. Likewise my wife, Mary, shall have peaceable dwelling in the house I now live in, with gardens, orchards, etc. Grazing and hay for two cows on three small parks and grazing for horses of Friends visiting her. Also turf for firing on the farm and liberty for life from molestation or rent; after her decease all above privileges and appurtenances to son, Tryal Edmundson; said son interest in farm of Tineel, excepting aforementioned reserves. Likewise the graveyard which I give to my Friends, the people in scorn called Quakers. To said son, Tryal, interest in grazing on derry Lennoys, and to his children, forty pounds sterling to be improved by their father and divided to them or survivors with profits.

To children of unhappy son, William, forty pounds sterling, executors to pay it to their father to improve it and give greater part to good and gentle, and lesser to wicked and forward.

To children of unruly son, Samuel, forty pounds sterling to be paid to father when will proved.

To children of foolish and disobedient daughter, Hindrance Seale, Jane, Thomas, Martha, Elizabeth, James, Gregory, £10 sterling each, to be improved by executors with advice of Trustees.

To grandson, William Seale, apprentice with Michael Lightfoot, £15 sterling due on bond from Richard Grey and William Bushell of Mountmellick, executors, to improve till apprenticeship ends.

To rebellious daughter, Anne Moore, wife of Lawrence Moore, deceased, her three daughters, Ann, Anna, Rebecca, £10 sterling.

'To my seven children,' William, Samuel, Tryall Edmundson, Mary Fayle, Susanna Sheldon, Hindrance Seale. Anna Moore, £5 sterling each.

Son-in-law, Eleazar Sheldon, to account for substance already given in trust for children. All above donees to discharge with quietness receipt of legacies.

To children of step-son-in-law, Thos. Strangman, Thos. and Susanna Strangman, two guineas to be improved by their grandfather, Thomas Ashton.

Executors : George Rooke of Meath Street, Dublin, Tryall Edmundson.

Observers : James Hutchinson of Knockballymagher, Thomas Winslow of Birr, Richard Eaves of Ballymoyle, Joshua Strangman of Mountmellick.

Dated 19th October, 1710.

Witnesses : Richard Grey, Richard Eaves, Thomas Wilkinson, Richard Clarke.

174. ELLY, ABIGAIL, City of Cork.

Widow of William Richard Elly of Dublin.

Brother James Beale of Cork Trustee and Executor to receive dividends from St. George Steam Packet Company and to pay same in equal moieties to mother Susanna Lecky and sister Susanna Beale, but transferring one half of said property in said Company to brother Robert John Lecky after Mother's death and to allow said sister to dispose of the other half as she thinks fit, verbally or in writing. Residue to Mother for sole use and disposal.

Dated 3rd 12th month 1835.
Witnesses : William Harvey, John Lecky. (Original signatures.)
L.L.389.

175. FENNELL, JOSHUA, of Kilcommon.

EXTRACT OF WILL

Confirms to the Monthly Meeting of the people called Quakers of Co. Tipperary the burying place on the lands of Ballibrado by a lease renewable from William Austin. Will dated 15th November, 1761.

176. FULLER, ABRAHAM, City of Cork, Linen-Draper.

Money bequests to brother Joseph Fuller, sole executor, to sister Martha Ashton wife of Joshua Ashton (to whom part debt remitted) to niece Martha Fuller annuity up to age of 21 years when she is to receive capital of £250 unless she marries without consent of executor.

To testator's mother-in-law Blessing Bewley his household goods now in her house. To sister Susanna Allen silver coffee pot. Leases and other assets to said Joseph Fuller.

Dated 5th, 4th month, 1763.

Witnesses : Walter Kelly, Ambrose Greenhow.

178. HIETT, James, of Cork City.

To only son Samuel, sole executor, property in Marybone Lane, County of City of Dublin, held by lease from Isaac Roberts ; property in Grattan Street, Cork, subject to payment of bequests in money to daughters Hannah, Mary, Martha, Sarah, Elizabeth and Jane.

Dated 3rd July, 1792.

Witnesses : West Darby, John Pilkington, and Priscilla Hunter.

177. GARRATT, JOHN, City of Cork, Chocolate-maker.

Wife, Ann Garratt to have £40 per year and furniture of a room, payable by son Joseph Garratt to whom said money is to go after her death. Legacies to daughter Mary Bell of Dublin, grand-daughters Sarah Bewley of Dublin, and Ann Bell at eighteen years. To grandsons John Bell at twenty-one years, and Thomas Bewley at fourteen years, to fit him for an apprentice, with a provision that at twenty-one years his grandmother or Uncle Joseph is to give him £50, they are also to diet and clothe and school him until he is fourteen years. To half-brother Paul Garratt four pounds a year his care to be undertaken by testator's son William. Remainder to go to above named Joseph Garratt, a mahogany chest of drawers being reserved for son William who has had his share at marriage.

Dated 19th of 1st month called January, 1769.

Witnesses : John Corrin, Joseph Clarke, Ann Lawless.

George Randall and Joseph Abell overseers.

179. JACKSON, ERASMUS, of Mountmellick.

To niece Mary Jackson house in Mountmellick now in possession of Thomas Cantrill, with reversion to testator's nephew Nathaniel Jackson, sole executor and his heirs, to whom also all title, rights, etc., in lands of Drinah (held by lease from testator's father Robert Jackson) and all residue and remainder of effects.

Dated 5th February, 1759.

Witnesses : Thos. Strangman, Samuel Strangman, Tho. Mathews.

(Original signatures, including testator).

180. JACKSON, ROBERT, of Meath Street, Bookseller.

Acknowledgment of debts in favour of sister Rachel Maria Jackson, being monies given in trust for her by her father, by Joshua Webster and by Elizabeth Webster. Her maintenance at Mountmellick School had hitherto been paid by the interest from these sums. To her also title to property in Church Street. Other legatees Joshua Webster son of Israel Webster, Robert and Joshua Webster, sons of " my Grand-uncle Robert Webster, Mary Webster, alias Tuite, Forbes Ross, Peter

Wade, Joshua Clibborn, cousin Nathaniel Jackson (folio bible and needlework cover); William Gilbert Bookseller — he to put stock, etc. in order in return for £20 legacy, or failing him, Caleb Jenkin, Bookseller. To poor Quakers of City of Dublin. Two sons of Nathaniel Jackson of Mountmellick to have the copper plates for copperplate copy books.

Executor : Joshua Clibborn, Executrix : Sister Rachel Maria.

Dated : 3rd of 7th month (July), 1778.

Codicil 3rd, Mo. 1785, revoking part which makes Joshua Clibborn executor.

Memoranda signed by Samuel Bewley and John Shannon testifying to handwriting and signature of Robert Jackson.

Proved : Consistorial Court, 15th February, 1793.

181. LACKEY, JOHN, Kilkenny.

Wife Mary Lackey alias Chadwick, executrix, younger children unnamed.

Dated 3rd July, 1780.

Witnesses : John Bayder, Martha Reynolds, Elizth. Maher. Statement to the effect that a bond for £300 demised to testator by Elizth. Osborne Louise Whitley drawn on Thos. and John Rogers and John Dance should go to the discharge of debts.

182. LECKY, ANNE, of Youghal.

To nieces Elizabeth Clibborn £5, Anne Morris £10. Nephew John Morris and his daughter Anne £10 each. Nephew John Lecky £10, also named as co-trustee, with nephew Thomas Lecky, for £30 to be given as thought fit to niece Susanna Dudley, with reversion to her child or children. £10 each to nephews Thomas and William Lecky and £5 to James Lecky. To nieces Mary Anne Smyth, £50, with watch and wearing apparel. To Hannah Lecky £5. Grandnephews Robert Jacob and James Smyth £10 and £5 respectively, and to nephew John Lecky Poole £100. Residue on trust to nephews John, Thomas and William Lecky to be placed at interest for benefit of sister Hannah Poole with interest £10 p.a., in case of her death, to her husband Richard

Poole, and in case of her son John Lecky Poole, surviving her the residue to go to him, but in case of his predeceasing her same to be divided among legatees before named.

Executors : John, Thomas and William Lecky.

Dated 25th of 11th month, 1800.

Witnesses : Joseph Fisher, Edward Bateman.

Original signature of Ann Lecky, (Lecky Letters, No. 97).

183. MANDERS, JONATHAN.

Inventory of effects of, and debts due to. (Original).

Dated 17th of 9th month, 1786.

Cash £92 16s. Bag of wool, worth £57 19s. 4d. Cask of Metheglin £15, hogshead cider £2, Copper furnace with beams, scales and weights. £8, a Colt £5 7s. 3d. and another supposed to be worth £12 10s.

Debts due from Thomas Bennett, Stephen Elms, Wm. Price, Robert Parker, Rebecca Deaves, George Newenham, Timothy Sughrue, Wm. Thompson, John Anglin, " Bradshaw and Clark," Thomas and Elias Tolbots Bond.

184. MARTIN, SAMUEL, Aghford, Co. Wexford.

Farm stock to be sold immediately after death. To sister Sarah, widow of Joseph Poole of Growtown. To the children, Jacob, Samuel, Sarah, Abigail and Elizabeth, of my brother, Jacob Martin of (name missing) Mills, £200 to be divided. To my nieces, Margaret Martin of Growtown, £150, and Sarah Doyle of Youlgrove, Co. Wexford, £20, daughters of brother, Josiah Martin ; nephew Thomas Martin of the City of Cork, son of said Josiah Martin, £50. To Isaac, Josiah, Thomas, Mary, Elizabeth and Eleanor Martin of Aghford, children of brother Isaac Martin, deceased, £10 each on attaining age of 21 years, or on marriage. To brother Josiah Martin of New Ross, an annuity of £2 10s. 6d. To Richard Poole of Growtown, £50, and to nephew Jacob Poole of Growtown, executor and residuary legatee, £100 and all residue, etc.

Dated 4th August, 1810. Pr. Consist. Court of Ferns, 18th August, 1810.

Witnesses : John Sparrow, Patt. White, Jane Williams.

185. MOORE, ELIZABETH, widow, of Newtown Hill, near Tramore, Co. Waterford.

Confirmation of Deed of Assignment of Cottage at Newtown Hill, owned by Testator to Mary and Anne Mowbray (Spinsters of said Newtown Hill) or the survivor or assignee. Also to said Mary and Anne Mowbray ten pounds each and all furniture, linen and wearing apparel in equal division. To Sarah Goouch and Jacob Penrose, junior, ten pounds each. To nephew Isaac Carroll and nieces Elizabeth and Emilie Frances Carroll and Anna Jackson all residue of whatever kind in equal shares.

Executors : Reuben Harvey Jackson, of Cork, Jacob Penrose, junior of Tramore, Solicitor, Sarah Goouch of Tramore.

Dated 28th August, 1866.

Witnesses : Patrick Boyce, John Driscoll.

Codicil, leaving to Mary and Anne Mowbray another £20.

Codicil, dated 10th June, 1867.

Witnesses to codicil : Patrick Boys, (sic), John Driscoll.

Will and Codicil proved : Prerog Court, 11th January, 1869.

H.M. Court of Probate, District Reg., Waterford.

186. PEARCE, RICHARD.

Intending to make journey by sea for Ireland.

To daughter, Prudence, £200 more than already given ; daughter Sarah £400 at age of 21 years, or at marriage, provided such marriage is with consent of brother, Thomas or Samuel Turner, William Edmondson, brother (ms. torn), brother and sister Cooke, and Thomas (torn) or any three of them, £200 at time of marriage and £200 two years later if alive or if has left a living child. If my wife, Sarah, be with child the child is to have £200 at seven years old.

For a meeting place and for poor Friends £20 as Friends think fit belonging to the Limerick Meeting. To Ann Keny and Dick French £2. To (torn) of the Friends 10/- a person. Remainder to son Thomas Pe(arce). Overseers William Edmondson, Brother Cuppage, Thomas Wight, James Craven, Thomas Phelps. If son cannot administer without an oath then Emlyn Symon White to do so ; and if in doubt to leave matters to above five persons—" to all which in short (the wind and weather being now fair) I conclude."

Dated 3rd August, 1681.

Witnesses : William Alloway, Henry Joyner (his mark), M. Morgan (his mark).

187. PEARCE, THOMAS, of Idston, Berkshire.

Wife, Katherine Pearce, freehold lands in Idston with reversion to son, Thomas Pearce and his heirs. Also the great hall and parlour two butteries, chambers called the long loft, and red, green and brocade chambers; the paled garden with liberties of ingress, egress and regress and way to and from oven, well and kitchen and use of backside to have and hold for life if Joseph and Charles Pearce do so long live; also household stuff upon the farm. To my eldest son, Thomas Pearce, freehold land in Marston, parish of Highworth. Son Charles Pearce, son Richard Pearce, (land in Scawenhampton), son Thomas Pearce leasehold land in Ashbury and Idston. Daughters Martha, Elizabeth, Katherine, Mary, Margaret, forty shillings apiece. Godchildren which are of my sons and daughters twenty shillings apiece. To all servants 5/- apiece.

Executor, son Thomas Pearce. Overseers son-in-law, John Phillips and John Kent.

Dated last day of January, 1664. Pr. 15th April, 1665.

Witnesses: Francis Pearce, T. Stratton, Wm. Stratton, William Oram.

188. PEDLOW, JAMES, Lisacurran.

To my four sons, Edward, Thomas, Joseph, John all freehold property share and share alike, if inclined to sell must do so only to each other, the one that gets the mansion house paying others a fair share. To three daughters, Ann, Jane and Sarah (a minor) £10 each. Daughter Shusey. To sons Henry and James and daughters Mary and Isabella one British shilling each. Crops either in or on the land to be sold.

Executors: John Greer of Tannaghmore Lodge, and son Edward.

Dated 10th May, 1821.

Witnesses: James Boyes, John Boyce, junior, James Francis (solicitor).

189. PHILLIPS, THOMAS, City of Cork, Cooper.

To James, son of John and Mary Phillips ten guineas for his care and attention. To Hannah daughter of said John and Mary, gold locket buttons. To poor cousin Thomas Hill of Cork, comber, suit of old warm clothes, six pairs coarse stockings, all old shoes, six coarse shirts, six cravats, old loose coat and three guineas. To John Phillips watch and to his wife Mary silver ewer(?). All the residue, money and effects, linen, etc., to be equally divided between cousins John Abbott of Cork, merchant, William Abbott of ditto, carpenter, Sarah Meyer and Hannah Stafford sons and daughters to late cousins John and Mary Abbott, deceased, but bed, chest and chest of drawers to Hannah Stafford, being poorest.

Executors : Ebenezer Pike and Cooper Penrose both of City of Cork.

Dated 24th March, 1765.

No witnesses.

Endorsed : "Acknowledged by the Testator as his hand and seal and published as his last will and testament this 2nd day of January, 1769. in presence of Ebenezer Pike, Jas. Fisher."

190. PIKE, WILLIAM, of Cork City, Merchant.

Inventory of goods sent to registrar of Cork Diocese, by his widow, Deborah :—n.d.

Furniture of parlour, back parlour, kitchen and above stairs, including walnut dining table, cane bottomed chairs, brass, silver, china (specified), dog-wheel and rack, 3 guns, etc.

(William Pike died 1755.)

191. PIM, ANTHONY.

My wife, Elizabeth, house in which we reside (place not specified), sons, Thomas Thacker Pim, Samuel Pim, John T. Pim, Charles A. Pim, George Pim, and Sylvanus Pim, daughters Anne Jacob and Mary Robinson, son-in-law, William Robinson. Interest in Blue Yard concerns and Bayfield. Barnland held from Warburton. Acherogar and New Park held from Lord Maryborough. Interest in Timber yard, under lease from John Gatchell. Interest in 20 patriotic shares.

Executors : Sons, Thomas T. and Samuel Pim and son-in-law, Wm. Robinson.

Dated 28th January, 1842.

Witnesses : William Thacker, Thomas Fayle.

Codicil as memoranda (witnessed by Thomas Delaney and Thomas Fayle) on Will leaves garden at back of dwelling-house to wife, being held under lease at £2 per annum from the Marquis of Drogheda.

192. PIM, CHARLES, of Mountrath, Queen's County.

To son Charles house, furniture, chandling and soap boiling utensils with tenement adjoining all at Mountrath; also title etc., to lands at Clonbarrow now in possession of testator and of Laurence Kavanagh. To son John Pim (under 21) house appurtenances profits, etc., of house where John Melbourne now lives (no location given) with reversion in case of death before majority, to said son Charles Pim. Parts of lands of Rushin, (Queen's Co.) and profits thereon, to which testator is entitled to be put in Trust to son Charles for use of " my brother Jonathan Pim and my sister Mary Roberts during their respective lives." Money bequests to sons Charles, John and Francis £200 each, and all residue of whatever kind to be divided equally with reversion to survivor or survivors.

Executors : Son Charles Pim, James Pim of Mountmellick.

Dated 6th October, 1815.

Witnesses : I. Calcutt, Tom Knaggs and Richard Morris.

Codicil incorporated in Probate dated 20th January, 1821 demising all the business property formerly given to son Charles, to the three sons equally for a period of three years, during which they are to carry on the business after which time each to be at liberty to pursue his own business.

Codicil witnessed by : Robert Knaggs, Anty. Deverell, Thos. Borrows.

Proved Prerogative Court, 16th March, 1821.

193. PIM, MARY, of Rushin in Queen's Co.

Widow of Tobias Pim, late of Rushin.

To stepsons James and John Pim and to own eldest and third sons Charles and Jonathan Pim, five shillings and fivepence each. To second son Thomas Pim and to niece Mary Powell equal division of all ready money. To grandson Tobias under 21 years, son of Thomas Pim right and title to all lands, etc., of Nurney, Kildare and Rushin acquired by late husband's will, with reversion to Thomas Pim in case of death of Tobias. Remainder to said Thomas and Mary Powell.

Executors : " sons Charles Pim, Jonathan Pim and Thomas Pim."

Dated 15th March, 1747.

Witnesses : Joshua Edmundson, Francis Russell, Jo. Calcutt.

Proved Prerogative Court, 9th August, 1749.

194. PIM, MARY, of Mountrath, Queen's Co.

To daughters Alice Simmons, Mary Roberts and Jane Shannon and Catherine Calcutt, £2 5s. 6d. ; £80, £80 ; £40 respectively. To son Charles Pim £40. To sons Thomas Pim and Jonathan Pim £160 in equal shares, this to remain in executors hands until such time as said sons shall change their conduct for the better, in the opinion of their friends and the two executors. If they fail to do so the capital is to remain with executors and be ' dealt out in weekly portions as a subsistance for them.' To grandson Joshua Peet £20.

Executors : Son Charles Pim. Son-in-law William Shannon.

Dated 16th March, 1794.

Witnesses : William Molloy, John Wyly, Jno. Jackman.

Proved in Prerogative Court 8th January, 1801.

195. POOLE, JACOB, Growtown, Wexford, (copy).

Lands of Little Killiane and Ballykelly and Growtown to brother-in-law, James Webb, City of Dublin, cousins Joseph Williams of Randall's Mills, friend Thomas Thompson of Cooladine, both Wexford, as Trustees and Executors. To my dear wife, Mary Poole, £80 annually as per marriage settlement of 1813, and, as trustee for son, Joseph Poole a minor, interest in lands of Growtown, house and furniture and £180 annually. Daughters Sarah, Deborah and Eliza. All children to be educated and maintained out of interest on above lands, failing which lands and furniture of Growtown to be sold except for books and furniture needed for son Joseph. If wife remarries said annuity of £180 to be divided between said children and any as yet unborn, son or sons, for purpose of apprenticeship, only until the age of 21 years ; executors to pay reasonable apprenticeship fees. Daughters' proportion of this to cease on marriage.

To each daughter £600 on marriage (if with consent of executors, failing which £10 annually for life), and to daughter Sarah an additional £200 sterling on marriage.

To every son £800 at 21 years.

Cousins Jane Williams of Randall's Mills, Sarah Abigail and Elizabeth Martin of Enniscorthy.

Dated 29th of 9th month, 1824.

Witnesses : Susannah Phillips, Patrick Martin, Penelope Stephens.

Codicil 22/10/1827.

By which son Jacob born after making said will is to be considered as included in it.

Sum allowed for children's maintenance increased to £250 per annum.

Bequests to daughters, Deborah and Eliza to be increased by £50 each unless marrying without consent of executors, when amount aforesaid to be increased from £10 to £15 in justice. Reversion of son Joseph's bequest to go to Jacob after which to be divided among daughters.

Executors to have power to sell lands of Ballykelly to discharge bequests.

Joseph Bewley, son of Samuel, an additional Trustee and Executor.

Witnesses : Jane Sparrow, Martha Sparrow, Thomas S. Crane, Susannah Phillips.

196. POOLE, JONATHAN, of Growtown, Wexford.

Son of Joseph. To be buried at Corlican.

Brothers, Joseph Poole (executor), Richard Poole, brother (in-law), Samuel Williams. Sisters, Sarah, Elizabeth, Jeane, Dorothy and Mary. Cousin, Thomas Poole, son of Thomas, Cousin Margaret Poole, daughter of William Poole, deceased. To the poor Friends of Forrest and Lambstown Meeting thirty shillings as Friends shall think proper.

Dated 3rd May, 1764. Pr. Consist. Court 31st August, 1764.

Witnesses : Jonathan Poole, Laurence Watson.

197. POOLE, JOSEPH, Growtown, Wexford.

To be buried at Corlican in a decent but not expensive manner. Wife Sarah Poole, otherwise Martin, father, Joseph Poole, the elder, sons Joseph and Jacob Poole, minors. Father-in-law Jacob Martin and Isaac Cullimore of Neemstown, Wexford, executors. Niece Elizabeth Fawcett. The lands of Growtown, Ballykelly (Wexford) and of Little Killean. The latter formerly in possession of Nicholas Barrington and his son, John Barrington, by whom they were leased to Andrew Martin in trust for testator.

Date : 31st January, 1775 (unsigned).

Witnesses : Matthew Evans, John Eustace, Benj. Wilson.

198. PURVES, THOMAS, of Wexford (copy).

Appoints as trustees executors Joseph Morrison of Ballintore and Francis Davis, Junior of Kilcarberry, both of Wexford, to administer following trusts :—

Interest on 1,500 new 3% Government Stock for use of his wife Sarah for life. Following her decease £500, part of said stock to be paid to Trustees of British and Foreign Bible Society £500 to Trustees of Yearly Meeting of the Religious Society, of Friends in Ireland for Mission work, failing which to any other Benevolent purpose desirable to said Yearly Meeting Committee of Soc. of Friends in Ireland; remaining £500 of said stock also to first Yearly Meeting Committee after said wife's decease, for benevolent purposes as they shall approve "in their enlarged capacity." House, tenements and gardens at Spawell Road, Wexford to wife for life and afterwards to Trustees of the Monthly Meeting of the Society of Friends of Co. Wexford, the profit thereon to be applied to use of said Meeting. Said property not to be sold and no lease made for a longer period than thirty years. To trustees of schools in Syria approved by the Yearly Meetings Committee in Ireland the interest on £500 stock of Midland Great Western Railway.

Executors : Samuel Davis of Killabegs, Francis Davis of Hollymount, both Co. Wexford.

199. ROWSOM, SAMUEL, City of Cork.

All wearing apparel to father James Rowsom. Uncle John Wright to be paid all other substance for use of said father and of mother, payment to be made from time to time. James Doyle, executor to receive debts due from Joseph Fisher and Francis Malone, both of Youghal.

Memoranda of effects :— 3 coats and vests, 2 prs. breeches, 14 shirts, 3 cravats, 9 prs. stockings, 4 wigs, 2 prs. shoes, 1 pr. boots, 2 hats, 1 whip and a pair of spurs, 1 gun, small bit of bandel lining, a night cap and a wallet, 2 prs. buckles.

Dated : 29th of 11th month, 1755.

Witnesses : Henry White, Mickey Mahony.

200. SINDERBEE, RICHARD, City of Cork, Merchant.

To sister Elizabeth Griffiths, widow, sole executrix, the leasehold interest on the South Marsh, commonly called the Rape Marsh in the City of Cork held by lease of the late William Dunscombe. Reversion to niece Rebecca Griffiths and her heirs, with reversion, should she leave no heirs, to the Men's Meeting of the People called Quakers and their successors, subject to annuity of ten pounds to cousins George Sinderbee of the Parish of Westbury in Great Britain. Future possessors of the aforesaid premises to have power to lease such at improved yearly value.

Dated 8th May, 1756.

Witnesses : James Gibbs, Roger Power (Not Pub.).

Codicil, dated August 10th, 1770 by which James Gibbs is to receive £30 per annum and garden at Sunday's Wells, leased from Thos. Wily.

An erasure in this will includes the names of cousins Charles Sinderby, brother to above George, and cousin Francis son of William Sinderby of Monmouth.

201. SLEIGH, SARAH, City of Cork, Widow.

Sole beneficiary daughter Sarah Sleigh, except for £2 5s. 6d. to son Richard Sleigh, to be paid as soon as convenient after decease.

Executors : said daughter Sarah Sleigh, William Pike of Cork.

Dated : 13th July, 1755.

Witnesses : James Hull Lawton, Wm. White, Rob. Deane.

Inventory of goods of above, made 23rd of 8th month, 1755 :— Household articles including 6 oak cane chairs, cane couch and ' squab,' sideboard or Beaufet, brass, copper, pewter, etc., houshold linen.

202. SPARROW, ALEXANDER, of Castledermot.

To wife (ms. torn)ry Sparrow, Executrix, freehold dwelling house in Castledermot, houses occupied by James Dillon and Edward Killagrew, household goods. Cabins and gardens in S . . . (torn) and holdings of Walter Howland, John Carnon, Edward Stanton, Saml. Hawkins, Patrick Dorrien, William Mackey, Walter McDonnell, and the park or meadow behind said holdings commonly called the faw or calf park. The two little parks behind the orchard with adjoining land, bounded by the lands of Richard Ennis and Robert Parke ; or in lieu of above to receive £40 sterling p.a. paid half yearly out of benefit of lease in lands of St. John with sole reversion to sons Alexander, executor and James. James also to receive, 3 months after testator's decease three hundred pounds sterling, raised from leases in Levitstown, St. Johns and Roscolbin, and twenty pounds sterling yearly, beginning five years after testator's decease from lands of St. Johns and Roscolbin.

Daughter Jane Jackson, seven pounds and a piece of plate. Sons in law Timothy Forbes, Wilson Haddaway, Hugh Russell, Nathaniel Jackson, daughter in law Rebecca Higgins, grandsons Richard Sparrow ten pounds at 21 years and Alexander son of son Samuel deceased. All residue to son Alexander.

Dated : 8th March, 1722.

Witnesses : Peter Gross, Arthur Whitnell, John Bennett.

203. SPARROW, WILLIAM, Cooles, Co. Wexford, 1725.

See Eustace and Goodbody : *Quaker Records, Dublin, Abstracts of Wills*, No. 185.

CULLIMORE, JOHN, Old Booley, Co. Wexford.

To be buried at Corlican.

Executors " my dear wife," " my son, John, my friend, Joseph Poole, son Francis £5 on demand thereof. Sons Daniel and John £100 each, son Richard one shilling." Remainder of effects and stock and reversion of leases to be equally divided between " wife and sons, Jonathan, Thomas, George and Mary Cullimore," provided said children are dutiful and careful to manage for their mother.

Dated 11th of 8th month, 1733. Pr. Consist. Court, 11th October, 1737.

Witnesses : William Craven, Edward Carey, Jonathan Sparrow.

204. SUTTON, MARY, Mountmellick.

To Rachel Maria Jackson of Dublin all books, to Deborah Richardson white counterpane. Brother Francis Sutton of Haverfordwest one shilling. To Robert Goodbody an oak nest of drawers and to William Goodbody a desk received from his uncle. Nathaniel Jackson and his wife, Mary. Robert Jackson and his wife Mary, Robert Thacker, executor £2 5s. 6d. to buy a seal and £50 in trust to pay interest thereof to Elizabeth daughter of Nathaniel Jackson at twenty-one years, or on marriage, with reversion to her sisters Anna Maria and Frances Jackson. Also £50 in trust for Joshua Ridgeway with reversion to above Anna Maria and Frances, daughters of Nathaniel and Mary Jackson. Remainder to Hannah Jackson and Mary Thacker.

Dated : 1st January, 1813.

Witnesses : George R. Penrose, R. Thacker.

205. WEBSTER, ELIZABETH, of Meath Street, Dublin.

Money bequests to brother Henry Martin of Philadelphia (to be paid as annuity), granddaughter Rachel Jackson, grandson Thomas Jackson. Elizabeth Pleadwell, Rebecca Cantrell, Ann Sixsmith, Israel Webster, Israel Sharp, Dorothea Ward, Alice Groves, James Moor, Samuel Moor, Mary Fitzpatrick. To the children of Connell Moor deceased. To the Women's Meeting of Quakers in the City of Dublin £5 for division among widows not otherwise provided for. House linen and china to granddaughter. Desk and books to grandson. Remainder of furniture and plate between two grandchildren if they wish after valuation. To son-in-law Isaac Jackson watch, silver buckles and cane. Wearing apparel, linen and woollen to Rebecca Cantrell and Ann Sixsmith aforesaid. Residue to grandchildren.

Executors : Grandson Robert Jackson and Cousin Henry Clibborn of Wheelan, Co. Kildare.

Dated : 20th of 7th month, 1770.

Witnesses : Thomas Barrington, Jonathan Hill.

Proved Prerogative Court, 9th January, 1775.

206. WHITE, ANN, City of Cork, Widow of Daniel White of Bandon.

Unconditional legacy of £20 to granddaughter Dinah White eldest child of Hannah White widow of Thomas White (James), son Joshua White and nephew James Abell executors, also trustees for an unspecified sum anticipated as an asset on the death of testator's brother-in-law Henry White of Elmgrove, North Liberties of Cork.

Daughters Mary and Miriam White to receive interest from £900 of said legacy the remaining beneficiaries being James, Ann, John and Sarah White, the four younger children of said Hannah White and said son Joshua and daughter Hannah.

Dated : 6th June, 1792.

Witnesses : John Morris, Isaac Robinson.

207. WHITE, ANN.

Series of papers dealing with the Administration in 1819 to 1821 of the will of Ann White (died 1814) in the Consistorial Court of Waterford.

List of legatees : Grandniece Dinah White, Niece Hannah White, Nephews, Thomas and Benjamin, Grandnephews Henry, son of Thomas White, Walter, son of Benjamin White.

Probate in Prerogative Court Dublin, dated 15th (blank) 1821.

208. WHITE, DINAH, City of Waterford.

Sisters Anne Waring, Sarah White of Ballitore, nieces and nephews. Hannah, Anne, Thomas, Henry and Elizabeth White, children of brother James White of Ballitore ; Joseph, Hannah, Elizabeth, Maria and Thomas White Waring, children of sister Anna Waring, grandchildren of Thomas White ; Hannah Elizabeth and John Taylor White, children of brother John White of Cork. Above legatees to receive specified items of silver, china, furniture and books. Books include Spectators, Guardians and Tatlers, Gough's History (of Friends) and Bowdlers Essays. Bequests in money to above named with addition of brother-in-law Thomas Waring of Waterford, Aunt Mary White of Ballitore and Lydia, James and Maria White children of brother James. Shares in Waterford Gas Co., Severn Steam Packet from Cork to Bristol ; Lee Steam Packet ; National Insurance Co.

Executors : Thomas Waring, James White, John White.

Dated 7th of 2nd month, 1832.

Witnesses : George White, John G. O'Brien.

Proved in Consistorial Court, Waterford, 10th October, 1834.

209. WOODCOCK, FRANCIS, of Noreville, Queens Co.

Ten pounds to his old servant Judith Burgess, and remainder in toto to wife Mary Woodcock, including annuity from second Clonmel annuity Company.

Executors : Wife, William Walpole of Ashbrook.

Dated 12th of 1st month, 1844.

Witnesses : Robt. Perry, Rob. Rhodes.

Proved in Prerogative Court, 6th January, 1848.

210. WRIGHT, JONATHAN, of Edenderry, King's Co.

To nephew Samuel Hudson of 19, Castle Street, Dublin, draper, all real and personal estate of which testator is possessed or entitled to. Executor said nephew.

Dated 12th December, 1879.

Witnesses : Thomas Home, Robert Jackson.

An unidentified Inventory, probably that of one of the Davis family of Cork.

Stock in Tanyard and Chandlery including utensils £2,733 3s. 3d. Leases mentioned from George Newsom, T. Wyly at Farrinclay, Rd. Sargin and Edward Hatton and " Ground on the common set to Popham and Quarey.

Legacies to R. Davis, S. Manders, O. Valu, Jn. Davis and issue. N. B. Rachel Davis may will £300 (part of £700 bequeathed) remaining £400 to revert to her son John Davis.

Dated 20th of 7th month, 1791.

DEEDS AND OTHER LEGAL DOCUMENTS
A.

211. Indenture dated 12th of 3rd mo. (called) May, 1669 between William Mayne of City of Dublin, carpenter, and James Fade, miller, Robert Turner, linen draper, Samuel Claridge, merchant, all of said city ; Phillip Dymond, George Webber both of Cork, merchants ; William Edmondson of Rosenallis, Queen's Co., husbandman, Abraham Fuller of Lehensie, Queen's Co., yeoman, George Gregson of Lisnagarvie, Co. Antrim, merchant, and Thomas Holme of Bregurteen, Co. Wexford, yeoman, by which said William Mayne leased lands known as Baron's Inn garden, Bride Street, suburbs of Dublin " with liberty of egress and ingress for all Friends (called Quakers) " and liberty to build thereon, to the above as Trustees.

(Note this is the land on which the first Meeting House of the Society of Friends was built in Dublin, at the corner of Bride Street and Bride Alley. The deed was found a few years ago acting as binding to a Co. Wicklow minute book).

212. Indenture and Conveyance by which John Robinson, Thomas Simmons, William Taylor, all of City of Dublin, and John Bewley of Harlem, County of Dublin, on behalf of the Religious Society of Friends sold property in St. Stephen's Green, Dublin, including a former Burial Ground to the Royal College of Surgeons in Ireland with reservations as to the use of part of the property defined by an annexed map (not now here). Title of property recited back to the year 1664.

Dated 22nd July, 1805.

Witnesses : Barth. Hatton, William Doherty.

The deeds reciting the purchase of this property by the Society of Friends in 1664 are in the Library of the Royal College of Surgeons in Ireland. There is a partial copy in the library at Eustace Street.

213. Indenture by which William Penn, Governor and Proprietor of Province of Pennsylvania, demised 10,000 acres in same formerly held by Sir Matthias Vincent of Islington, Middlesex and his heirs Vincent Vincent and Theodore Vincent, executors of the will of their mother Dame Mary Vincent, to Joseph Pike of Cork, Ireland.

Dated 12th December, 1698.

Witnesses : E. Suegemia (?), H. Springett, Wm. Martin, Edward Singleton, endorsed lease Governor Penn., Vincent Vincent et. al. to Joseph Pike. Recorded in the Rolls office of Philadelphia in Book 23, vol. 2, p.278, 279 2nd day of 8th month, 1700, before Thomas Storey.

214. Indenture by which William Penn, senior and William Penn, junior, the son and heir of his mother Gulielma Maria Penn, formerly Springett, sold the land of Coolcore, barony of Deece, Co. Meath now tenanted by Daniel Powell, to Thomas Cuppage, of Lambstown, Co. Wexford.

Dated 4th August, 1708. Original signatures.

Witnesses : Robt. West, Cha. Collins, Fr. Gooldey.

B.

215. (1) Lease of land at Lurgan : William Brownlee and John Nicholson, jur. to John Walter (34). 1718.

(2) Certificate of Registration Timahoe Meeting House, Co. Kildare (93). 1719.

(3) Transfer of Balliachien (Rathfryland) Meeting House : Mordecai Barrow to Thos. Greer and counterpart of same (30 & 31). 1722.

(4) Lease of Tullylish (i.e. Moyallen) Meeting House (28). 1737.

(5) Lease of land at Mountrath, Richard Despard to Charles Pim (35). 1738.

(6) Lease of lands of Ballyraggan and Knockfield, Co. Kildare, Earl of Kildare to John Lecky (90). 1746.

(7) Lease of land at Mountrath, Earl of Mountrath to Charles Pim (40). 1749.

(8) Same by Richard Despard to Charles Pim (39). 1756.

(9) Lease of lands and property at Redcastle, Queen's Co., Arthur Broom of Redcastle to Charles Pim of Mountrath (48). 1756.

(10) Copy : Memorial of Registration of land at Mountrath, W. Burros, jr., and Charles Pim (38). 1756.

(11) Re-lease by John, James and Robert Lecky to James Malone of lands of Ballyraggen and Knockfield, Co. Kildare (91). 1758.

(12) Lease of Tullylish (Moyallen) Meeting House (29). 1760.

(13) Lease of land at Mountrath : Earl of Mountrath to Charles Pim (37). 1763.

(14) Lease of lands of Suffin near Parsonstown by Sir William Parsons to William Usher (62). 1767.

(15) Lease of Roscrea Meeting House (Tipperary) by John Damer of Dorsetshire to Tobias Pim of Fancrott (King's Co.), John Pim and Joseph Robinson of Roscrea, Tipperary, ground in Abbey Street, Roscrea, known as Old Tenter at angle of Castle Pleasure Garden for purpose of building Meeting House (96). 1773.

(16) Lease of Balliachien Meeting House (Rathfryland) : Samuel Waring to Henry Greer and Thomas Christy and copy of same (32 & 33). 1774.

(17) Receipt from Richard Roberts to executors of Charles Pim (59). 1774.

(18) Marriage Settlement of Robert Goff and Mary Woodcock (25) précis below. 1777.

(19) Lease of lands at Mountrath Earl of Mountrath to Charles Pim (36). 1781.

(20) Indentures of Conveyance of land by representatives of Charles Pim to Charles Pim junior at Clonbarrow to Mary Pim at Rushin and to Edward Peet at Derryluskey, all in Queen's Co. (49-53). 1781.

(21) Insurance policies made by (a) John Grubb, (b) Sarah, (his widow) on Anner Mills, Clonmel with the Royal Exchange Co. (86-88). 1783, 1788, 1810.

(22) Two copies : lease of Toberhead Meeting House, Co. Antrim by Gervais Johnston to Joseph Richardson, Thomas Phelps and John Handcock (26 & 27). 1784.

(23) Deed of Annuity by Joseph Robinson to John Pim (95). 1793.

(24) Lease of house in Rathdowney, Queen's Co., from Joseph Palmer of Cuffsborough, Queen's Co., and Humphrey Palmer of Rathdowney (23). 1793.

(25) Quittance of property rights from Thos. and Bridget Walpole to John Kelly, executor to Martin Costigan (60) (no lands cited). 1793.

(26) Attested copy of lease of ground by William Hill of Limerick to the Right Reverend John Young, Roman Catholic Bishop of Limerick (98). 1796.

(27) Conveyance and Declaration of Trust : Joseph Jackson of Tincurry, William Fennell of Rehill and George Fennell of Maginstown, all in Tipperary, convey lands formerly held by the Loobys of Garryroan, Tipperary, and Meeting House thereon to Solomon Watson of Summerville, Benjamin Grubb, Samuel Rigg and Richard Sparrow, all of Clonmel, for use of the Society of Friends (63 & 64). 1796.

(28) Lease of land and house in Ballitore : Abraham Shackleton to Mary and Susanna Bewley (21). 1801.

(29) Memorial of Registration of deed Arthur Broom and Charles Pim of lands near Mountrath including Derryluskey, Rushin, Clonbarrow and Swinney's Farm (47). 1802.

(30) Power of Attorney : John, James and Hannah Pim to Charles Pim (57). 1803.

(31) Copies of Deeds concerning the tenure of Corporation Mills, Clonmel, between David and John Malcomson 1808, and an ejectment order by the Earl of Glengal to Michael Casey, 1819 and copy of lease by Earl of Glengal to David Malcomson of same property (100-103).1820.

(32) Lease Robt. Phelan of Ballinacurragh, Co. Wexford to Francis Woodcock, Enniscorthy, of lands of Tomalossett, Bantry, Co. Wexford (17). 1809.

(33) Marriage Settlement Francis Woodcock of Tomalossett to Mary Neale (24) précis below. 1812.

(34) Lease Abraham Shackleton to James White of property in Ballitore, Co. Kildare (83). 1816.

(35) Bond : John Richardson of Mountrath to Mary Richardson of Dublin (53). 1818.

(36) Indentures of Conveyance of land by Charles Pim, jr., to Francis Pim of lands in Clonbarrow (55), 1820, and of lands to Mary White of a house in Mountrath (54), 1821, and to Wm. Bowes of ditto (56), 1835.

(37) Counsel's opinion re (a) payment of tithes 1833, (b) Ballybrado and Woodhouse Burial Grounds (82 & 79). 1846.

(38) Decree to Benjamin Haughton and others for possession of a dwelling house in Meath Street, Dublin, held by Samuel Bewley and others (81). 1850.

(39) Lease by Charles Pim to Charlotte White of lands in Mountrath (22). 1858.

(40) Miners' Rights at Gold Diggings at Ararat, Australia, to Reuben F. Alexander (14). 1860.

(41) Lists made in 1878 of Trusts for the monthly Meetings of Lurgan, Grange, Lisburn. Schedule of Legacies of Ulster Provincial School and Deed for payment of Trusts for same and return of Trust Properties for Brookfield (Antrim) School (73-78). 1878.

DEEDS AND LEGAL DOCUMENTS

C.

216. (1) Deed by which Anthony Sharp demised the freedom and liberty of the window lights on the west side of the Quaker Meeting House in Meath Street to Thomas Ashton on behalf of the Society of Friends for ever. 1697.

(2) Memorandum to George Rooke concerning lives in lease of widow Bell's house in Newmarket, namely Henry and Elizabeth Burcham, Joseph Beaseley, son of Edward Beasley of Dolphin's Barn; also of ground in Meath Street and Duncombs Lane from Bernard Brown, Samuel Roper, Isaac Roberts, Phillip Martin. 1715.

(3) Memorandum by which John Fuller set to Rachel Carleton a house and ground lately set to Adam Bloomfield. 1760.

(4) Summons for non-payment of tithes addressed to Mrs. Grubb, Anner Mills, Clonmel. 1814.

(5) Auctioneer's Bill for distrained goods belonging to Mr. Webb, Cornmarket (Dublin). 1848.

(6) Bond for payment of £20 from Mary Lee and Edwd. Blackwell to Isaac Jackson, Printer, Dublin, for payment for 1107 pounds weight of lettertype; original signatures. 1755.

(7) Bill of Exchange : Samuel Grubb, Clonmel, to William Colville, Dublin. 1780.

(8) Bill of Exchange drawn on William Balfour of Messrs. Forster, Lubbock, Bosanquet & Co., London to Jacob Hancock junior dated from Fort St. George. 1792.

(9) Note fixing a fair rent for Clonmel Meeting House by Robert Davis with James Douglas. 1827.

(10) Receipt from Henry Grattan to the Hon. David La Touche. 1774.

(11) List (only) of deeds to Clonmel Meeting House and Tipperary Friends reciting back to 1705. 1780.

LEGAL DOCUMENTS

D.

Bundle of Deeds etc., relating to EUSTACE STREET and SYCAMORE ALLEY

217. (1). Indenture between Joseph Maddock and John Stevens, William Brookfield, Joseph Fade and Paul Johnston respecting a house and plot of ground on west side of Eustace Street. 1712.

(2). Lease from Jo. Fade and Paul Johnston to Mrs. Goold of house in Eustace Street. 1735.

(3). Indenture made between Richard Leland and Robert Jaffray, Robert Clibborn, James Forbes and William Greenhow for renewal of name of life in lease to replace that of Robert Strettell deceased with that of Joshua Forbes, son of above James Forbes. 1762.

(4). Indenture by which Robert Clibborn, Robert Jaffray and Joseph Barcroft leased to Thomas Matthews premises on the west side of Eustace Street. 1765.

(5). Indenture made between John Leland and Robert Jaffray, Robert Clibborn, James Forbes and William Greenhow for renewal of life in lease to replace that of Joseph Maddock, deceased, with that of James Forbes junior, son of James Forbes. 1769.

(6). Indented Articles of Agreement between Robert Clibborn and Joseph Barcroft and Francis Christian to settle a suit pending in the High Court of Chancery for the prevention of making window openings in that part of the house of Francis Christian which overlooks the premises of the Quaker Meeting House, and to claim damages for encroachment and building on same, and for the pulling down of the gables and wall of the Little House, or School house. (Plan formerly Annexed). 1770.

(7). Indenture made between Robert Clibborn, Joseph Barcroft, both of Dublin, and Experience Cooper of Cooper's Hill, Queen's County, for renewal of life in an unspecified lease. Endorsed " renewal of this sent 1797 by Thomas Fayle to John Gray. 1833 John Gray told me he has it not, John Doyle." 1770.

(8). Indenture by which Thomas Matthews, surveyor, leased to Ralph Ward, secretary to the Commissioners for stamping vellum and parchment, a house on the west side of Eustace Street. 1774.

(9). Indenture between Major General John Leland and William Jackson, Samuel Russell, Joseph Williams, William Knott, Thomas Nicholson and John Wilson, all of Dublin, for renewal of lives in lease to replace the name of Joshua Forbes by that of the Duke of York. 1791.

(10). Indenture made between William Taylor, Isaac Simmons, Thomas Simmons, John Robinson, Joshua Edmundson and William Alexander, all of Dublin, and Sarah Clibborn of Moate, Westmeath, for replacement names of lives of Robert Jaffray and Joshua Forbes, both deceased, by those of George, Prince of Wales and Frederick, Duke of York, in lease unspecified, 1797.

(11). Deed of conveyance by which Thomas Matthew, junior, son of Thomas Matthew, sold premises on the west side of Eustace Street, formerly held by his father to John Robinson, Thomas Simmons, William Taylor and Robert Clibborn as Trustees for the Society of Friends. 1799.

(12). Bundle of deeds, leases, etc., relating to the purchase in 1809 by the Religious Society of Friends of the premises on the west side of Eustace Street, Dublin, formerly known as the Eagle tavern. These recite back to the year 1787 when the said premises were leased by Mary Reid, widow of William Reid, senior, to James Bennett, from whom they were purchased in 1809. The lease of 1787 cites the names of Denis Crossen, former lessor, and gives a list of fitments let with the two houses comprising the property.

The death of Richard Read, one of the testators, grandson of William Read, senior, during the Peninsular War, and the difficulty of proving his estate caused an accumulation of documents relating to Court searches which are preserved here. A copy of the will of William Read, senior, dated 11th July, 1774 is annexed.

To my wife, Mary Read, rents and profits of two houses in College Green, one in Eustace Street and one in College Green, all in Dublin, with reversion to children, if any, of son William, failing whom to above said granddaughters, daughter and son-in-law, Ann and Thomas Batty and their daughters, minors, Mary and Ann Batty. To my son, William Read £1,000 and one half of my stock in trade.

Trustees son-in-law Thomas Batty and friend Patrick Trevor, merchant of the city of Dublin.

Witnesses : Alexr. Durdin, Richard Martin.

Proved in Prerog. Court, 8th March, 1777.

(13). A deed of 1763 recites back to 1724 the title of William Reid to the above premises. They were formerly owned by John Barclay who leased the premises to David La Touche, now, 1763 in possession of Sankey Denis executor to Henry Barton who leased them to William Reid. Property defined as bounded on North by little lane leading to Quaker Meeting House and by Widow Goold's house, west by Quaker Meeting House, east by Eustace Street, south by Abel Strettle's house.

(14). Indenture by which John Robinson, Thomas Simmons and John Bewley, all of Dublin, leased premises on the West side of Eustace Street to Charles Brown jeweller. 1813.

(15). Indenture by which William Harding, John Valentine, Stephen Dalton, James Webb and John Knott, all of Dublin, as Trustees for the Society of People called Quakers leased to Abraham Campion, jeweller, the house on the West side of Eustace Street known as No. 3. Property bounded on the West by the house and property belonging to the " Society of Sycamore Alley Meeting House." 1814.

(16). Copy of above with, on the back, terms of a full surrender of premises by Abraham Campion. 1818.

(17). Indenture by which the house called No. 5 on the West side of Eustace Street was assigned by George, Charles and Frances Brown, and Henry Stock to George Edwards, bookseller, all of Dublin, reciting the names of former lessees as John Robinson, Thomas Simmons and John Bewley. 1815.

(18). Indenture made by William Read for mortgage of a house in Eustace Street with William Frederick Lover. 1817.

(19). Counterpart of above. 1817.

(20). Lease of Warehouse and premises in Eustace Street made by William Harding, John Knott, James Webb, all of Dublin, and John Valentine of Wexford as Trustees for the Society of Friends, and John Adair of Eustace Street. The deed forbidding the use of the premises for any trades (specified by name) which might be a disturbance or unpleasant by reason of noise, smells or anything offensive. 1818.

(21). Indenture by which Esther Charlotte Litton leased property on the West side of Eustace Street to Jonathan Pim, William Birkett junior, John Knott, Joshua Taylor, James Webb and John Webb as Trustees for the Society of Friends, Charlotte Litton being sole representative of the late Benjamin Chetwood and his wife, Anne, otherwise Eustace, by whom the property had been leased in 1712 to Joseph Maddock whose estate is now legally vested in the said Trustees. 1820.

(22). Assignment of a house in Eustace Street to George Edwards, bookseller, by Joshua Fayle, John Knott, James Webb, John Webb, William Birkett and Jonathan Pim as Trustees. 1821.

(23). Surrender of premises near Sycamore Alley by Anne Clibborn to Isaac and Thomas Simmons, John Robinson and William Alexander as Trustees with recitation to previous ownerships by John Barcklay. 1712.

(24). Indenture by which William Harding, Stephen Dalton, John Knott and James Webb, all of Dublin, as Trustees for Society of Friends leased to Stephen Cowan, goldsmith, of Dublin, house and property known as No. 4 Eustace Street. 1823.

(24a). Counterpart of above.

(25). Indenture made by same Trustees leasing to Richard Beilby and Maxwell McMaster the warehouse and property known as No. 5 Eustace Street, formerly let to John Adair and lately to George Newcomb. 1823.

(26). Indenture by which same Trustees (William Harding now of Leeds, England) leased to Richard William Osborne the house No. 5 Eustace Street, now a warehouse. 1828.

(27). Indenture by which Daniel Litton as heir to Esther Charlotte Litton demised to Jonathan Pim, William Birkett junior, John Knott, Joshua Fayle, James and John Webb as Trustees for the Society of Friends his interest in the premises in Eustace Street demised in 1712 to Joseph Maddock.

(28). Indenture by which renewal of lease of house in Eustace Street was made between William Bell, of Bellview, Queen's Co., and his wife, Charlotte, formerly widow of Ambrose Harvey of Dublin, and above Trustees. This recites the lease of the property to 1770 when Robert Jaffray and Abigail his wife set the property then held by Richard Tucker, to Francis Christian. By the will of Abigail Jaffray the property became vested in Abigail Hautenville who in 1818 renewed the lease to William Read. 1835.

(29). Small bundle of copies of deeds of assignment, costs etc., relating to Eustace Street property. 1849-1875.

LEGAL DOCUMENTS

E.

218. Bundle of documents 1713-1780 relating to land leased to Thomas Lackey otherwise Leckey of Clonmel, his son John Lackey, physician, his son John Leckey whose widow Mary (Chadwick) Leckey sold the premises to Joseph Grubb. Lands known as Stretches or Stritches Island westwards of the Bridge of Clonmel held by Joseph Comerford from Duke of Ormond and released to Thomas Lackey 1713. Other lessees include Samuel Gordon, Francis Collett, Patrick Sweeney, Joseph Grubb.

Bundle relating to premises on the Quay at Clonmel tracing the ownership from Joseph Grubb and Patrick Sweeney through Maria Despard, formerly Lackey, and Francis Despard to Catherine Wright, formerly Despard. This includes abstract of the title of the Reverend Timothy O'Connell and the Reverend Thomas McDonnell to the house known first as the State House, later the Infirmary.

219. Bundle of Indentures of lease of the Meeting House of Mountmellick, Queen's Co. dated (a) 1716 (reciting land demised by Arthur Lord, Viscount of Ely, in 1697) between Tobias Pladwell of Mountmellick and John Barecroft of Arkill, Kildare, farmer, Henry Ridgeway, Joshua Strangman, both of Mountmellick, and Gershon Boat of Mountrath. (b) 1735 Conveyance by Joshua Strangman senior of Mountmellick and Gershon Boat[e] of Tullylusk, Kildare, to William Ridgeway, Joshua Strangman junior, John Ridgeway of Ballycarrol, Queen's Co., James Pim of Rushin, ditto and Joshua Pim of Mountrath. (c) 1825 Renewal of Lease by Moses Pim of Lackey, Queen's Co., to James and Anthony Pim and Robert Goodbody, all of Mountmellick. (d) 1857 Conveyance of same premises by John Pim of Lackey and Robert Goodbody of Drayton Villa, Clara, to Anthony Pim, Samuel Bewley Pim both of Mountmellick and Jonathan Goodbody of Charlestown, Clara, with right of way to garden reserved to said John Pim.

220. Bundle of deeds and papers relating to Carlow Monthly Meeting include:

(a). Indenture made 1756 between William Fownes, Dublin and John Atkinson, Barberstown, Co. Kildare, of lands of Blackdown, Kilteel, Co. Kildare, formerly owned by Patrick Nowlan, deceased, and now by his widow, Elizabeth Nowlan.

(b). Indenture dated 1740 between William Archbold, Davistown, Kildare, and William Gill of Ballitore, lands of Moyl Abbey, Co. Kildare. Witnessed by Francis Lewis and Thomas Boake.

(c). Bundle of deeds relating to Killconner Meeting House, lying on the lands of the Great Park field belonging to Kilconner Mansion House, reverts to original deed made by Samuel Watson of Kilconner to Trustees for the old Meeting House lying opposite the said Mansion House. 1761, 1776, 1824, 1842, 1907.

(d). Copy of Memorial of lease of Carlow Meeting House. 1711.

(e). Inventory of papers belonging to Carlow Monthly Meeting. c.1837.

(f). Lease of Sir William Fownes to John Atkinson of land in Blackdown, Co. Kildare. 1756.

(g). Lease of land and premises in Castledermot by George Mason to Thomas Duckett and Gregory Russell reciting back to lease made to former by the Earl of Kildare in 1698 in which statement is made that the half-yearly rent is to be paid " at Strongbow's tomb in Christ Church, Dublin." Includes reservations made by deed (date unspecified) by which part of property is leased by George Mason to Abell Strettell, Joshua Beale and Thomas Duckett as Trustees for a Quaker Meeting House. 1706.

LEGAL DOCUMENTS

F.

INDENTURES OF APPRENTICESHIP

221. James Mason to George Grubb 1782, Daniel Kent to John Johnson, master of brig asa (facsimile) 1786, Joseph Hughes to Thos. White, 1785, John Jellico to Samuel Wilson, 1793. Thomas Jellico to John Wilson, 1795, Lawson Reeves to John Wilson, 1797. John Reeves to Samuel and Richard Grubb, 1804, William Reeves to Dennis Newsom, 1807, T. J. Haslam to Committee of Lisburn School, 1840, T. Walpole to A. White, 1850. The certificate (facsimile) of Friends in Limerick is enclosed with Daniel Kent's Indenture ; it includes signatures of " the Protestant clergy and Quakers of that city."

222. A Marriage Settlement made 12th April, 1770 between Robert Goff, of Dublin, and Mary Woodcock and Robert Unthank of the City of Dublin, grandfather of Robert Goff, whose daughter, Elizabeth Fletcher, has a right to property. Trustees Jacob Goff and Samuel Woodcock, both of Corlican, Co. Wexford. Lands of Corboymer, Corboybeg and Cornemayo, otherwise lower Corboy all in Co. Longford, in possession of Robert Unthank. Lands demised in 1754 by Richard Bourchier, mariner, of Bengal, East Indies, to Robert Unthank, situated in Francis Street and Limerick Alley, Dublin. Lands belonging to Robert Goff, Ballymakane, Co. Wexford. Original signatures. Witnesses John Green and William Woodcock.

223. A Marriage Settlement made 3rd November, 1812, between Francis Woodcock of Tomalossett, Co. Wexford, and Mary Neale and her father, Richard Neale of Meelick Mill in Queen's County, miller. Trustees Jacob Poole of Growtown, and William Woodcock of Tomalosset, brother of Francis. Recites lease made by Cadwallader Edwards senior and junior and Eliza (Donovan) Edwards, wife of Cadwallader the elder, to Samuel Woodcock, now deceased, in the year 1793. Concerns lands of Clonmore, Co. Wexford, formerly owned by Richard Donovan. Includes Ann Edwards, 3rd daughter of Cadwallader senior. Original signatures. Witnesses Ben Williams and John Baker.

PORTFOLIOS

224. A set of 33 portfolios in the library contains several hundreds of documents of a miscellaneous nature ranging from the 17th to the 20th century.

They are all indexed and catalogued. A full list is in each portfolio. Further material is in process of filing in a similar manner.

Portfolios are briefly classified as follows :

1. (a) Dreams and Visions, (b) Travel, (c) Certificates of removal, etc.

2. Testimonies to persons deceased 1672-1945, Convincements 1693-1793 and Dying Sayings 1722-1795.

3*. (a) "Thomas Wilson" Collection of letters, (b) Original miscellaneous Letters 1698-1888.

4. Copies of letters (some contemporary) 1699-1868.

5. Documents and letters relating to education 1719-1858.

6. Epistles to and from individual Friends and to and from Meetings on religious matters ; also Meeting pronouncements on various subjects 1690-1826.

7. (a) Legal documents 1697-1781. (b) Matters relating to Meeting houses and Residences 1694-1876. (c) Miscellaneous unclassified documents (1663-1872).

8. (a) Miscellaneous original letters 1794-1803. (b) Meeting pronouncements, certificates, etc., 1668 (a copy of letter re London Yearly Meeting) to 1841 (b).

9. General personal letters and memoranda 1694-1851 and three copies of 17th century letters, two from Anthony Sharp to Thomas Sharp, and to English Friends, one from John Perrott to Henry Cromwell.

10. Meeting Epistles and Minutes, home and abroad ; miscellaneous Meeting letters, etc.

11. A stitched bundle of 18th century manuscripts, including an account of the preservation of Friends during the rising of 1798 ; a letter describing the visit of Emperor of Russia to Friends (1814) and an account of an escape from sea robbers. Copies of epistles and miscellaneous letters.

12. Miscellaneous manuscripts and letters, mainly of 18th century. Includes some letters and manuscripts of Mary Leadbeater. Notes on Nicholson and Gooch families.

13. Contains in addition to 18th, 19th and 20th century material, thirteen photostats of letters relating to Ireland between 1654 and 1659. These are taken from the originals in the Swarthmore Collection of Letters of Early Friends in the library of Friends House, London.

*14. 135 letters pertaining to the Newsom family of Edenderry (1788-1840).

*15. 40 letters and documents pertaining to the Poole family of Co. Wexford 1661-1824.

*16. A collection of 17th and 18th century papers relating to Bandon, Meeting, Co. Cork.

*17. Letters relating to the disunity from the Society of Friends of Peter Nicholson 1753-1770.

18. Original papers of "Sufferings" of Friends, 17th and 18th century.

19. Miscellaneous 17th, 18th and 19th century documents, including copy of the order of James II for the release of Friends in 1686 ; copy of epistle of George Fox 1669 ; copy of letter of William Penn 1704 ; certificates, letters, memorials, epistles etc.

20. Certificates for travelling in the ministry, various announcements, epistles 1714-1839, etc.

*21. Collection of letters and papers of the Goodbody and kindred families 1680-1850.

22. Mainly copies of marriage certificates 1837 to 1853, with some early ones ; also genealogical accounts of the Fuller, Neale and Jackson families ; abstracts of births and burials in Cork, Limerick, Tipperary, Waterford and Youghal Meetings, 1839-1850.

23 to 26. Certificates of removal and for travelling for the years 1830 to 1835 inclusive (mainly Dublin).

27. Dublin Monthly Meeting papers of a miscellaneous nature for the years 1834 and 1835.

28 to 34. The same for the years 1836, 1837, 1838, 1839, 1840, 1841 and 1842. These include treasurers' accounts, library reports, certificates, papers of dis-unity, applications for membership, letters, etc.

All portfolios are catalogued in the general card index.

*Those marked with an asterisk have been noted elsewhere in this volume.

MAPS AND PLANS

225. Map of Friends' Meeting Houses in Ireland showing days of Meetings, 1794.

Travelling map of the British Isles used by Joseph Pease, showing Meetings, c.1840.

Plan of Rosenallis (Queen's Co.) Burial Ground, with names up to about 1856.

Plan of Friends' old Burial Ground in Parliament Street, Waterford and papers concerning same, dated 1914.

Map of Newgarden Friends' Burial Ground, Co. Carlow, revised 1883.

Map of Suir Island School premises, n.d. (used in 1906).

Map, with ornamentation, of the lands of Ballynockin, King's Co., held by Jeremiah Hanks. Surveyed 1783 by James Parr.

Map of Dublin (printed by J. Kirkwood, Dublin), 1841.

Map of Aungier St., Dublin, n.d. (includes Lord Longford's house).

Plan for Railway Station, Kingstown, made by Samuel Roberts, 1844.

MISCELLANEOUS

DOCUMENTS CONCERNING BANDON MEN'S MEETING (PORTFOLIO 16)
1702-1727

226. A bundle of fragile material relating to Bandon Meeting, (Co. Cork), which was established about 1655. The Meeting House was built in 1728.

Four indented deeds by William Murray to Robert Arnell and Joshua Taylor in April, 1727, and to Jonas Devonshire, November, 1727.

Copy of heads of lease by Earl of Cork to William Murray, 1722.

Copy of lease of graveyard by Abra. Savage to Thos. Knight, March, 1702-3.

Two copies of searches for license for Meeting place in Bandon, 1720.

Letters (two autographed Thos. Wight).

Seven intentions of marriage 1710-1724.

Seven Papers of Sufferings.

One testimony of Disunity, 1704.

Loose Minutes of Bandon Men's Meeting, 1706-1714, with which are a few genealogical details of the families of Massey, Abbott, Morris, Knight and Abbey.

226 (contd.). Folder of Photostats presented by Northern Ireland Public Records Office, of early 18th century material relating to Friends' in Co. Cavan.

Collection of Marriage Certificates—17th-20th century.

Large collection of Photographs named, of Friends, Meeting Houses, Friends Residences, Burial Grounds, etc.

UNSORTED MATERIAL

227. Dublin Monthly Meeting Records : 1843-1848.

Bundle of Miscellaneous letters 1830-1832, and notes on Gaynor family.

Miscellaneous fragments of Cork, Tipperary, Mountrath, Clonmel and Moate Meeting Records, 18th century.

Bundle of Sufferings.

Bundles of Testimonies.

Bundle of Commonplace books and isolated pedigree material, etc.

Bundle of original National Meeting Proceedings from 1671-1780.

Bundles of Monthly Meeting original papers of 18th century.

228. 17th CENTURY LETTERS etc.

(An addition to those already mentioned in the text mainly in Grubb Collection).

John Perrot	to Henry Cromwell	1656	Copy
A. Sharp	to Thos. Sharp	1694	,,
G. Fox	to Friends in Ireland	1685	,,
S. Cheevers	to Deb. Sandham	1664	,,
J. Locke	to R. Brecon & R. Collier	1669	,,
J. Crook	to Isaac Pennington	c.1660	,,
F. Howgill	to Thos. Aldam	1665	,,
Tobias Pleadwell testimony	to Wm. Capton	1672	Original
Wm. Edmundson testimony	to Abraham Fuller	1694	Copy
Moate Meeting testimony	to Abraham Fuller	1694	,,
Testimony	to Deborah Sandham	1695	,,
Convincement	of John Watson	1693	,,
Convincement	of Ellis Lewis	1698	,,
James Dickinson	to Thomas Wilson	1699	Original

Thos. Story	to Geo. Rooke & Thos. Wilson	1695/6	Original
Sam Waldenfield	to Thos. Wilson	1695	,,
Geo. Rooke	to Thos. Wilson	1696	,,
George Rooke	to ————	1698	,,
Rich Waller et al	to Margaret Fox	1658	Photostat
Rich Waller et al	to Margaret Fox	1657	,,

Facsimilie copies of William—Hannah Penn letters :

List of Friends visiting Carlow, 1695-1735.

Letters and Papers relating to Limerick Friends :

Meeting for Suffering to Friends in Ireland, 23 signatures 1692.

John Bowron	to Geo. Fox	1659	Photostat

Building of Lurgan Meeting House, List of Subscribers, 1694.

Sam Buckley	to Margaret Fox	1656	Photostat
Jonathan Burnyeat	to Wm. Brookfield	1708/9	Original
Ed. Burrough	to Mgt. Fox, Dublin	1655	Photostat
Ed. Burrough	to ,, ,, Waterford	1655	,,
Rich. Clayton	to ,, ,, Dublin	1658	,,
,, ,,	to ,, ,, Lurgan	1655	,,
,, ,,	to ,, ,, ,,	1655	,,
,, ,,	to ,, ,, ,,	1656	,,
Wm. Edmundson	to ,, ,, ,,	1656	,,
Thos. Loe	to Geo. Fox	1660	,,
Thos. Marford	to Geo. Fox et al Waterford Prison	1659	,,
Wm. Penn (Epistle)		1698	Copy
R. Roper	to Mgt. Fox Waterford	1657	Photostat
Robt. Salthouse	to Mgt. Fox Dublin	1658	,,
John Stubbs	to Mgt. Fox ,,	1656	,,
Rich. Waller	to ,, ,, ,,	1656	,,
Doc. signed by James I, Protection to Friends (original in T.C.D.)		1689	,,
Epistle of George Fox concerning marriage of kindred		1683	,,
Inventory of goods of Isabel Carleton		1697	,,
S. Cheevers	to Deborah Sandham, Colchester Gaol	1664	,,
J. Lock	to R. Brecon & R. Collier	1669	,,
J. Crook	to Isaac Pennington	c.1660	,,
F. Howgill	to Thos. Aldam	1665	,,
Some of the heads on which George Fox spoke at Yearly Meeting		1690	,,

229. LISTS, INVENTORIES ETC.

in the Historical Library, 6 Eustace Street, Dublin,
of material in other sources

Correspondence of the Greer family of Dungannon, 1717-1891. See Appendix II. Calendar

Letters of Elizabeth Goff and her family of Horetown, Co. Wexford—see Appendix II. Inventory

Correspondence of the Greeves—O'Brien families of Dungannon, Armagh and Lisburn, and of America, between 1818 and 1869.

Most of the letters are written by John Greeves and his family to his daughter, Ann, who married William O'Brien, son of Daniel and Mary (nee Wright) O'Brien of Carlow in 1818 and emigrated with him to America. John Greeves died in 1843 after which the letters are less frequent. Three inserted trees trace the descents of the Greer-Greeves, the Malcomson-Bell and the Christy-Sinton family connections.

The first of the family of Greer or Greve to settle in Ireland was Henry who with his wife, Mary Turner, settled at the Redford Altnavannog, Tyrone in 1653. From his eldest son James is descended the family of Greer and from the second, Robert, the Grive, now Greeves family.

Three volumes, 146 letters, copied and presented to the library by Col J. R. H. Greeves in 1956, the originals being now in America. Typescript

Letters of the Heazelton family of Co. Tyrone, 1802-1826, with family tree, see No. 111. Abstracted and copied by J. R. H. Greeves and presented to the library 1960. Typescript

Letters and papers of the Heather family of Co. Tyrone, 1829-1851 with family tree abstracted and copied by J. R. H. Greeves and presented to the library 1960, see No. 11. Typescript

Ackworth School Archives presented by Friends' House Library, London 1965. Catalogue

Ackworth School, Yorkshire, was founded by the Society of Friends in 1778 in buildings purchased from the Governors of the London Foundling Hospital. This catalogue of material includes educational papers, committee records, diaries, letters, accounts, portraits, prospectuses, maps, registers, school magazines, etc., etc., forming a record of the school since its inception. Also 61 papers of the records of the Foundling Hospital and a history of the same.

Abstract of Robson Mss. vol. 37 at Friends' House, London. Brief extracts from the collection known as the Robson Mss. presented to the Library of Friends' House, London, in 1905. Gives authors and recipients of letters, all of Quaker interest between 1669 and 1786.   Inventory

Two only 17th century. Presented by Friends' House Library, London.

Abstract of Robson Mss. vol. 94 at Friends' House, London.   Inventory

As above. Correspondence to and from Samuel Fothergill (1715-1772) between 1737 and 1771. There are a few Irish references in each of above items. Presented by Friends' House Library, London.

Abstracts of Harvey Mss. vol. I at Friends' House, London. 91 documents dating 1655-1843.   Inventory

Minutes, letters, epistles, testimonies, etc., presented by Friends' House Library.

Papers from the library of John Stephenson Rowntree of York (1834-1907). Mainly concerning analysis of registers of births, marriages and deaths and other statistics. Presented by Friends' House Library.   Inventory

Letters, dreams and visions at Friends' House, London.   Inventory

A collection dating from 1657-1781 including several letters of early Friends.

Digest of Cork Meeting Books made by Russell Mortimer 1964.   Typescript

List of microfilms of Ireland Yearly Meeting Archives at Friends' House, London.

List of documents relating to the famine of 1846-1849. Placed in the Public Record Office, Dublin in 1933 by the Religious Society of Friends' in Ireland.

List of Mss. documents relating to Friends in the National Library of Ireland.

APPENDICES

ON

NORTHERN IRELAND RECORDS

BY

B. G. HUTTON, B.A., DIP.ARCH.ADMIN.

I

ULSTER PROVINCE MEETING

According to Wight and Rutty the " first settled meeting of the people called Quakers in Ireland " was established at William Edmundson's house in Lurgan, Co. Armagh, in 1654. A former Cromwellian soldier, Edmundson had been convinced by the preaching of James Naylor and came to Ireland in 1652. Although William Edmundson moved to Co. Cavan in 1655 the Lurgan meeting flourished and the next few years saw the formation of a considerable number of meetings throughout the Province. At Grange near Randalstown; at Toberhead near Magherafelt; at Ballyhagen near Kilmore in Co. Armagh; at Lisnagarvey or Lisburn; at Belturbet in Co. Cavan; at Grange near Charlemont in Co. Tyrone, etc. The earliest surviving records of the Ulster Province Meeting which came to embrace the above-mentioned constituent meetings are contained in a minute book, 10/11/1674—2/7/1693. The original volume is in Friends Meeting House, Dublin, although a photostat copy is available in the Public Record Office of Northern Ireland with the reference T.1062/47. The early meetings appeared to have been held in rotation between Ballyhagen, Lurgan and Lisburn, with Ballyhagen featuring most prominently. Much of the early business is concerned with sufferings, and the Province Meeting seems to have had a reasonable measure of administrative control even at this early date over the widely scattered meetings. The first few entries in 1674 and 1675 give details of attendance and subscriptions from meetings described as :—Lurgan, Ballyhagen, Lisnegarvey, Grange, Cavan, Antrim, Magherafelt, Grange beyond Charlemont, and Carrickfergus. Following this first Ulster Province Meeting minute book there is a gap of a year until the main and virtually unbroken series of minutes begins in 1/10/1694.

It is difficult to be precise about the exact status of some of the smaller constituent meetings in the late 17th century, and indeed several of them became extinct. But from the 18th century the following meetings for which records survive can properly be described as constituent Monthly Meetings of the Ulster Province:—Lisburn, Lurgan, Grange near Charlemont, Richhill, Ballyhagen, Antrim, Cootehill.

It is important to note that all the original surviving records of the Ulster Province Meeting and its constituent meetings are in Friends' Meeting House, Railway Street, Lisburn, with the sole exception of the first minute book of the Ulster Province Meeting. In recent years these volumes and loose papers were arranged and catalogued according to a pattern quite independent of the records in Dublin. But the references given provide an accurate finding aid to the archive at Lisburn.

In the following pages an asterisk indicates that photostat as well as microfilm copies of the Quaker records at Lisburn are in the Public Record Office of Northern Ireland. Copies on microfilm only are marked with a dagger (†).

ULSTER PROVINCE/QUARTERLY MEETING

Minutes of Province/Quarterly Meeting	10/11/1674 - 2/ 7/1693 Dublin*
,, ,, ,, ,,	1/10/1694 - 14/ 7/1717 Q/1/1*
,, ,, ,, ,,	26/ 8/1717 - 28/ 2/1750 ,, /2*
,, ,, ,, ,,	6/ 5/1751 - 17/11/1770 ,, /3†
,, ,, ,, ,,	12/ 2/1785 - 8/ 6/1801 ,, /4
,, ,, ,, ,,	7/ 9/1801 - 3/ 3/1823 ,, /5
,, ,, ,, ,,	8/ 3/1824 - 9/ 6/1845 ,, /6
,, ,, ,, ,,	3/ 3/1834 - 5/ 6/1840 ,, /7
,, ,, ,, ,,	8/ 9/1845 - 6/ 3/1865 ,, /8
,, ,, ,, ,,	2/ 3/1846 - 31/12/1860 ,, /9
,, ,, ,, ,,	8/ 9/1856 - 18/ 6/1866 ,, /10
,, ,, ,, ,,	4/ 3/1861 - 7/ 1/1877 ,, /11
,, ,, ,, ,,	18/ 3/1878 - 28/10/1918 ,, /12
,, ,, ,, ,,	6/ 1/1919 - 17/ 3/1956 ,, /13
Rough Minutes of Province/Quarterly Meeting	13/ 7/1754 - 29/11/1755 Q/2/1
,, ,, ,, ,,	/ 2/1756 - 3/ 9/1758 ,, /2
,, ,, ,, ,,	15/ 1/1763 - 26/11/1768 ,, /3
,, ,, ,, ,,	26/ 2/1763 - 7/ 3/1767 ,, /4
,, ,, ,, ,,	11/ 7/1767 - 17/11/1770 ,, /5
,, ,, ,, ,,	5/ 9/1796 - 5/12/1808 ,, /6
,, ,, ,, ,,	8/ 6/1818 - 8/12/1823 ,, /7
,, ,, ,, ,,	8/ 3/1824 - 3/ 3/1828 ,, /8
,, ,, ,, ,,	/ 9/1840 - 8/12/1845 ,, /9
Women's Minutes of Province/Quarterly Meeting	18/ 2/1792 - 17/12/1801 Q/3/1A
	9/ 5/1794 - 8/ 5/1801 ,, /1B
,, ,, ,, ,,	7/3/1825 - 4/ 3/1839 ,, /2
,, ,, ,, ,,	3/12/1827 - 4/ 9/1854 ,, /3
,, ,, ,, ,,	20/ 3/1882 - 21/ 3/1898 ,, /4

APPENDIX I 181

Ministers' and Elders' Minutes of Province/Quarterly Meeting	14/10/1758 - 20/4/1764	Q/4/1A
" " " "	1/ 3/1823 - 8/ 6/1850	,, /1B
" " " "	11/11/1852 - 9/ 9/1866	,, /2
" " " "	7/ 6/1862 - 25/10/1882	,, /3
" " " "	6/ 1/1883 - 20/ 1/1900	,, /4
" " " "	17/ 3/1900 - 9/ 6/1928	,, /5
" " " "	15/ 9/1928 - 3/ 1/1948	,, /6
" " " "	21/ 2/1948 - 14/ 3/1958	,, /7
Mostly copies of Yearly Meeting Ministers' and Elders' Proceedings	c.1890	,, /8
Marriage certificates	17/ 9/1731 - 2/11/1786	Q/5/1
Marriage register	20/ 2/1812 - 19/ 7/1848	,, /2
Book of Sufferings	1748 - 1809	,, /3†
Register of births and burials	1841 - 1858	,, /4
Proceedings of Yearly Meeting	2/ 3/1807 - 8/ 9/1823	,, /5
Proceedings of Yearly Meeting, with minutes of Committee of Ulster Provincial School	8/12/1823 - 4/ 6/1827	,, /6
London Epistles	2/6 /1823 - 2/ 3/1835	,, /7
Miscellaneous papers relating to the building of Megaberry Meeting House, and to the carrying of firearms	late 18c.	,, /8
Papers relating to apprenticeship	late 18c.	,, /9
Papers relating to Quaker usage	late 18c.	,, /10
Papers relating to discipline	late 18c.— mid 19c.	,, /11
Epistles, mainly from Dublin and London Women's Yearly Meeting	mid 19c.	,, /12
Tithe Sufferings	1706 - 1711	,, /13
Copies of London Yearly Meeting Minutes	1675 - 1745	,, /14
" Discipline " volume, i.e. Minutes and Christian advices from Dublin Half-Yearly Meeting.	from c.1676	,, /15
,, ,,	,,	,, /16
Yearly Meeting marriage advices	1808	,, /17
Treasurer's account Book	1814 - 1879	,, /18
Report of Library Committee	1854	,, /19

LISBURN MONTHLY MEETING

Although the Lisburn Meeting had its origins as early as 1654 the earliest surviving minutes begin in 1675. At that date the meetings appeared to have been held in the houses of Anthony Richardson, John Greer and Richard Boyse. It was not until c. 1690 that a permanent Meeting House was acquired. Membership was drawn from the Lisburn area and in the 18th century the constituent meetings included Ballinderry, Hillsborough, and even Newtownards. The minute books are concerned with routine disciplinary business, although the first volume concludes with copies of late 17th century removal certificates and of title deeds to the burial ground at Magheramesk. The subsequent records of the Lisburn Meeting are equalled only by those of Lurgan Meeting as a remarkably fine and complete series.

Men's Minutes	8/ 2/1675 - 26/ 4/1735	LBM/1/1†
,, ,,	2/ 8/1735 - 18/ 8/1782	,, /2†
,, ,,	5/ 9/1782 - 18/ 5/1815	,, /3
,, ,,	15/ 6/1826 - 18/ 2/1836	,, /4
,, ,,	17/ 3/1836 - 16/ 1/1845	,, /5
,, ,,	13/ 2/1845 - 15/ 7/1858	,, /6
,, ,,	14/10/1858 - 12/ 3/1868	,, /7
,, ,,	16/ 4/1868 - 12/ 4/1877	,, /8
,, ,,	17/ 5/1877 - 18/10/1888	,, /9
,, ,,	13/12/1888 - 12/ 2/1903	,, /10
,, ,,	12/ 3/1903 - 16/12/1915	,, /11
,, ,,	13/ 1/1916 - 12/11/1925	,, /12
,, ,,	17/12/1925 - 4/ 6/1938	,, /13
,, ,,	16/ 7/1938 - 15/ 8/1946	,, /14
,, ,,	14/ 9/1946 - 13/ 8/1953	,, /15
Men's Minutes (rough)	26/ 8/1762 - 8/ 9/1763	LBM/2/1
,, ,, ,,	20/ 9/1764 - 17/12/1765	,, /2
,, ,, ,,	18/12/1771 - 20/ 4/1775	,, /3
,, ,, ,,	14/ 5/1775 - 22/ 5/1777	,, /4
,, ,, ,,	9/ 1/1783 - 24/11/1785	,, /5
,, ,, ,,	18/12/1785 - 20/11/1788	,, /6
,, ,, ,,	15/ 5/1794 - 18/ 1/1798	,, /7
,, ,, ,,	15/ 2/1798 - 14/ 7/1803	,, /8
,, ,, ,,	18/ 8/1803 - 16/ 7/1807	,, /9
,, ,, ,,	13/ 8/1807 - 18/ 4/1811	,, /10
,, ,, ,,	16/ 5/1811 - 16/12/1813	,, /11
,, ,, ,,	13/ 1/1814 - 16/ 7/1818	,, /12
,, ,, ,,	13/ 8/1818 - 12/12/1822	,, /13
,, ,, ,,	16/11/1823 - 13/ 5/1826	,, /14
,, ,, ,,	13/10/1839 - 9/ 8/1857	,, /15
Women's Minutes	12/ 9/1793 - 12/ 2/1800	LBM/3/1
	8/ 8/1813 - 8/ 3/1857	,, /2

APPENDIX I

Ministers' and Elders' minutes	24/ 3/1791 - 17/ 5/1838	LBM/4/1
,, ,, ,, ,,	9/ 8/1838 - 5/ 8/1852	,, /2
,, ,, ,, ,,	11/11/1852 - 12/ 5/1862	,, /3
,, ,, ,, ,,	11/ 8/1862 - 9/12/1872	,, /4
,, ,, ,, ,,	10/ 6/1873 - 9/ 6/1892	,, /5
,, ,, ,, ,,	27/11/1879 - 25/10/1900	,, /6
,, ,, ,, ,,	25/ 8/1892 - 25/ 5/1905	,, /7
,, ,, ,, ,,	31/ 8/1905 - 29/11/1923	,, /8
,, ,, ,, ,,	13/ 3/1924 - 15/11/1934	,, /9
Record book	1703 - 1842	LBM/5/1
Record book	1766 - 1820	,, /2
Birth notes	1812 - 1854	,, /3
Birth certificates	1854 - 1952	,, /4
Burial notes	1812 - 1854	,, /5
Burial certificates	1856 - 1897	,, /6
Marriage register	1817 - 1846	,, /7
	1847 - 1904	,, /8
	1905 - 1937	,, /9
Testimonies of denial	late 18c.	,, /10
Removal and disownment certificates	c.1830	,, /11
Settlement and removal register	1820 - 1856	,, /12
Settlement and removal certificates	1856 - 1883	,, /13
Removal register	1865 - 1904	,, /14
Disownment and admission register	1842 - 1903	,, /15
Various epistles	late 18c.	,, /16
Dublin Yearly Meeting	c.1755	,, /17
Rules and Advices Record book of Sufferings	1811 - 1861	,, /18
Proceedings of Quarterly and Yearly Meetings	1835 - 1856	,, /19
List of members	c.1813	,, /20A
List of members	late 19c.	,, /20B
Treasurer's account book	1799 - 1834	,, /21
Proceedings of Quarterly Meeting	1866 - 1922	,, /22
Quarterly Meeting minutes	1870 - 1905	,, /23
"Poor" Committee minutes	1806 - 1832	,, /24

LURGAN MONTHLY MEETING

The Lurgan Meeting was established in 1654 but again, like Lisburn, the surviving minutes commence only in 1675. The first meeting was of course held in William Edmundson's house and certainly from 1675 meetings were being held at the houses of Robert Hoope, Mark Wright, Thomas Calvert, Francis Robson and Roger Webb. But a Meeting House evidently existed prior to 1691 when the minutes refer to the purchase of timber to enlarge the Meeting House. In 1697 when a new Meeting House was completed, a reference is made to the former building as being " too little and going to decay." The new Meeting House was built " upon a tenement called Madden's tenement on the S end of the town of Lurgan upon a copyhold lease from Esq. Brownlowe, in the name of Robert Hoope being for this meetings use." Robert Hoope heads the list of contributors as the " chief promoter overseer and contriver," with £40, although more than 130 individuals contributed over £200, some giving as little as a 1/- according to their means. Many of the decisions reached by the Meeting are described in considerable and illuminating detail, which make the first minute book of the Lurgan Meeting probably the most informative of any of the records at Lisburn. The following topics are all touched upon :—accurate keeping of records, marriage, drinking, extravagant dress, fornication, apprenticeship, education, honesty in trade, financial assistance to fellow Quakers, sufferings especially in 1689, settlement of disputes between relatives and neighbours, maintenance of Trust property, and even the apprehension of counterfeit Quakers—" be advised that lately a man pretending to be a friend, at Corke, is run away and proved a mere cheat, a shoemaker by trade, about 50 years old, middle stature, slender body, thin visage, paile countenance, having a light collored Perriwig (somewhat short) he wears moustaches and a short chin beard, his eyes very gray and of a dead look, a sharp nose with a little rising in the midle, his voice low and not clear. His cloak and other apparel was about light brown. He had with him a son of about 10 or 11 years of age. His name is Richard Clemens."

Men's Minutes		1675 - 1710	LGM/1/1†
,,	,,	3/11/1710 - 8/ 3/1752	,, /2†
,,	,,	12/ 4/1752 - 14/ 2/1779	,, /3†
,,	,,	25/ 4/1779 - 10/ 6/1789	,, /4
,,	,,	17/ 3/1798 - 20/11/1819	,, /5
,,	,,	18/12/1819 - 14/ 9/1822	,, /6
,,	,,	19/10/1822 - 20/ 1/1827	,, /7
,,	,,	17/ 2/1827 - 14/ 7/1832	,, /8
,,	,,	18/ 8/1832 - 5/ 5/1842	,, /9
,,	,,	9/ 6/1842 - 14/12/1860	,, /10
,,	,,	18/ 1/1861 - 12/ 5/1875	,, /11

APPENDIX I

Men's Minutes—contd.	14/ 7/1875 - 17/ 6/1891 LGM/1/12
,, ,,	5/ 7/1891 - 16/ 5/1906 ,, /13
,, ,,	13/ 6/1906 - 11/ 9/1918 ,, /14
,, ,,	16/10/1918 - 13/ 9/1933 ,, /15
,, ,,	15/11/1933 - 14/ 4/1954 ,, /16
Men's Minutes (rough)	25/ 5/1777 - 17/ 3/1789 LGM/2/1A
,, ,, ,,	17/ 3/1798 - 6/ 5/1801 ,, /2/1B
,, ,, ,,	14/ 5/1803 - 19/ 5/1804 ,, /3
,, ,, ,,	16/ 6/1804 - 18/ 5/1805 ,, /4
,, ,, ,,	15/ 6/1805 - 26/ 2/1806 ,, /5
,, ,, ,,	17/ 5/1806 - 18/ 3/1809 ,, /6
,, ,, ,,	20/ 5/1809 - 15/ 6/1811 ,, /7
,, ,, ,,	17/ 8/1811 - 17/ 4/1813 ,, /8
,, ,, ,,	11/ 5/1813 - 19/ 4/1817 ,, /9
,, ,, ,,	17/ 5/1817 - 14/ 9/1822 ,, /10
Women's Minutes	20/ 9/1794 - 16/ 7/1796 LGM/3/1
,, ,,	20/ 8/1796 - 16/ 4/1803 ,, /2
,, ,,	18/ 5/1849 - 18/ 3/1864 ,, /3
Record Book " No. 1 "	1674 - mid 18c. LGM/5/1*
Record Book " No. 2 "	mid 18c.-early 19c. ,, /2
Birth notes	1809 - 1885 ,, /3
Burial notes	1812 - 1844 ,, /4
Marriage certificates	1715 - 1811 ,, /5*
Marriage notes	1812 - 1848 ,, /6
Marriage certificates	1869 - 1906 ,, /7
Removal certificates	1796 - 1862 ,, /8
Removal certificates	1864 - 1894 ,, /9
Removal and admission certificates	1863 - 1883 ,, /10
Acknowledgment of removals	1809 - 1891 ,, /11
Testimonies of disownment	1688 - 1796 ,, /12
List of members	c.1810 - c.1883 ,, /13
Sufferings	1812 - c.1868 ,, /14
Parcel of " Marriage Papers "	pre-1884 ,, /15
Stubs of marriage and burial certificates	modern ,, /16

GRANGE NEAR CHARLEMONT MONTHLY MEETING

The meeting which was settled at Grange in Co. Tyrone in 1660 or 1662 was known as " Grange near Charlemont " or " Upper Grange " to distinguish it from the meeting already established at Grange near Randalstown in Co. Antrim or " Lower Grange." A very adequate brief account of the establishment and history of this meeting has been compiled by George Chapman. The Grange Meeting was joined to Lurgan from 1795 to 1809 for " business," and in 1920 merged with Richhill to become a Preparative Meeting.

Men's Minutes	13/ 2/1726 - 12/ 1/1770	GM/1/1
,, ,,	26/ 1/1776 - 9/ 7/1779	
,, ,,	13/ 4/1787 - 20/11/1793	,, /2
,, ,,	20/11/1793 - 23/ 9/1795	,, /3
,, ,,	18/10/1815 - 24/ 3/1824	,, /5
,, ,,	21/ 4/1824 - 22/12/1847	,, /6
,, ,,	19/ 1/1848 - 8/11/1882	,, /7
,, ,,	6/12/1882 - 7/11/1915	,, /8
,, ,,	5/12/1915 - 4/12/1955	,, /9
Men's Minutes (rough)	18/10/1809 - 20/11/1816	GM/2/1
Women's Minutes	23/10/1822 - 23/ 3/1837	GM/3/1
,, ,,	24/ 5/1837 - 20/ 9/1854	,, /2
,, ,,	22/11/1854 - 5/ 8/1885	,, /3
Ministers' and Elders' Minutes	18/ 2/1829 - 11/ 5/1842	GM/4/1
,, ,, ,, ,,	17/ 8/1842 - 11/ 8/1847	,, /2
Record book	1686 - 1784	GM/5/1
Record book	c.1812	,, /2
Accounts	1899 - 1948	,, /3
Register of births	1812 - 1923	,, /4
Burial notes	1813 - 1854	,, /5
Register of burials	1813 - 1923	,, /6
Marriage certificates	late 18c.	,, /7
Marriage certificates	1813 - 1848	,, /8
Testimonies of denial	late 18c.	,, /9
Removal certificates	1861 - 1879	,, /10
Register of removal certificates	1865 - 1909	,, /11
Testimonies of disunity, removals and sufferings	1810 - 1861	,, /12
List of members	late 18c.	,, /13
List of members	1846 - 1883	,, /14
Accounts	c.1746	,, /15
Accounts	1833 - 1864	,, /16

APPENDIX I 187

BALLYHAGEN MONTHLY MEETING

Although the meeting at Ballyhagen near Kilmore in Co. Armagh was one of the earliest founded, the minutes survive only from 1705 and imperfectly. In 1793 the old meeting house at Ballyhagen was abandoned and the present meeting house in Richhill town took its place. Tradition has it that some records were destroyed by damp in the old meeting house.

Of the surviving records the most striking are the late 17th century and early 18th century wills, many with inventories, which have been described by J. R. H. Greeves in the Irish Genealogist, Vol. 2, pp.228-239. The importance of the inventories must not be overlooked since they provide a unique and very detailed picture of the Quaker community as farmers and weavers.

Men's Minutes	1705 - 1734	BM/1/1†
,, ,,	15/ 4/1781 - 25/ 6/1793	,, /2
Women's poor relief	1695 - 1745	BM/3/1
Loose wills with inventories	late 17c.-early 18c.	BM/5/1*
Family lists	c.1680 - 1790	,, /2
Marriage certificates	1692 - 1789	,, /3*
Book of testimonies	1708 - 1813	,, /4

RICHHILL MONTHLY MEETING

Men's Minutes	20/ 1/1842 - 22/ 1/1863	RM/1/1
,, ,,	19/ 2/1863 - 7/12/1882	,, /2
,, ,,	11/ 1/1883 - 10/ 3/1892	,, /3
,, ,,	8/ 1/1891 - 5/ 3/1903	,, /4
,, ,,	9/ 4/1903 - 10/ 5/1917	,, /5
,, ,,	7/ 6/1917 - 9/ 3/1921	,, /6
,, ,,	6/ 4/1921 - 5/12/1945	,, /7
Men's Minutes (rough)	22/ 8/1793 - 20/ 8/1795	RM/2/1
,, ,, ,,	22/ 9/1796 - 24/ 7/1800	,, /2
,, ,, ,,	24/ 3/1803 - 1/ 3/1804	,, /3
,, ,, ,,	—/ 4/1818 - 24/ 8/1820	,, /4
,, ,, ,,	23/11/1820 - 23/10/1823	,, /5
,, ,, ,,	20/11/1823 - 23/ 6/1825	,, /6
,, ,, ,,	23/ 2/1832 - 24/ 5/1838	,, /7
,, ,, ,,	22/11/1839 - 20/ 1/1848	,, /8
,, ,, ,,	9/ 5/1872 - 11/12/1890	,, /9

Women's Minutes	25/ 1/1866 - 6/11/1879	RM/3/1
,, ,,	8/ 1/1880 - 8/12/1887	,, /2
Ministers' and Elders' Minutes	5/ 3/1914 - 12/ 9/1952	RM/4/1
Register of marriages	1847 - 1913	RM/5/1
Birth notes	1812 - 1919	,, /2
Abstracts of births	1812 - 1878	,, /3
Abstract of burials	1812 - 1920	,, /4
Burial certificates	1812 - 1920	,, /5
Marriage entries	1816 - 1850	,, /6
Papers relating to disownment	18c.	,, /7
Testimonies of disunity	1815 - 1869	,, /8
Applications for membership	1817 - 1870	,, /9
Copies of Quarterly Meeting and Yearly Meeting Proceedings	1807 - 1825	,, /10

ANTRIM MONTHLY MEETING

A meeting was settled at Antrim in 1669; it was discontinued in 1844.

Men's Minutes (rough)	7/ 2/1740 - 4/ 9/1763	AM/2/1
,, ,, ,,	16/10/1763 - 24/ 5/1773	,, /2
,, ,, ,,	31/ 9/1772 - 24/12/1775	,, /3
,, ,, ,,	1/ 9/1776 - 5/ 1/1777	,, /4
,, ,, ,,	10/ 9/1780 - 13/11/1785	,, /5
,, ,, ,,	25/12/1785 - 1/ 1/1790	,, /6
,, ,, ,,	12/ 2/1790 - 12/ 8/1791	,, /7
,, ,, ,,	23/ 9/1791 - 8/ 3/1793	,, /8
,, ,, ,,	12/ 4/1793 - 9/ 5/1794	,, /9
,, ,, ,,	6/ 6/1794 - 7/ 9/1798	,, /10
,, ,, ,,	12/10/1798 - 10/ 5/1801	,, /11
,, ,, ,,	11/ 6/1801 - 12/11/1801	,, /12
Papers relating to births, burials, marriage and disownment	1758 - 1798	AM/5/1

COOTEHILL MONTHLY MEETING

The Cootehill Monthly Meeting was settled in 1692 and took the place of the earlier Cavan and Belturbet meetings. During the period of the sole surviving minute book, 1766-1796, Cootehill embraced also the meeting at Oldcastle. In 1796 Cootehill was united with Grange near Charlemont. The original meeting house at Cootehill was erected c.1720 and demolished c.1920.

Men's Minutes	14/ 5/1766 - 2/ 3/1796	CM/1/1

II

The following details relate to collections of Quaker material in the Public Record Office of Northern Ireland from private sources. These are originals (D.), photostats (T.) or microfilm (Mic.).

F. USSHER GREER, LISNANANE, CO. TYRONE

c.200 documents. Title deeds and leases relating to the Greer family property, including linen interests, in Dungannon and Dublin, etc., 1690-1845. D.645.

V. McG. GREER, MONEYMORE, CO. LONDONDERRY

c.1,000 documents. Correspondence of the Greer family of Dungannon, Co. Tyrone, 1717-1891. The letters which form the main section of this collection were written to and by the second Thomas Greer, 1724-1803. The family owned a bleach green known as New Hambro or New Hamborough at Dungannon, in partnership with Messrs. Wakefield, Pratt and Meirs of London. During 1776 this partnership was dissolved and Thomas Greer entered into partnership with Wakefield and Bell and together they ran the bleach green until 1796. Shortly afterwards the Greers and the Wakefields had a final disagreement and Thomas Greer and Son decided to trade with the firm of Hayters. Linen trade was also carried on with America through Samuel and John Morton of Philadelphia, the first flax seed being imported in 1757. Trading was hampered towards the end of 1770 by a glut of linen in Philadelphia and also by ill feeling over the tax levied by the British Government on certain goods exported to America. The Greer family were Quakers and made numerous religious visits to England and Scotland as well as throughout Ireland; these visits together with current religious disputes within the Quaker movement are discussed at length. D.1044.

J. S. W. RICHARDSON, BESSBROOK, CO. ARMAGH

c.100 documents. Letters of Elizabeth Goff and her family, Horetown, Co. Wexford which contain much relating to the meetings and organisation of the Society of Friends, 1768-c. 1840; they include:— a detailed description of a journey from Quebec to Toronto and Kingston made by emigrant Friends, c.1823; anti-Slavery petition from Friends in Moyallen, Co. Down, c.1824. D.1762.

MISS MURIEL RICHARDSON, BELFAST

8 documents. These include the correpondence between James N. Richardson, Lisburn, Co. Antrim and Edward Pease, Darlington,

Yorkshire, 1833-1847. The letters are principally concerned with family affairs and with the Society of Friends, and include a comment on the future of Quakerism in Van Diemen's Land. T.1489.

J. S. W. RICHARDSON, BESSBROOK, CO. ARMAGH

c.150 documents. These include the correspondence between Elizabeth Goff, Horetown, Co. Wexford and numerous relatives, 1760-1814. The letters are principally concerned with family affairs and with the Society of Friends but there is some reference to the impact of the 1798 Rebellion upon Dublin. T.1621.

JOHN DOUGLAS, BELFAST

Volume containing the out-correspondence, accounts and memoranda of Robert Bradshaw of Dublin and Milecross, Co. Down, 1784-1792; the early years provide details of Bradshaw's interest in the flax seed trade but eventually the entries become concerned exclusively with Quaker trust affairs. Mic.99.

H. BASS, LISBURN, CO. ANTRIM

c.50 documents. Correspondence of Isaac Bass of Lisburn in 1837 which is concerned with family affairs and Quaker administration and which includes a number of letters from relatives in Brighton. Mic.111/2.

NAMES OCCURRING

IN

IRISH QUAKER REGISTERS

A

Abbott	Albright	Anderton	Arthur
Abell	Alcock	Andrew	Aschcroft
Abraham	Alders	Annesley	Asco
Abram	Alderworth	Ansley	Ashbey
Acritt	Aldridge	Anston	Ashton
Acton	Alexander	Anyon	Aske
Adams	Allan	Archdall	Askey
Adamson	Allason	Archbold	Astick
Addey	Allen	Archer	Aston
Adgett	Allerdice	Ardill	Atenborough
Adkin	Allerdyce	Ardry	Atherton
Adkins	Alleyn	Arey	Atkins
Adridge	Allison	Arley	Atkinson
Aery	Allment	Arnell	Atteridge
Agnew	Alment	Arnold	Audlam
Aickin	Alloway	Armour	Auldridge
Alberson	Allwood	Armstrong	Auliffe
Albey	Anderson	Armstronge	Ayers

B

Babington	Barclay	Bateman	Beetham
Badcock	Barcroft	Bates	Beevan
Baddily	Bardin	Batters	Belchy
Baily	Barecroft	Bayes	Bell
Baines	Barger	Baylee	Bellwood
Bake	Barker	Baynham	Belshaw
Baker	Barlow	Baynton	Benat
Bagalley	Barnard	Beale	Benfield
Bagnall	Barnes	Bealey	Benit
Bagnell	Barns	Beamish	Benn
Bagwell	Barr	Beard	Bennett
Balding	Barras	Beasley	Bennis
Baldwin	Barrett	Beates	Bentham
Balfore	Barrington	Beats	Bentley
Balfour	Barrow	Beatty	Benson
Ball	Barry	Beaty	Bermingham
Ballintine	Barten	Beavan	Bernard
Balster	Barton	Beaver	Berry
Bamfield	Barwick	Beck	Best
Banbrick	Bass	Beckett	Bevan
Bancroft	Bastiville	Beckitt	Bevans
Banfield	Batch	Beeby	Beverly
Banks	Batchelor	Beech	Beverstock
Barber	Bate	Beesley	Bevin

B — *contd.*

Bewley	Bobicar	Braithwit	Brunskill
Bickes	Boddy	Brameree	Brunette
Bickett	Bold	Bramery	Bryan
Bickhouse	Boles	Brannan	Bryans
Bighton	Bolster	Brannen	Bryant
Bigland	Bolton	Breading	Buckley
Biker	Bomford	Breatherick	Budd
Billing	Bond	Breathericke	Bull
Bilote	Boomar	Breenan	Bulla
Binns	Boomer	Brenan	Bullack
Biott	Booth	Brereton	Bullagh
Birbeck	Boothe	Britt	Bullock
Birch	Borula	Brewer	Bullough
Birchall	Borradale	Brewster	Bullow
Bird	Boswell	Breyan	Bunce
Birkbeck	Bottom	Brice	Bunton
Birket	Bouchier	Bridge	Burdek
Birkett	Bould	Bridges	Burford
Birt	Boulles	Brien	Burgess
Bishop	Bourd	Briggs	Burk
Black	Bourn	Brinan	Burke
Blackbourn	Bourras	Britt	Burn
Blackburn	Boushier	Britten	Burne
Blades	Bowen	Britton	Burns
Blain	Bowles	Broadhead	Burnside
Blair	Bowman	Broadhurst	Burnyeat
Blackman	Bowmer	Brockbank	Burrow
Blakeburne	Bows	Brocklebank	Burrows
Blakely	Boxer	Brocklesby	Burt
Blakeney	Boyce	Broderick	Burton
Blamire	Boyd	Brogdale	Bury
Blanch	Boyland	Brogden	Busbee
Bleak	Boyle	Brookfield	Bushbee
Blethin	Boys, Boyes	Brooking	Bushby
Blodwick	Brackles	Brookings	Bushell
Bloomer	Braddock	Brooks	Busse
Bludwick	Bradford	Brounfield	Bustard
Boadle	Bradhurst	Brown	Butcher
Boake	Bradley	Browne	Butler
Boales	Bradshaw	Brownlee	Buttermoth
Boardman	Brady	Brownloe	Butterworth
Boate	Bragg	Brownlow	Byrd
Bobear	Braithwait	Brumskill	Byrn
			Byrne

C

Caddow	Caulfield	Clegg	Conry
Cain	Cavenagh	Cleland	Constable
Caine	Cecill	Clemens	Constant
Caldwell	Chadwick	Clements	Conway
Callison	Chaffin	Clemmins	Cook
Callow	Chamberlain	Clemmons	Cooke
Calvard	Chamberlin	Clendenan	Cooley
Calverly	Chambers	Clendennan	Coomb
Calvert	Champion	Cleod	Coombs
Cambridge	Chancy	Clerk	Cooper
Campbel	Chanders	Clibborn	Cope
Campbell	Chandlee	Clibborne	Copeland
Canning	Chandler	Cliborn	Coppock
Canter	Chandley	Cliffton	Corbatt
Cantrell	Chapman	Clifton	Corblett
Cantrill	Chard	Close	Cordiner
Cape	Charles	Clower	Corfield
Capel	Chase	Cluthbart	Corles
Caple	Chaunders	Coakley	Corlett
Capper	Chaytor	Coakly	Corliss
Capton	Cheater	Coale	Cormack
Card	Cheator	Coates	Cormick
Carduffe	Cherry	Coborne	Cornock
Carey	Chesney	Cockrane	Cornthwaite
Carleton	Chester	Cole	Cornwall
Carlile	Chesterman	Coleman	Corren
Carlton	Chesworth	Collegon	Cosbee
Carlyle	Cheter	Collett	Cosby
Carmichael	Chevers	Collier	Cotten
Carnahan	Child	Collins	Cotter
Carnes	Christian	Colman	Cottingham
Carr	Christy	Colvin	Cotton
Carrary	Chrubb	Conally	Coulton
Carrodus	Church	Conbourne	Courghee
Carroll	Clampit	Conelly	Coursey
Carter	Clancey	Coulan	Coursie
Cartwright	Clancy	Coulan	Courteney
Carty	Clare	Connell	Courtis
Casby	Clarenden	Conner	Courtney
Cash	Clark	Connolly	Cousin
Cassady	Clarke	Connor	Cove
Castle	Clarridge	Connors	Cowell
Castles	Clary	Conolly	Cowman
Castleton	Clatchy	Conraheey	Cowper
Caufield	Clayton	Conran	Cowsnock

C — contd.

Cox	Creagh	Cross	Cumberland
Coyle	Creavan	Crothers	Cummins
Cozins	Creeth	Crouch	Cumpston
Crabb	Creevy	Crow	Cunningham
Craddock	Creiagh	Crowley	Cuppage
Crafford	Creith	Crubb	Cupton
Craft	Crips	Crump	Currant
Craig	Critchett	Cuddy	Curled
Crampton	Croft(-s)	Cudmore	Curlote
Crane	Crone	Cuffe	Curry
Craper	Crooke	Cullamore	Curtis
Cratia	Crooks	Cullimore	Curtiss
Craven	Crookshank	Cullinore	Cuthbert
Crawley	Crosdale		

D

Dack	Delany	Donnella	Duckett
Dale	Delap	Donnellath	Ducker
Daley	Delapp	Doolittle	Dudley
Dallin	Dellany	Doran	Duepont
Dalton	Dennis	Dorcas	Duffy
Danelly	Dent	Doron	Dugan
Daniel	Denton	Dorson	Dugdale
Daniell	Derkindren	Douglas	Dugdill
Darbee	Desmanios	Dove	Duglass
Darby	Deverell	Dowd	Dun
Darker	Deverson	Dower	Dunbar
Darragh	Devitt	Dowdney	Duncan
Darton	Devonsher	Dowlen	Duck
Daughany	Dewras	Dowlon	Dunkly
Daunt	Deyell	Downes	Dunlop
Davenport	Dickinson	Dowson	Dunn
Davies	Dickson	Doyle	Dunne
Davis	Dillany	Dramsfield	Dupleax
Dawson	Dillon	Draper	Duplex
Day	Dinham	Drenan	Durrance
Deale	Dirkindren	Drennan	Durre
Deane	Dixon	Drewitt	Durrey
Dearman	Dobbs	Dring	Dwyer
Deaves	Dobson	Driver	Dye
Deeble	Dodd	Druitt	Dyer
Deery	Dollard	Drury	Dymock
Deeves	Donald	Ducat	Dymond
Delahunty			

E

Eagar	Edge	Ellott	Erbury
Earle	Edgeton	Ellwood	Erratt
Earls	Edmondson	Elly	Erritt
Easmond	Edmundson	Elmes	Errot
Eason	Edwards	Ely	Erwin
Easum	Egerton	Emerson	Eson
Eavins	Elders	End	Esson
Ebbs	Elicoate	England	Eustace
Ebton	Eliot	English	Eustice
Eburn	Ellicote	Englefield	Evans
Ecclenbrough	Ellinthorp	Enligh	Eveligh
Ecclenbur	Ellinworth	Ennis	Evens
Eccles	Elliot	Epye	Eves
Eddy	Ellis	Eratt	Evory (or Ivory)
Edens	Ellison		

F

Fade	Fendell	Flahy	Fountain
Fairbank	Fenix	Flanagan	Foutaine
Fairbridge	Fennell	Flanigan	Fowler
Fairbrother	Fenn	Fletcher	Fox
Fairley	Feren	Fling	Foy
Fallowfield	Ferguson	Flood	Frampton
Fanu	Ferley	Flower	Francis
Faren	Feron	Floyd	Frankland
Faris	Ferone	Foard	Franklin
Farley	Ferrar	Fogart	Frantham
Farlow	Ferrer	Fogarty	Franthem
Farmer	Ferris	Foley	Fredd
Farrell	Fetch	Foole	Freedd
Fawcet	Fieldhouse	Forbes	Freeman
Fawcett	Filer	Force	French
Fay	Fin	Ford	Frewen
Fayle	Finch	Forest	Frier
Fearen	Finlay	Forrester	Frith
Fearns	Finsley	Forse	Frizell
Fearnsley	(or Tinsley)	Forster	Frost
Fearon	Firth	Forsythe	Fry
Featherston	Fisher	Forth	Fryer
Featherstone	Fitt	Fosit	Fugard
Fell	Fitzgerald	Fossey	Fuller
Fendal	Fitzpatrick	Foster	Fulton
Fendall	Fitzwilliams	Fothergill	Furnas
			Fyance

G

Gale	Gilkes	Golphin	Gray
Galfin	Gill	Good	Gribbell
Gallaher	Gillan	Goodacre	Gribble
Gambel	Gillett	Goodbody	Gridley
Gamble	Gilling	Goold	Grierson
Gardiner	Gilmore	Goouch	Griffett
Garnet	Gilpin	Gordon	Griffin
Garnett	Gittas	Gove	Griffitts
Garratt	Gittos	Gorse	Griffiths
Garrett	Glaister	Cortrep	Grimes
Gaskin	Glaisyer	Gosling	Green
Gatchell	Glasford	Gossage	Greene
Gairn	Glester	Gouch	Greenhow
Gaw	Glorney	Gouge	Greenup
Gay	Glynn	Gough	Greenwood
Gaye	Goad	Goulbee	Greer
Gaynor	Goatly	Goulding	Greevan
Geale	Goatley	Gousden	Greeves
Gee	Godden	Gowan	Gregg
Geehan	Godfray	Gower	Gregson
Geoghegan	Godfrey	Gowin	Grogan
George	Godkin	Gover	Groomly
Getto	Godsell	Govier	Grove
Gibbs	Godwin	Grace	Groves
Gibson	Goff	Graham	Grosvenor
Gifford	Goin	Grailey	Grubb
Gihon	Going	Graily	Grumbley
Gilbert	Goldbey	Grandy	Grumbly
Gilberts	Goldberry	Grant	Grundy
Gilbertson	Goldby	Grattan	Guion
Gildersley	Goldbrough	Gratton	Gunson
Giles	Gollaher	Graves	Guy

H

Hadden	Halladay	Hancock	Harding
Haddock	Hallaway	Handcock	Hardy
Hadley	Halliday	Hands	Harford
Hadlock	Hallowday	Handy	Hargrave
Hadly	Haly	Hanks	Hargrove
Hadock	Haman	Hanna	Harkleey
Hagan	Hammon	Hannin	Harlan
Halford	Hammond	Hanning	Harland
Halfpenny	Hampton	Hardcastle	Harlin
Hall	Hamson	Harden	Harman

H — contd.

Harper	Healy	Hinkson	Hornbee
Harrington	Hearson	Hinshaw	Horton
Harris	Heather	Hinton	Hough
Harrison	Heatherington	Hitchcock	Houlden
Harrisson	Heathwood	Hix	Houlten
Harrold	Heaton	Hoare	Houlton
Harrow	Helm	Hobbs	How
Harry	Helton	Hobkin	Howard
Hart	Hender	Hobley	Howell
Hartey	Henderson	Hobson	Howes
Hartford	Hendren	Hodgins	Howet
Hartley	Henning	Hodgkinson	Howis
Harty	Henshaw	Hodgson	Howison
Harvey	Henry	Hodshon	Hows
Harwood	Hergrave	Hogan	Hoy
Haslam	Heritage	Hogg	Hoyland
Haslem	Heron	Holdbrook	Hubbard
Hassen	Herrin	Holden	Hubburd
Hastie	Hewgan	Holdsworth	Huddleston
Hasty	Hewit	Holland	Hudson
Hatton	Hewitt	Holliday	Hueson
Hattonville	Hews	Hollin	Hugan
Haughton	Hewson	Hollingsworth	Hughes
Haven	Hibbs	Hollond	Huleat
Hawkins	Hickman	Holloway	Hull
Hawks	Hiett	Holme	Hume
Hawton	Higginbotham	Holmes	Humphreys
Hay	Higgins	Holton	Hungerford
Haydock	Higginson	Hone	Hunt
Hayes	Hildreth	Honor	Hunters
Hayman	Hildrith	Hoope	Hurst
Haythornee	Hill	Hoopes	Huson
Haythornwaite	Hillary	Hootin	Hussey
Hayward	Hillery	Hoowe	Hust
Haywood	Himing	Hoowee	Hutchings
Hazleton	Hinchley	Hope	Hutchins
Head	Hind	Hopkins	Hutchinson
Headon	Hinds	Horn	Hutton
			Hynes

I

Ingham	Ingram	Innis	Irwin
Inglefield	Inman	Irvine	Ivory

J

Jackson	Jeffers	Jeoffers	Jolley
Jacob	Jeffrys	Jessop	Jolly
Jacobs	Jellico	Jessup	Jones
Jaffray	Jellicoe	Jiffard	Jopson
James	Jenkins	Jobson	Jordan
Janhert	Jenkinson	Johnson	Jourdane
Jay (see Gay)	Jenkison	Johnston	Joyce
Jebb	Jenkisson	Johnstone	Judd
Jeboe	Jennings	Joice	Julian

K

Kane	Kelsell	Kent	Kilgower
Kealey	Kelso	Kenway	King
Keasby	Kelsoe	Ker	Kinion
Kear	Kemp	Kerby	Kinning
Kearney	Kendal	Keringham	Kirby
Keating	Kendall	Kernaghan	Kirk
Keegan	Kendleside	Kernehon	Kirkpatrick
Keene	Kenion	Kerney	Kitchin
Keith	Kennan	Kerley	Kitching
Kelly	Kennedy	Kerr	Knight
Kell	Kennion	Keys	Knott
Kelsel	Kenny	Kid(alias Price)	Knowles
		Kilgour	Knox

L

Lackey	Lauders	Leaths	Levy
Laden	Laundy	Leavy	Lewis
La Grange	Laurence	Leaze	Leybourn
Laithwait	Lavender	Leckey	Leybourne
Lalor	Law	Lecky	Liddal
Lamb	Lawes	Lee	Liddon
Lamphier	Lawford	Leech	Lightfoot
Lancaster	Lawlor	Lees	Lill
Lane	Lawson	Lego	Lillburn
Langdon	Lawton	Leigh	Lilly
Langley	Laybourn	Lemax	Lindly
Langtree	Lea	Lemox	Lindley
Langtrey	Leadbeater	Lennax	Lindsey
Lantree	Leadman	Lennox	Lingwood
Lapham	Leake	Leonard	Linley
Larkin	Leaper	Lester	Linn
Lashills	Leary	Leveret	Linsey
Latty	Leathes	Leire	Lippey

L — contd.

Lisk	Lockington	Lowe	Lynam
Lister	Lodge	Lowry	Lynan
Littel	Loe	Lowther	Lynar
Little	Loft	Loyd	Lynas
Lively	Logan	Lucas	Lynass
Livingstone	Long	Luckas	Lynch
Lloyd	Longmire	Lund	Lynes
Lock	Lonsdale	Lunn	Lynn
Locke	Lovell	Luscombe	Lyons
Locker	Low	Lutis	Lyster
Lockhart	Lowden		

Mc, Mac

Macaboy	McCombe	Mackay	McMinn
McAdam	McConatty	Mackey	McNamara
McAllister	McConnell	McKee	McNeess
McAvoy	McCrandle	McKenny	McNeice
McBride	McCullogh	McKenzie	McNeill
McCabe	McCullough	Mackie	McQuaon
Macartney	McCutchen	Mackin	Macquay
Maccolum	McDermot	McKinnagh	McQuay
Macconaughty	McDonald	McKitrick	Macquillan
Maccue	McDonell	McKittrick	Macquillen
Maconaughty	McDowell	McLean	McQuillan
McClachy	McElroy	McLeland	McRannell
McClellen	McEvoy	Maclusk	Macristal
McClung	McGee	McMahon	Macullam
McClunn	McGilkrist	MacManus	Macullem
McClure	McGuire	McManus	McWharton
McCoen	Macinstry	McMeaken	McWilliams
McCollom	McIntire		

Mad, etc.

Madden	Maine	Manley	Mark
Madder	Maise	Manliff	Marriage
Madderow	Malcomson	Manliffe	Marsh
Maddock	Maley	Manly	Marshal
Magee	Mallagh	Mann	Marshall
Magill	Malone	Mannin	Martin
Maginnis	Manchester	Manseragh	Massey
Maguire	Manders	Mansergh	Mason
Maholam	Manes	Mara	Massy
Mahon	Manifold	Marchant	Mastin

M — contd.

Maston	Medcalf	Milton	Morison
Matchet	Medcalfe	Minnis	Morrice
Matchett	Mee	Miollis	Morris
Mather	Mellifont	Mison	Morrison
Matherine	Mellor	Mitchel	Morrow
Mathers	Menagh	Mitchelbourn	Morton
Mathes	Mercer	Mitchell	Moss
Mathew	Merchant	Mitten	Mosley
Mathews	Meredith	Mittin	Motteren
Matteshe	Merreweather	Mitton	Moughan
Matthews	Merrick	Mogford	Mountjoy
Matthias	Merrit	Molloy	Moxon
Maund	Merritt	Monk	Mulhall
Mawhart	Merrywether	Monke	Mullhall
Mawhorter	Messenger	Montgomery	Mulliken
Mawhuter	Metcalf	Montjoy	Mullikin
Mawman	Meyers	Moodey	Mullin
Max	Michaels	Moon	Mullins
Maxwell	Mickle	Moone	Mulloan
May	Middleton	Mooney	Mulloane
Mayfield	Midgly	Moonfield	Mullone
Mayne	Milbourne	Moor	Mumford
Maynes	Millhouse	Moore	Munday
Mayo	Millbourne	Moorehead	Mundy
Meade	Miller	Moorhouse	Munrow
Meader	Millhouse	Moran	Murdagh
Meador	Milliken	Morehead	Murphy
Means	Millner	Morehouse	Murray
Meares	Mills	Moren	Mussen
Mears	Milne	Morgan	Myles
Medallon	Milner		

N

Narney	Neville	Newly	Nixon
Nathill	Nevins	Newmarch	Nobbs
Naylen	Nevit	Newmarsh	Noble
Neale	Nevitt	Newsom	Noon
Neil	Newberry	Newton	Noris
Neill	Newbold	Neyne	Norman
Neland	Newenham	Neynoe	Norns
Nelson	Newlan	Nicholls	North
Nettleton	Newland	Nicholson	Northall
Nevel	Newlin	Nickson	Norton
Nevill	Newlon	Nicolson	Nottingham

N — *contd.*

Nowdon	Nugent	Nutly
Nowland	Nusom	Nuttel
Nowlon	Nuthill	Nutter

O

Oakley	Oder	Oliver	Ostell
Oakely	Odgers	O'Neill	Ottway
Obre	Odkins	Osborne	Otway
O'Brien	Odlum	Osburn	Owden
O'Callaghan	Ogdin	Osley	Owens
Oddie	Ogle	Ostel	

P

Padget	Pease	Pettigrew	Pledwell
Padgett	Peased	Pheir	Plerr
Padson	Peasley	Phelan	Plumber
Pagan	Peck	Phelps	Plumbsted
Page	Pedlow	Phillips	Plummer
Paine	Peel	Philpot	Poe
Paisley	Peale	Philps	Poel
Palmer	Peerson	Pickard	Poge
Panker	Peet	Pickering	Pollard
Panter	Peett	Pickett	Pollock
Parke	Peile	Pierce	Polloge
Parker	Peirson	Pierson	Pologe
Parr	Peisley	Pike	Poole
Parrot	Pelin	Pile	Poore
Parry	Pell	Pilkington	Pope
Parsons	Pellet	Pillar	Pore
Partridge	Pemberton	Pilsworth	Porter
Parvin	Pen	Pim	Pott
Pasco	Penn	Pimlett	Potter
Pasley	Pennington	Pimlott	Pounder
Patrick	Pennock	Pimm	Power
Patrickson	Penrose	Piper	Powell
Patridge	Pepper	Pitford	Poynter
Patterson	Percival	Pits	Pratt
Pattison	Perfett	Pitts	Prescod
Paul	Perrin	Place	Preston
Peacock	Perrot	Plant	Price
Pearce	Perry	Plasted	Prigg
Pearse	Peterson	Pleadwell	Prince
Pearson	Petticrew	Pleadwells	Pringle

P — *contd.*

Pritchard	Prouse	Purcell	Purves
Pritchet	Prout	Purdie	Purvis
Procter	Prush	Purdy	Pye
Proctor	Pulford	Pursell	Pyle

Q

Quin
Quinn

R

Rackley	Read	Ridgeway	Rossell
Radford	Reading	Rigby	Round
Rafter	Realt	Rigg	Rountree
Raines	Reap	Rigge	Rourk
Raitt	Reddinge	Riland	Rourke
Rake	Reddock	Riley	Rons
Ramsay	Ree	Roase	Rouse
Ramsbotham	Reed	Robbin	Routh
Ramsey	Reeves	Roberts	Rowland
Randall	Reid	Robertson	Rowley
Randell	Refford	Robeson	Rowntree
Randle	Reford	Robins	Rubie
Rankin	Rennix	Robinson	Rubotom
Ransom	Renny	Robson	Ruby
Ranton	Rest	Roche	Ruddock
Raper	Reylance	Rodam	Rudock
Ratcliffe	Reynolds	Roddom	Rumfet
Ratcliff	Rhames	Rodgers	Rumphit
Rathwell	Rhodes	Rodom	Rumphitt
Raw	Ribton	Roe	Rushworth
Rawlins	Rice	Rogan	Russell
Rawsom	Richardson	Rogers	Ryan
Ray	Richey	Rooke	Ryder
Raymond	Richy	Rorke	Ryland
Rayner	Rickets	Rose	Rylands
Raynor	Rickman	Rosemond	Rylins
Rea	Ridge	Ross	Rynelds

S

Sadler	Salverly	Sandham	Saunderson
Sadlier	(or Calverly)	Sandwith	Savage
Sain	Sames	Sargent	Savory
Sale	Sams	Satterthwaite	Sawyer
Salter	Sanders	Saul	Sayer
Saltmarsh	Sanderson	Saunders	Sayers

S — contd.

Sayright	Shore	Smith	Steer
Sayward	Short	Smithson	Stenness
Scafe	Shillingsworth	Snealson	Stephen
Scar	Shilly	Snelgrove	Stephens
Scarr	Shingleton	Snell	Stephenson
Sceife	Shinkwin	Softlaw	Stepney
Scofield	Shipsey	Softlow	Steven
Scott	Shute	Sotheran	Stevens
Scowcroft	Sibson	Southall	Stevenson
Scriven	Sides	Southbourne	Stewart
Seales	Siggins	Southwell	Stockbridge
Sealey	Sikes	Sowden	Stockdale
Sealy	Sill	Sparks	Stockton
Seamaden	Sim	Sparrow	Stoddart
Searle	Simkin	Speers	Stoit
Sears	Simons	Spence	Stokes
Seaver	Simmons	Sperry	Stolman
Sedgwick	Simpkin	Spiers	Stones
Seelby	Simpkins	Spillars	Storey
Seely	Simpson	Spindlow	Story
Selwood	Simson	Spires	Stotsbury
Sergeant	Sinclair	Spotten	Stott
Seton	Sinderby	Sprigg	Stout
Sewyer	Sing	Spring	Stoute
Seymour	Sinklar	Sproule	Stoyt
Shackleton	Sinkler	Sproules	Strangman
Shanly	Sinton	Sprowle	Strangwidge
Shannon	Sissemore	Spurrit	Strettell
Sharp	Sixsmith	Squibb	Strettle
Sharpe	Sizemon	Stacey	Strickland
Sharpless	Skeife	Stafford	Stringer
Sharpley	Skelcock	Stamp	Stubbs
Shaw	Skelton	Stamper	Sturge
Shean	Skinner	Stanfield	Sturgess
Sheen	Slade	Stanford	Sturmy
Sheills	Slaide	Stanhope	Sudgeon
Sheldon	Slater	Stanton	Suliot
Shelly	Slee	Starkey	Sumerford
Sheperd	Sleigh	Starr	Summers
Shepherd	Slingsby	Start	Sutcliff
Sheppard	Slythe	Steacey	Sutton
Shepperd	Smallhorn	Stead	Swaffald
Sheridan	Smallhorne	Stedman	Swaffild
Sherrad	Smallman	Steele	Swainson
Sherwood	Smallwood	Steenson	Swan

S—contd.

Swanson	Sweethen	Swifield	Sykes
Swayfield	Sweetman	Swinerten	Symkin
Swayne	Swenerton	Syberry	Synge

T

Tabirkin	Thirkilde	Todd	Trait
Tackaberry	Thistlethwaite	Todhunter	Tranham
Taggart	Thomas	Toghill	Trapnell
Tailford	Thomlinson	Tolerton	Treanor
Talbot	Thompson	Tomey	Treavor
Tallee	Thomson	Tomkins	Tregelles
Tallford	Thornberry	Tomlinson	Trembell
Tally	Thornburgh	Tooly	Trenham
Tame	Thornbury	Toomey	Trenor
Tankard	Thorndall	Toomy	Tristrem
Tanner	Thorndell	Toovey	Troges
Tatnell	Thornton	Toppin	Trotter
Taverner	Thorp	Tottenham	Trueman
Tavernor	Thorpe	Tottersell	Trumbull
Taylor	Thredwell	Tough	Trump
Tegart	Thwaites	Tourneiur	Tuart
Tellford	Thwayts	Townsill	Tuckett
Tennant	Thyne	Toursill	Tucker
Terry	Tibbs	Towell	Tuft
Tessyman	Tillesley	Towels	Tuke
Tew	Tillsy	Towle	Turner
Thacker	Timmons	Townsend	Turtle
Thackeray	Timons	Tracey	Tute
Thackray	Tinekin	Trafford	Twinem
Thatchell	Tinsley	Tragus	Tyers
Theobald	Tippier	Trail	Tylor
Thirkild	Tison	Trainer	Tyson

U

Ultrim	Unthank	Urin	Utram
Ultrum	Uprichard	Usher	

V

Valentine	Veasey	Verso	Vipond
Vallis	Veek	Vick	Vipping
Vance	Verman	Vicke	Vippond
Vanner	Verne	Vickers	Vivers
Varman	Vernon	Vipon	Vousdon
Vaston			

W

Waddy	Watts	Whithill	Wilson
Wade	Wear	Whiting	Wilmer
Wainwright	Webb	Whitton	Wilmot
Waite	Webber	Whitsitt	Wilsmith
Wakefield	Webster	Whitsitte	Wilson
Walbrook	Weild	Whitten	Wily
Walby	Weilly	Whittfield	Winder
Waldron	Weir	Whittle	Window
Walker	Welch	Wickham	Winnington
Wall	Weld	Wicklaff	Winsloe
Wallace	Weldon	Wickliff	Winslow
Wallis	Welsh	Wicklow	Winter
Walpole	Weltch	Widdas	Winthrop
Walpoole	West	Widdes	Wisely
Walsh	Westcomb	Widdos	Wish
Walshe	Westman	Widdows	Witherell
Walter	Weston	Widows	Witherelt
Walton	Wetherald	Wiggelsworth	Wood
Ward	Wetherel	Wigglesworth	Woodas
Wardell	Wethereld	Wigham	Woodcock
Wardle	Wetherell	Wight	Woodhouse
Ware	Wettington	Wiglesworth	Woods
Waren	Whallen	Wigmore	Woodward
Warham	Whalley	Wilcocks	Woodworth
Warin	Wharton	Wilcox	Woolley
Waring	Wheddon	Wild	Wormel
Warner	Wheeler	Wilkins	Warrell
Warren	Wheelright	Wilkinson	Worsell
Warriner	Wheldon	Willan	Worswell
Warwick	Whellock	Willball	Worth
Waseley	Whinnery	Willcocks	Worthington
Wasley	Whinry	Willen	Wren
Wastle	Whitaker	Williams	Wrest
Waterhouse	White	Williamson	Wright
Waters	Whitehead	Willin	Wyley
Watson	Whiteside	Willis	Wylie
Watt	Whitfield	Wills	Wynne
			Wyre

Y

Yare	Yeates	Young
Yauhert	Yeats	

Z

Zane	Zanes

INDEX

Testators' names are in heavy type.
The list of surnames in pp. 193-207 have not been indexed.

A

Abbey, family mentioned : 226.
Abbott, family mentioned : 226.
—— John : 189.
—— Mary : 189.
—— William : 189.
Abell Abraham : 139.
—— Elizabeth (nee Beale), (wife of Richard Abell) : 146.
—— Elizabeth Ridgeway : 160.
—— Elizabeth (nee Morris) : 139.
—— family : 110.
—— James : 92, 96, 114, 206.
—— James (1751-1818), Diary of : 133, 137.
—— James, Testimony to : 108.
—— Jane : 154, 160.
—— —— (1787-1852) : 133, 146. Extracts from Memoranda.
—— John : 160.
—— John : 116.
—— John (1791-1861), Journal of : 133 154.
—— Joseph : 177.
—— Joshua : 154, 160.
—— Margaret (Beale) : 154.
—— Mary : 136.
—— Richard : 92, 136, 146, 154, 160.
—— —— (1750-1801), Journal of visit to London Yearly Meeting : 133, 139.
—— Sarah : 146, 154, 160.
Abernethy, Dr. : 101.
Accommodation in London, Cost of : 105.
Account Book, Tipperary : 16.
Accounts, Carlow : 6.
—— Committee (Minutes of : 7.)
—— Cork Treasurer's : 14.
—— Dublin Men's Meeting : 7.
—— Moate Men's Meeting : 9.
—— Munster Province : 13.
—— Poor fund : 17.
—— Tipperary : 17.
—— Waterford Men's Meeting : 17.
—— Limerick Women's Meeting : 15.
—— Yearly Meeting : 2.
Acherogar, (Leix) : 191.
Ackworth School (Yorkshire) : 229.

Active—(Vessel) : 86.
Adair, John : 217, (20), (25).
Adams, name mentioned : 108.
Addey, Lizzie Poole (1818-1886), Her recollections : 149.
Advices, Christian : 1, 2, 3, 14.
Affairs and Wills (Books for) : 7.
Africa, Interior of, Journey to : 106.
Aghford, Co. Wexford : 184.
Agricultural Labourers : 82.
Agricultural School : 132.
Aldborough (Aldeburgh), Suffolk : 99.
Alexander, George, mentioned : 106.
—— Reuben F. : 215, (40).
—— Samuel : 80.
—— William : 217, (10).
Allegiance, Act of (1774) : 63.
Allen, Rebecca : 161.
—— Susanna : 176.
—— William : 28, 82, 105.
—— —— mentioned : 103.
Alloway, William : 186.
Alment, Elizabeth : 162.
—— James Doyle : 162.
—— John : 162.
—— Joseph : 162.
—— Mark : 162.
—— Sarah : 162.
—— William : 162.
Alpaca : 28.
Altnavannog, Co. Tyrone : 12.
America, Commodities from : 84.
—— Journey to mentioned : 106.
—— Secession among Friends in : 102, 157.
—— Civil War, comments on : 110.
American Meetings : 2.
Amethyst, vein of, in Cork : 88.
Aungier Street, Dublin, Map of : 225.
Anglin, John : 183.
Anglo-Chinese War : 118.
Annals of Ballitore : 54, 55, 125, 143, 147.
Anner Mills (Clonmel) : 22, 68, 74, 76, 79, 80, 84, 89, 92, 142.
—— —— Insurance on : 215, (21).
—— —— House : 81.
Annesley, Francis : 72.
Anti-Slavery, Agitation in Cuba : 118.

209

INDEX

ANTI-SLAVERY Meetings : 100, 102.
—— —— Mentioned : 150.
—— —— Petition from Moyallen : A.II.
—— —— Society in Ireland : 57.
ANTRIM Monthly Meeting Records : AI.
APPEAL, to London Yearly meeting: 115.
APPL·CATIONS, (membership) : 11.
APPRENTICESHIP INDENTURES : 221.
ARARAT, Australia, Miners rights at Gold Diggings of : 215, (40).
ARCHBOLD, WILLIAM : 220.
ARKHILL, Edenderry, Offaly : 24.
—— Registration of Meeting House at : 24.
ARMSTRONG, HENRY : 118.
ARNELL, ROBERT : 226.
ASHBRIDGE, AARON : 135.
—— ELIZABETH (1713-1755), Account of early life by herself : 133, 135.
ASH, JONATHAN : 162.
ASHBROOK, (Queen's Co. ?) : 209.
ASHBURY (Berks ?) : 187
ASHFORD (Kent) : 99.
ASHTON, JOSHUA : 176.
—— MARTHA : 176.
—— THOMAS : 173, 216.
Asia, BRIGANTINE : 221.
ASTRONOMY, Letters on : 38-40, 63.
ATHLONE (Co. Westmeath) : 9.
ATHY (Co. Kildare) : 3, 6, 18, 30, 36, 167.
—— Assizes mentioned : 59.
ATKINSON, JOHN : 220. (a) (f)
ATTORNEY GENERAL, Papist appointed : 106.
AUSTELL (Cornwall) : 99.
AUSTIN, WILLIAM : 175.

B

BACKHOUSE, J. : 106.
—— JAMES, Journey to New South Wales.
BACON HOGS, Prices of : 86.
BAGWELL, Col. : 82.
—— JOHN : 166.
BAKER, ANNA M. : 66.
—— JOHN : 223.
BALFOUR, A. : 54.
—— WILLIAM : 216, (8).
BALLIACHIEN (Co. Down) : 215 (3), (16). *See* RATHFRILAND.
BALLIBRADO (Co. Tipperary) : 175.
BALLINABARNEY (Wexford) : 11.
BALLINACURRAGH, Co. Wexford : 215.
BALLINACLASH (Co. Wicklow) : 12.
BALLINACLAY, Co. Wexford : 11, 118.
BALLINAKILL (Queen's Co.) : 10, 23, 167.

BALLINTORE (Co. Wexford) : 11, 24, 198.
BALLITORE, Co. Kildare : 6, 18, 21, 27, 36, 42, 58, 110, 121, 132, 167, 208, 220.
—— Annals of : 54, 55, 125, 143, 147.
—— Inn : 59.
—— Lease : 215, (28), (34).
—— Lease of Land and House : 215.
—— School : 54, 88, 132, 143, 147.
—— School, Letters from Pupils : 132.
—— School, Magazine Produced by Boys : 132.
BALLYBRADO BURIAL GROUND (Co. Tipperary) : 215, (37).
BALLYBRUMHILL (Co. Carlow) : 95.
BALLYCANE (Co. Wicklow) : 12.
BALLYCARROL, Queen's Co. : 10, 219.
BALLYHAGAN (Co. Tyrone) Monthly Meeting Records : A1.
BALLYHOOLY (Co. Cork) : 63.
BALLYKEALY, Carlow : 63.
BALLYKEANE MEN'S MEETING : 12.
BALLYKELLY (Wexford) : 195, 197.
BALLYKENEGAN, Co. Wexford : 172.
BALLYMAKANE, Co. Wexford : 222.
BALLYMORE EUSTACE (Co. Kildare) : 38.
BALLYMOYLE (Queen's Co.) : 173.
BALLYMURRAN BURIAL GROUND : 12.
BALLYMURRY (Nr. Moate) : 9.
BALLYNOCKIN, (King's Co.) Map of lands of : 225.
BALLYRAGGAN, Co. Kildare, lease of lands of : 215, (6).
BALLYVADEN (Tipperary ?) : 95.
BALTIMORE, U.S.A. mentioned : 157.
—— Letter from : 118.
BANDON (Co. Cork) : 206.
"—— and the West" (Meeting) : 13, 14.
—— Meeting : 14, 224 (16), 226.
—— Men's Meeting Minutes : 226.
BANK FAILURES : 63, 99.
BANK NOTES, Engraving of : 86.
BANKRUPTCY, Commissioners in : 87.
BANKS, E. W. mentioned : 156.
BANTRIE, BARONY OF (Co.Wexford) : 11.
BARBERSTOWN, Co. Kildare : 220.
BARCLAY, DAVID : 79.
—— JOHN ED. : *Letters of Early Friends* : 82, 106.
—— JOHN (Dublin) : 168, 217, (13), (23).
—— ROBERT : 79.
BARCROFT, JOHN : 24, 108.
—— JOSEPH : 217, (4), (6), (7).
—— Name mentioned : 24.
—— WILLIAM : 10.
BARECROFT, JOHN : 219.
BARDFIELD (Essex ?) : 102.

BARGIE (Co. Wexford) : see FORTH AND BARGIE.
BARLEY, Price of : 85.
BARNARD, HANNAH : 76, 140.
BARNES, WILLIAM : 124.
BARNLAND (? Leix) : 191.
BARON'S INN (Dublin) : 7.
—— —— Garden : 211.
BARRINGTON, JOHN : 55, 197.
—— NICHOLAS : 197.
—— THOMAS : 205.
BARRONSTRAND STREET (Waterford) : 17.
BARROW, Mordecai : 215, (3).
BARTON, HENRY : 217, (13).
—— SARAH : 172.
BASS, H. (Lisburn) : A. II.
—— ISAAC : A. II.
BATEMAN, EDWARD : 181.
BATES, ELISHA, Baptism of : 105.
BATES, WIDOW : 168.
BATH (Somerset) : 29.
BATTY, ANN (nee READ) : 217, (12).
—— MARY : 217 (12).
—— THOMAS : 217, (12).
BAYDER, JOHN : 182.
BAYFIELD (? Queen's Co.) : 191.
BAY OF BULLS (Newfoundland) : 85.
Beacon to the Society of Friends : 105.
BEAL, BENJAMIN : 170.
—— RACHEL : 170.
—— SAML. : 170.
BEALE, JAMES : 174.
—— JOSHUA : 57, 220.
—— name mentioned : 18.
—— SUSANNA : 174.
BEASELEY, EDWARD (Dublin) : 216.
—— JOSEPH : 216.
BECK, THOS. : 99.
BEDFORD, DUKE OF : 82.
BEEF, Price of : 100, 101.
BEES : 52.
BEGGARS : 103.
BEILBY, RICHARD : 217 (25).
BELFAST : 160.
—— Public Record Office at AII.
BELL, ANN : 177.
—— CHARLOTTE : 217 (28).
—— JOHN : 106, 177.
—— MARY : 177.
—— Widow : 216.
—— WILLIAM : 217 (28).
BELL-MALCOMSON, Pedigree : 229.
BELLAMY, ADDY : 92.
BELLVIEW, Queen's Co. : 217 (28).
BELLEVIEW PARK see Boythenrath (Co. Tipperary).
BENGAL, East Indies : 222.
BENNETT, JOHN : 202.
—— JAMES : 217 (12).
—— THOMAS : 183.
Bennis, William : 163.
BERKSHIRE : 187.

BERNARD, Saint : 63.
BESSBROOK, (Co. Armagh) : AII.
BEVINGTON, HANNAH : 30.
BEWICK, WILLIAM, his descriptions of birds : 105.
BEWLEY, ANN, (Cork) : 164.
—— ANNE (nee Gough) : 61.
—— BLESSING : 176.
—— ELIZA : 160.
—— FANNY : 63.
——— GEORGE (of Edenderry) : 134.
—— JOHN : 217 (14) (17).
—— JOHN (of Harlem, Co. Dublin) 212.
—— JOHN (of Mountmellick) : 61.
—— JOSEPH : 116, 195.
BEWLEY, MARY (Cork) : 164.
—— MARY : 215 (28).
—— MARY (nee Gough) : 35.
——— MUNGO : 35, 61.
—— SAMUEL (1785) : 180, 195.
—— SAMUEL (1850) 215, (38).
—— SAMUEL, his tea auction : 105.
—— SARAH : 164, 177.
—— SUSANNA : 215 (28).
—— THOMAS : 30.
—— **Thomas** : 164, 177.
" B-H " (see Hannah Barnard).
BIANCONI Cars mentioned : 155.
Biographies of Irish Friends : 143.
—— Cottage : 143.
BIRBECK, MORRIS (sen.) : 22, 33.
—— Family : 33.
—— name mentioned : 29.
—— WILLIAM : 22.
BIRKETT name mentioned : 29.
—— WILLIAM (jun.) 217 (21), (22), (27).
BIRMINGHAM (Warwickshire) : 107.
BIRR, (King's Co.) : 10, 173.
BIRTH NOTES, see each Meeting.
BIRTH REGISTERS, see each **Meeting**.
BLACKDOWN, Kilteel, Co. Kildare : 220.
BLACKMORE, H. : 166.
BLACKROCK : 26.
BLESSINGTON, (Co. Dublin) : 38.
BLESSINGTON in Fingal : 169.
BLEW COAT HOSPITAL, Dublin : 168.
BLOOMVILLE (Queen's Co.) : 58.
BLACKWELL, EDWARD : 216.
BLOOMFIELD, ADAM : 216.
BOAKE, JANE (later Haughton) : 34.
—— name mentioned : 18, 24.
—— THOMAS : 220.
BOARD OF WORKS : 110.
BLUE YARD CONCERNS (Mountmellick): 191.
BOARDMAN name mentioned : 18.
BOAT,(E), GERSHON : 219.
BOATS, steam : 102.
BODDY, WILLIAM : 68.

BOLES, ABIGAIL, nee Craven later Watson : 121.
—— ANN : 166.
—— John : 165, 166.
—— JOHN, (jun.) : 121.
BOOK BINDING : 38.
Book of Extracts : 104.
BOOKS, distribution of printed : 3.
BORDEAUX (France) : 63.
BORRIS in Ossory (Queen's Co.) : 23.
BORROWS, THOS. : 192.
BOSTON, " Cousin " : 168.
BOSTON mentioned : 149.
BOTANICAL Lectures : 28.
BOURCHER, RICHARD, mariner : 222.
Bowdlers Essays : 208.
BOWES, WM. : 215 (36).
BOX, ELIZA : 54.
BOYCE, JOHN, jun. : 188.
—— PATRICK : 185.
BOYD, name mentioned : 64.
BOYES, JAMES : 188.
BOY(E)S, RICHARD : 7.
BOYLE, JAMES of Pennsylvania ⸝-144.
—— MARTHA (nee Williams) : 144.
BOYNE, Battle of : 123.
BOYTHENRATH *alias* BELLEVIEW PARK (Co. Tipperary) : 95.
BRADFORD, M. : 29.
—— name mentioned : 29.
BRADSHAW, ROBERT : AII.
BRADSHAW & CLARK (Messrs. ?) : 183.
BREGURTEEN, Co. Wexford : 11, 211.
BRIDE'S ALLEY (Dublin) : 7.
BRIDE STREET, Dublin : 211.
BRIEN, HONOR : 172.
BRIGHT, JOHN : 110.
BRIGHTON (Sussex) : 99, AII.
BRINKLEY, J. : 63.
BRISBANE, SIR THOMAS : 63, 88.
BRISTOL mentioned : 108.
BRITISH and Foreign Bible Society : 198.
BRITISH ISLES, Travelling map of : 225.
BRITISH QUEEN (steamship) : 106.
BROADBENT, SARAH : 84.
BROAD-OAK, near Lisnagarvey, Co. Antrim : AI.
BROOKFIELD SCHOOL (Antrim) : 132, 215 (41).
BROOKFIELD, WILLIAM : 217 (1).
BROOM, ARTHUR (of Redcastle) : 215 (9), (29).
BROUGHAM, LORD : 103.
BROWN, BERNARD : 216.
—— CHARLES, jeweller : 217 (14).
—— FRANCES : 217 (17).
—— GEORGE : 217 (17).
—— HANNAH : 22.
BROWNE, ROBERT : 76.
BROWNLEE, WILLIAM : 215 (1).
BRUSNA FLOUR MILLS : 140.
BULLOCKS, prices : 84.

BUONAPARTE (NAPOLEON) : 86.
BURCHAM, ELIZABETH : 216.
—— HENRY : 216.
BURDER, BENJAMIN, Baker : 168.
—— HENRY : 168.
—— JOHN : 168.
BURGESS, JUDITH : 209.
BURIAL GROUNDS Care of : 5.
BURIAL NOTES, see each meeting.
—— Registers, see each Meeting.
BURKE, EDMUND : 22, 63, 132, 143.
BURLINGTON Co., America, (freeholders and officers of) : 72.
BURROS, WILLIAM jun. 215 (10).
BURTON, ALDERMAN, of Carlow : 134.
BURY St. Edmunds (Suffolk) : 96, 98, 100.
BUSHELL, WILLIAM : 173.
BUTCHER, M. and Sons : 116.
BUTLER, P. : 166.
BUTTER, how sold : 99.
—— Trade : 86, 97, 100.
—— Recession of Trade : 105.
BUXTON, HOWELL : 99.
BYRD, WM. : 99.
BYRON, Lord : 51, 52.

C

CABLE to America, Laid 1856 : 155.
CAHIR (Co. Tipperary) : 16.
CALCUTT, CATHERINE : 194.
—— I. : 192.
—— Jo. : 193.
CALVERT, ADAM : 88.
CAMBRIDGE, PETER : 43, 167.
—— Family mentioned : 46.
CAMDEN Street School, Dublin : 4, 131.
CAMPION, ABRAHAM, Jeweller : 217 (15), (16).
CANAL at Athy : 36.
—— Travel : 30.
CANDLER, JOHN mentioned : 106.
CANDLES, Dipt. : 85.
—— Mould : 85.
CANTRILL, GODFREY : 10.
CANTRELL, REBECCA : 205.
CANTRI(E)LL, THOMAS : 179.
CAPITAL Punishment, Attitude of Tory Party to : 104.
CAPPER, SAMUEL : 107.
CARBUTT, EDWARD : 55.
CAREY, EDWARD : 203.
CARLETON, Aunt : 62.
—— DEBORAH : 46.
—— ELIZABETH (later Shackleton) : 21.
—— JOHN : 167.
—— JONATHAN : 167.
—— RACHEL : 216.
—— SAMUEL : 46.
—— **Samuel** : 167.

—— THOMAS : 54.
CARISLE (Cumberland) : 26.
CARLOW : 3, 6, 24, 85, 110, 134, 167.
—— Meeting Accounts : 6.
—— —— House : 220.
—— Monthly Meeting : 6, 220.
—— Women's Meeting : 6.
CARNEY, JOHN : 166.
CARNON, JOHN : 202.
CAROLINA (U.S.A.) : 75.
CARRICK ON SUIR (Co. Tipperary) : 64, 69.
CARROLL, ELIZABETH : 185.
—— EMILIE FRANCES : 185.
—— ISAAC : 185.
CARTER, ABBY : 53.
CASEY, MICHAEL ejectment order, Clonmel : 215(31).
CASH Book, Men's, Dublin : 7.
CASHEL (Co. Tipperary) : 16, 95.
CASHEL, Archbishop of : 63.
CASTLEDERMOT (Co. Kildare) : 3, 202, 220.
CASTLESALEM (Co. Cork) : 14.
CASTLE Street, Dublin : 210.
CATHOLIC Emancipation : 103.
CAUL, EDWARD : 172.
—— MARY (nee Cullimore) : 172.
CAVAN (Co.), Friends in : 226.
CENTRAL Relief Committee of Society of Friends : 110.
CERTIFICATES : see each Meeting.
CERTIFICATES, Marriage : 16, 224 (22), 226.
CERTIFICATES, Ministers : 2.
CERTIFICATES of Removal : 7, 8, 9, 10, 11, 14, 15, 16, 17.
CHANDLEE, Deborah (nee Shackleton) : 19, 21, 23, 27, 28, 29, 30, 31, 36, 42, 45, 52, 147.
Chamberlain, ELIJAH : 168.
—— JONAS : 166.
—— RICHARD : 162.
CHANDLEE, DEBORAH (later Johnson) : 23, 53.
—— JANE : 31, 53.
—— JOHN 167.
—— MARY : 28, 52.
—— name mentioned : 53.
—— Thomas : 18, 28, 30, 47, 52, 167.
—— THOMAS, junior : 18, 38, 45.
—— THOMAS of Fermoy : 90.
CHARD, ARTHUR : 116.
CHARITABLE School (Clonmel) : 66.
CHARITIES, Clonmel : 64.
CHARLEBURY (Oxon) mentioned : 106.
CHARLES I : 70.
CHARLES II (Ann Wright's visit to): 95.
CHARLES X of France, arrival in England 103.
CHARLES, GEORGE : 217 (17).

CHARLEVILLE (Co. Cork) 13, 14.
CHARLTON, ROBERT : 77.
CHARTER Schools, Irish : 104.
CHELMSFORD, (Essex) : 96, 99, 100, 101, 102, 103.
CHELSEA HOSPITAL : 135.
—— Pensioners : 51.
CHESHIRE, mentioned : 135.
CHESTER BAR : 22.
CHESTER, RICHARD : 22.
CHETWOOD, ANNE (nee Eustace) 217 (21).
—— BENJAMIN : 217 (21).
CHICHESTER (Sussex) : 99.
CHOLERA 77, 103.
CHOLERA, Deaths from : 104.
CHRIST CHURCH, Dublin, Strongbow's : tomb in, : 220.
CHRISTIAN NAMES, insertion of additional : 87.
CHRISTIAN, FRANCIS : 217 (6), (28).
CHRISTIANSTOWN, Registration of Meeting House at : 24.
CHRISTY, DEBORAH : 167.
—— Family mentioned : 46.
—— JOHN : 54.
—— MARGARET : 25, 167.
CHRISTY-SINTON, Pedigree : 229.
—— THOMAS : 215 (16).
—— —— Bequest of : AI.
—— —— of Rochester, mentioned : 99.
CHURCH RATES : 103.
CIRENCESTER (Glos.) : 86.
CLADDAGH, Galway, Attempted establishment of Fishing industry at : 116.
CLAMPITE, MARY : 172.
CLAPHAM mentioned : 99, 106.
CLARA (King's Co.) : 9, 140, 158.
CLARE ISLAND (Co. Mayo) : 110.
CLAREMONT, Institution for the Deaf : 28, 52.
CLARENDON, LORD : 110.
CLARIDGE, SAMUEL of Dublin mentioned 211.
CLARKE, ISABEL, of Carlisle : 134.
—— JOSEPH : 177.
—— RICHARD : 173.
CLARKSON, THOMAS : 28.
CLASHAWAUN JUTE WORKS : 158.
CLIBBORN, ANNE : 217 (23).
—— ELIZA (recollections) 94.
—— ELIZABETH : 181.
—— ELIZABETH (nee Grubb) : 77, 80, 81, 94, 158.
—— ELIZABETH (Grubb) (1780-1861) Journal of : 133, 142.
—— Family of Anner Mills : 81, 114.
—— HENRY : 205.
—— JOHN : 9.
CLIBBORN, JOHN BARCLAY : 68, 79, 80, 142, 158.

—— Joshua : 24, 180.
—— Name mentioned : 23, 40, 81.
—— Robert : 217, (3), (4), (5), (6), (7), (11).
—— Sarah : 217, (10).
Clise, Mr. (? McClise), his pack of cards : 86.
Clogheen (Tipperary) : 44, 45, 58, 79.
Clonbarrow (? Queen's Co.) : 192.
—— Conveyance of land at : 215, (20) (36).
Clonbrogan (Co. Tipperary) : 165.
Cloneheen (Co. Tipperary) : 95.
Clonmel (Co. Tipperary) : 16, 21, 23, 36, 84, 95, 96, 97, 100, 106, 107, 218, 130, 166.
—— Annuity Company : 209.
—— Annuity Society : 163.
—— Bridge of : 218.
—— Charitable School : 66.
—— Charities in : 64.
—— Corporation Mills : 215, (31).
—— Infirmary : 218.
Clonmel literary institute : 66, 67.
—— Lying-in Institution : 65.
—— Meeting House, heating of: 103.
—— Meeting Records : 227.
—— Mendicity Institute : 87.
—— Quay at : 218.
—— Rents in : 105.
—— Savings Bank : 82.
—— Sunday and Day School : 67.
Clonmore (Co. Wexford) : 223.
Clothes List (School) : 62.
Coaches, Steam : 102.
Coal, Price of : 108.
Coalbrookdale, Iron Works at : 96.
—— mentioned : 106.
Coastal Trading Vessels : 108.
Coggleshall (Essex) : 102, 105.
Coghill's Court (Dublin) : 7.
Cohannan and Culnagew, farms at : 112.
Coin Collecting : 86.
Coins, Design for Irish : 63.
Colchester (Essex) : 97, 102.
Coleman, Mary : 172.
Coleraine (Co. Londonderry) : 24.
College Green, Dublin : 95, 217 (12).
Collett, Francis, mentioned : 218.
Collins, Cha., original signature 1708: 214.
Colonial and British Register : 100.
Colville, William (Dublin) 216.
Comet, 1819 : 63, 173.
Comerford, Joseph : 218.
Commonplace Books : 227.
Compendium of Irish Biography, A: 149.
Conditions and Prospects of Ireland 1848 : 110.
Congenies (France), Quaker colony at: 107.

Conran, Elizabeth : 169.
—— Henry : 169.
—— James : 169.
—— John : 61, 96, 169.
—— Louisa : 61, 96.
—— Magdalen : 169.
—— Mary : 169.
—— Robert : 169.
—— Sophia 169.
Convincements : 224, (2).
Conway, Lord : 7.
Cooke, ? Sister : 186.
Cooladine (Co. Wexford) : 11, 59, 195.
Coolcors, Co. Meath : 214.
Coolegegan (? Kildare) : 20.
Cooles, Co. Wexford : 203.
Cooper, David : 170.
—— Experience : 172, 217, (7).
—— John : 170.
Cooper's Hill (Queen's Co.) : 217.
Cootehill (Co. Cavan) Monthly Meeting Records : AI.
Cope, Thomas, of Philadelphia : 110.
Copper Sheeting, price of : 52.
Corbally (Limerick) : 160.
Corban, Thomas : 22.
Corboy Beg (Co. Longford) : 222.
Corboymor, Co. Longford : 222.
Cork : 13, 14, 26, 83, 110, 160, 162, 163, 164, 174, 176, 177, 178, 184, 185, 189, 190, 199, 200, 201, 206.
—— City, Anti-Slavery Meeting : 88.
—— County : 13.
—— Diocese : 190.
—— Earl of : 226.
—— Infirmary (Appeal for) : 57.
Cork Institute, Royal : 63.
—— Meeting Books Digested : 229.
—— Meeting Records : 227.
—— Men's Meeting : 136.
—— Monthly Meeting : 5, 108.
—— Printer : 1.
—— Tonnage of Ships at : 88.
—— Women's Meeting : 13.
Corlican, Co. Wexford, 196, 197, 203, 222.
Cornemayo (otherwise Lower Corboy) (Co. Longford) : 222.
Corn Laws : 110.
Cornmarket (Dublin) : 216.
Corn, Price of : 97.
Corporation Mills, Clonmel, tenure of : 215, (31).
Corrin, John : 177.
Costigan, Martin : 215 (25).
Cottage Dialogues : 55, 143.
—— *Biographies* : 143.
Cotton, Arrival from America : 86.
—— Drying of : 85.
—— Growth : 88.
—— Prices : 18.
—— Trade, Wages in : 61.

INDEX

COURTENEY, TOBY : 24.
COWAN, STEPHEN, goldsmith : 217, (24).
COWPER, WILLIAM : 52.
Cows, Purchase of : 95.
COWSHED, New type of : 108.
COX, THOS. : 168.
CRABBE, GEORGE : 143.
—— JOHN : 123.
—— THOMAS : 123.
CRANE, name mentioned : 120.
—— THOMAS S. : 195.
CRAS, JACOB : 91.
CRAVEN, ABIGAIL, see BOLES, ABIGAIL.
—— JAMES : 186.
—— WILLIAM : 203.
CRAWLEY, BENJAMIN, Builder of Dublin 134.
CRAWSHAW, ETHEL : 122.
CRETAN, DR. : 28.
CREWDSON, ISAAC : 105.
CROKER, CROFTON : 63.
CROMWELL, HENRY : 224 (9).
CROOK, mentioned : 99.
CROSS CHANNEL ROUTE, Steamboats on: 100.
CROSSEN, DENNIS : 217, (12).
CROTCH, WILLIAM : 96, 140.
CRUMLIN, House at : 38, 39.
CUFFSBOROUGH, Queen's Co., Joseph Palmer of : 215, (24).
CUBAN AND SPANISH AFFAIRS, Comments on : 118.
Cullimore, Daniel : 171, 203.
—— ELIZABETH : 171, 172.
—— FRANCIS : 203.
—— George : 172, 203.
—— ISAAC : 171, 197.
—— JOHN : 171, 203.
—— JONATHAN : 203.
—— MARY : 172, 203.
—— PETER : 172.
—— RICHARD : 203.
—— RUTH : 171, 172.
—— THOMAS : 203.
CULNAGEW AND COHANNAN, Farms at : 112.
CUPPAGE, " Brother " : 186.
—— ROBERT : 11.
—— THOMAS : 214.
CZAR OF RUSSIA : 77.

D

" DADD'S " (in Naas) : 30.
DALKEY (Co. Dublin) : 41.
DALTON, ELIZABETH : 172.
DALTON, STEPHEN : 217, (15), (24).
DAMER, JOHN, of Dorsetshire : 215 (15)
DANCE, JOHN : 182.
DANNAHY, JNO. : 63.
DARBY, DEBORAH : 114.

DARBY, WEST : 178.
DARCY, Rev. JOHN (Church of Ireland, Galway) ; 116.
DARLINGTON (Yorkshire) : AII.
—— mentioned : 99.
DARTNELL, ROGER : 63.
DARTON, MESSRS. (Publishers) : 106.
DAVIS, Farrily of Cork, Inventory : 210.
—— FRANCIS : 198.
—— JOHN : 210.
—— JONATHAN : 60.
—— JNO. : 61.
—— MARY : 54.
—— MARY (later MERRYWEATHER) : 60.
—— RACHEL : 210.
—— ROBERT : 216.
—— SAMUEL : 198.
DAVISTOWN, Kildare : 220.
DAWSON, ELISHA : 105.
DAWSON, name mentioned : 18.
DEAL, Price of : 108.
DEANE, ROB : 201.
DEATH PENALTY, Petitions against : 103.
DEATHS, Records of, see each Meeting.
DEAVES, family mentioned : 109.
DEAVES, REBECCA : 183.
DEECE, Co. Meath, Barony of : 214.
DEEDS, Carlow (Schedules of) : 6.
—— Cork : 14.
—— Dublin : 7.
—— Edenderry : 8.
—— Tipperary : 16.
—— Waterford : 17.
—— Wexford : 11.
—— Wicklow : 12.
DEERSKINS, Arrival from America : 86.
DELANEY, THOMAS : 191.
DENIALS, Certificates of : 7, 8, 9, 12, 15, 17.
DENIS, SANKEY ? : 217, (13).
DENT, DAVID, his school : 86.
DENTIST, Earnings of : 102.
DEPTFORD (Wilts.) : 168.
DERRY LENNOYS (sic. Queen's Co.?) : 173.
DERRYLUSKEY, Queen's Co. : 215 (20).
DESPARD, FRANCIS : 218.
—— MARIA (LACKEY) : 218.
—— RICHARD : 215 (5), (8).
DEVERELL, ANTHY : 192.
DEVONSHIRE HOUSE : 76.
DEVONSHIRE, JONAS : **226.**
DEXTER, JAS. : 30.
DIACULUM, a Palliative, 1775, : 20.
DIALECT, Forth-Bargy : 124.
DICKENSON, JAMES : 117.
DIGGIN, name mentioned : 120.
DILLON, JAMES : 202.
DILLWORTH, name mentioned : 29.
DISCIPLINE, Book of (1811) : 1.
DISCIPLINE, Committee replies on : 4.

DISOWNMENT PAPERS, 1680 : 11.
DISUNION, Certificates of : 10, 14, 16, 17, 226.
DISUNITY, Testimony of : 226.
DIVIDED THOUGHT AMONG FRIENDS : 104.
Divine Protection by Dinah Goff, 1857 : 109.
DIXON, SARAH : 160.
DOBBS, DR. JOHN : 121.
DOCTOR OR PHYSICIAN, Legal title of : 106.
DOHERTY, WILLIAM : 212.
DOLPHIN'S BARN : 216.
DOLPHIN'S BARN LANE BURIAL GROUND (Dublin) : 7.
DOLPHINS BARN LANE, Concerns in : 169.
DONOUGHMORE, LORD : 63.
DONOVAN, RICHARD : 223.
DORRIEN, PATRICK : 202.
DOUGLAS, JAMES : 216.
DOUGLAS, JOHN M. : 159, AII.
DOVER, Holiday in : 100.
DOWLING, JOHN : 53.
—— MALACHI : 53.
DOYLE, JAMES : 59, 199.
—— JOHN : 217 (7).
—— SARAH : 184.
—— Sisters : 53.
—— name mentioned : 18.
DREAMS and VISIONS : 224 (1), 229.
DREAPER, JAMES : 162.
—— SAM : 162.
DROPSY, Cure for : 108.
DRINAH (? DRINAGH), Queen's Co. : 179.
DRISCOLL, JOHN : 185.
DROGHEDA, Marquis of : 191.
DUBLIN : 3, 7, 21, 168, 174, 177, 195, 204, 205, 207.
DUBLIN CASTLE : 82.
—— College of Surgeons : 7.
—— Eagle Tavern : 7, 217 (12).
—— Friends' Institute : 157.
—— Journal : 63.
—— Map of : 225.
—— Meath Street : 3.
—— Men's Meeting : 7.
—— Monthly Meeting : 7, 10.
—— Monthly Meeting (list of Mss. of : 7.
—— Monthly Meeting Papers : 224 (27).
DUBLIN MONTHLY MEETING, Repayment of money to : 160.
—— Records of Seventeenth Century : 7.
—— Women's Meeting : 7.
—— Yearly Meeting : 106.
DUCKETT family : 132.
—— name mentioned : 18, 49.
—— THOMAS : 220.
DUDLEY name mentioned : 23.

—— MARY : 92, 96, 114.
—— ROBERT : 54, 73, 75, 92.
—— SUSANNA : 181.
DUNCOMBS LANE (Dublin) : 216.
DUNGANNON (Co. Tyrone) : 46, AII.
DUNGARVAN (Co. Waterford) : 106.
DUNLAVIN (Co. Wicklow) : 38.
DUNMOW (Essex) : 102.
DUNSCOMBE, WILLIAM : 200.
DUNSINK OBSERVATORY : 63.
DURDIN, ALEXR. : 217, (12).
DURHAM : 99.
DURRANCE, ANNE, of Carlisle (later Gill) 134.
DYING SAYINGS : 224, (2).
DYMOND, PHILLIP, of Cork, mentioned : 211.

E

EAGLE TAVERN, Dublin : 7, 217, (12).
EARLHAM (Home of the Gurney family): 77.
EASTERN ENGLAND, Religious Visits to : 99.
EAVES, RICHARD : 173.
ECLIPSE OF SUN (1769) : 38.
—— —— —— (1737) : 39.
—— —— —— (1817) : 86.
EDENDERRY (Co. Kildare) : 3, 8, 10, 21, 24, 117, 210.
—— Men's Meeting : 8.
——mentioned : 108.
—— School : 88, 128.
—— Women's Meeting : 8.
EDERMINE (Wexford) : 11.
EDGEWORTH, MARIA : 55.
EDDYSTONE LIGHTHOUSE, Dues for : 120.
EDMONDSON, see EDMUNDSON.
EDMUNDSON family mentioned : 109.
—— HINDRANCE (later Seale) : 173.
—— JOHN : 8.
—— JOSHUA : 193, 217, (10).
—— MARY : 173.
—— SAMUEL : 173.
—— TYRAL : 173.
—— WILLIAM : 3, 8, 10, 122, 123, 186, 211.
—— William : 173.
—— —— : AI.
EDUCATION, Documents relating to : 95, 128 *et seq.*, 224, (5).
—— Joint Committee for : 129.
—— Rules for Provincial School : 4.
—— Ulster School Report : 2.
—— of Youth : 5.
EDWARDS, ANN : 223.
—— CADWALLADER, junior : 223.
—— —— senior : 223.
—— ELIZA (nee Donovan) : 223.
—— GEORGE (Bookseller) : 217, (17), (22).

EILES, MAJOR : 63.
ELECTRIC EXPERIMENTS : 63.
ELIOT, JOHN : 22.
—— J. : 92.
—— M. : 92.
ELLWOOD, JONATHAN : 139.
—— THOMAS : 95.
Elly, Abigail : 174.
ELLY, WILLIAM RICHARD : 174.
ELMGROVE, North Liberties, Cork : 206.
ELMS, STEPHEN : 183.
ELY, LORD : 61.
EMPRESS OF RUSSIA : 39.
ENGLAND, Friends from : 13.
ENGLISH, THOMAS : 9.
ENGRAVING OF BANK NOTES : 86.
ENNIS, RICHARD : 202.
ENNISCORTHY, (Wexford) : 11, 85, 172, 195, 215, (32).
EPISTLES (Devotional) : 1, 2, 13, 224, (6).
—— (Devotional Women's) : 2.
ESSEX, Meetings in : 100.
ETHER as Medicine : 28.
——for relief of gout : 85.
EUSTACE, ANNE, alias CHETWOOD : 217, (21).
—— JOHN : 197.
—— P. BERYL : 7.
—— SUSANNAH : 87.
—— SUSANNAH FENNEL : 87.
EUSTACE STREET, DUBLIN, Bundle of Deeds relating to : 217.
EUSTACE STREET MEETING (Dublin) Built : 7.
EVANS, JOSEPH : 99.
—— MATTHEW : 197.
—— SAMUEL : 163.
EXETER : 19.
EXETER HALL, Temperance Meeting in : 103.
EXETER MEETING Certificate from Friends of : 117.
EXTRACTS, Book of 1.
EYE, Cure of swelling around : 136.
EYRE CHILDREN : 44.

F

FADE, JAMES, OF DUBLIN, mentioned, 211.
—— JOSEPH, 217 (1) (2).
FALMOUTH, mentioned, 76, 10
"FAMILY LISTS" : 4, 8, 10, 14, 15, 17.
FAMILY VISITS : 13.
FAMINE, Relief work : : 64, 158.
—— —— Central Committee for : 150.
FANCROFT, (King's Co.) : 215 (15).
FARRINCLAY (? Cork) : 210.
FATHER MATTHEW : 106, 149, 150.
FAW OR CALF PARK : 202.

FAWCETT, ELIZABETH : 197.
FAWCETT, SARAH see PHILLIPS, SARAH.
FAYLE, C. : 53.
—— JOSHUA : 217, (22). (27),
—— MARGARET ANNE : 28.
—— MARY : 173.
—— ROBERT : 31, 38.
—— THOMAS : 28, 191, 217 (7).
FELL name mentioned : 29.
FENNELL COLLECTION : 18.
FENNELL family mentioned : 63, 109.
—— GEORGE : 215, (27).
—— **Joshua** : 175.
—— name mentioned : 108.
—— WILLIAM (of Rehill) : 63, 215, (27).
FEMALE BOUNTY FUND : 13.
FENNER, R. I. : 169.
FERMOY (Co. Cork) : 90.
FERNS (Co. Wexford), Consistorial Court of : 184.
FIELDING (Shopkeeper) : 30.
FISH, Prices : 100.
FISHER family mentioned : 63.
—— JAMES : 163, 189.
—— JOSEPH : 181, 199.
FISHERIES, Department of : 110.
——and Oyster Beds : 110.
FITZGERALD, CHARLES : 163.
—— D. : 27.
—— family pedigrees : 159.
—— W. : 27.
FITZPATRICK, MARY : 205.
FITZSIMONS, JANE : 53.
—— SARAH : 53.
FLETCHER, ELIZABETH : 222.
FLOUR, Bad Sale of : 104.
"FLY" (Carriage) : 107.
FOLEY, DOREEN (Edmundson) : 173.
FOLKESTONE (Kent) : 99.
FORBES family mentioned : 109.
—— JAMES : 217, (3), (5).
—— —— (junior) : 217, (5).
—— JOSHUA : 217, (3), (9), (10).
—— name mentioned : 108.
—— TIMOTHY : 202.
FOREIGN MISSION WORK : 103.
FOREST (Co. Wexford) : 107.
FORREST (Co. Wexford) : 11, 71, 196.
FORSTER, JOSIAH : 103, 106.
—— LUBOCK, BOSANQUET & Co., of London : 216.
—— MATTHIAS : 123.
—— WILLIAM : 31.
FORTH AND BARGIE, Barony of : 11.
FORTH-BARGY, Dialect of : 120, 124.
FORT ST. GEORGE (?) : 216.
FOTHERGILL, ANNE : 84.
—— JOHN, physician : 50, 121.
—— SAMUEL : 229.
FOTHERGILL, JOHN, physician : 50, 121.
—— SAMUEL (impression made on Admiral Tyrrell) : 29.

INDEX

FOULKES, RICHARD : 7.
FOUNDLING HOSPITAL, Dublin : 28.
FOWNES, SIR WILLIAM : 220.
—— WILLIAM : 220.
FOX, R. BARCLAY : 116.
—— GEORGE : 5, 95, 134.
—— —— (copy of Epistle of) : 95.
—— —— his book *A Warning to England* : 1.
FRAMPTON, RICHARD : 75.
FRANCE, Journey to, mentioned : 106.
—— Protestants in : 92.
FRANCIS, JAMES (Solicitor) : 188.
FRANCIS STREET, Dublin : 169, 222.
FRANKLIN, —— : 122.
Freeburg, 100 ton vessel : 104.
FREEHOLDERS, Disfranchisement of : 102.
FREEMAN, JAMES : 22.
FRENCH, DICK : 186.
FRENCH EMBARGO ON GOODS, 1795 : 85.
FRENCH, MRS. : 53.
FRENCH REVOLUTION : 143.
FRENCH SHIPS OF WAR, Losses by : 85.
FRIENDS' DECLARATION OF FAITH, 1680, Copy of : 114.
FRIENDS HOUSE, London, Library of : 224, 229.
FRIENDS' MEETING HOUSES IN IRELAND, Map of : 225.
FRIENDS' IN IRELAND, History of : 122.
Friendship, Sloop : 85.
FRIENDS' BOOKS, printing of : 1.
FRIENDS' (Poor) : 196.
FRIENDS TRAVELLING, Hospitality for : 5.
FRIENDS VISITING IRELAND : 94.
FRY, ELIZABETH : 77, 100, 101, 106.
—— —— Visit of, to Ireland : 142.
—— —— Visit to Queen Victoria : 106.
—— JOHN : 22.
FULLER, ABRAHAM, of Lehensie, Queen's Co., mentioned : 211.
Fuller, Abraham : 176.
FULLER, DEBORAH : 24, 26.
—— ELIZABETH : 26.
—— —— (later Shackleton) : 21.
—— family mentioned : 24.
—— family genealogy : 224, (22).
—— HENRY : 24.
—— JACOB : 24.
—— JANE : 26.
—— JOHN : 216.
—— JOSEPH : 176.
—— MARTHA : 176.
—— THOMAS : 26.
FUNERAL CUSTOMS, Differences between England and Ireland : 98.
FURLONG, JOHN : 172.

GALWAY : 85.
GARNET, EDWARD : 129.
GARRATT, ANN : 177.
Garratt, John : 177.
GARRATT, JOHN : 162, 164.
—— JOSEPH : 177.
—— PAUL : 177.
—— WILLIAM : 177.
GARRETT, JAMES : 24.
GARRITT, JOE : 26.
GARRYMORE (Tipperary) : 12.
GAS FOR LIGHTING : 63.
GATCHELL, ANNE (nee JACKSON) : 20.
—— ELIZABETH (formerly Strangman) : 42, 161.
—— FRANCIS : 161.
—— GEORGE : 161.
—— HENRY 161.
—— ISABELLA : 161.
—— JAMES : 161.
—— JOHN : 191.
—— JONATHAN : 161.
—— —— (letters of) : 118.
—— JONATHAN JOSHUA : 161.
—— JOSHUA : 161.
—— MARY : 161.
—— MARY ANNE : 161.
—— Messrs. of Waterford : 118.
—— NATHAN : 161.
—— REBECCA : 161.
—— SAMUEL : 161.
—— and WALPOLE (firm of) : 118.
—— WILLIAM : 42.
GAYNOR family, letters and notes on : 227.
GEORGE IV, presentation of addresses to, in Dublin Castle : 82.
GEORGE, Prince of Wales : 217, (10).
GIBBS, JAMES : 200.
GIBSON, WILLIAM : 123.
GILBERT, WILLIAM : 180.
GILL, ANNE (nee Durrance) : 134.
—— JOSEPH, his journal (1697-1724) : 134.
—— WILLIAM, of Ballitore (Kildare) : 220.
—— —— of Skelton (Cumberland) : 134.
GILMORE, MARY (later Heather) : 111.
GLAYSIER, JOHN : 99.
GLENDRUID, CABINTEELY : 55.
GLENGAL, Earl of : 215, (31).
GLENVILLE, Co. Cork : 138.
GLOVEMAKING : 27.
GODFREY, JOHN : 166.
GODLEE, JOHN : 99.
GODWIN, THOMAS : 166.
GOFF, DINAH : 109, 149.
—— ELIZABETH : AII, 229.
—— Family letters.
—— JACOB : 109, 168, 222.
—— ROBERT : 215, (18), 222.

GOLD, Bought at Bank : 99.
—— Coined at Mint : 99.
GOOCH family, Notes on : 224. (12),
GOODBODY, ELIZABETH (PIM) (wife of
    Mark Goodbody) : 114, 140.
—— Family papers : 114, 224, (211).
—— —— mentioned : 81, 110.
—— JANE (PIM) : 140.
—— JONATHAN : 158, 219.
—— LEWIS F. : 158.
—— LYDIA (nee Clibborn) her diary :
    158.
—— MARGARET (PIM) : 140, 158.
—— MARK : 140.
—— OLIVE C. : 7, 127.
—— ROBERT : 114, 158, 204, 219.
—— —— Life of : 133, 140.
—— WILLIAM : 208.
GO(O)LD, Widow 217, (13).
GOOLD, Mrs. : 217, (2).
GOOLDE, FR. : 214.
GOOUCH, SARAH : 185.
GORDON, SAMUEL mentioned : 218.
Goughs History (of Friends) : 208.
GOUGH, JAMES : 22, 61, 84.
—— JOHN : 38, 48, 75.
—— MARY (later Bewley) : 35.
GOULDING, HUMPHREYS MANDERS : 160.
GOVERNMENT STOCK : 198.
GRACE CHURCH STREET MEETING (London) : 103.
GRAHAMSTOWN, South Africa : 118.
GRAINS, Prices of : 63, 86.
GRANGE LODGE, Mountmellick : 91.
GRANGE near Charlemont, Monthly
    Meeting Records AI.
GRANGE (Co. Armagh), Monthly Meeting 215, (41).
GRATTAN, HENRY : 216.
GRATTAN STREET, Cork : 178.
GRAY, JOHN : 217, (7).
GREAT LAKES mentioned : 157.
GREAT YARMOUTH (Norfolk) : 116.
GREEN, HANNAH : 26.
—— JACOB : 106.
—— JOHN : 222.
GREENHOW, AMBROSE : 176.
—— WILLIAM : 217, (3), (5).
GREENMOUNT LINEN SPINNING CO. : 157.
GREEN ROW SCHOOL (Cumberland) : 58.
GREENWOOD, BENJAMIN : 167.
GREER family mentioned : 81.
—— —— of Dungannon, Correspondence of : AIII.
GREER-GREEVES, pedigree : 229.
GREER HENRY : 215, (16), 229.
—— JAMES : AIII.
—— JOHN : 188.
—— or GRIVE, ROBERT : 229.
—— ROBERT J. : 129.
—— T. : 54.

—— THOMAS : 215, (3).
—— F. USSHER : AII.
—— V. McG. : AII.
—— WILLIAM : 229.
GREEVES, family correspondence : AII.
—— JOHN : 112, 229.
—— —— Greer Pedigree : 229.
—— J. R. H. 111, 112, AIII.
—— THOMAS, Correspondence of : 111.
GREGSON, GEORGE, of Lisnagarvie, Co.
    Antrim, (merchant) : 211. AI.
GRELLETT, STEPHEN, mentioned : 103,
    106.
GREY, RICHARD : 173.
GRIESEBANK, Ballitore : 62.
GRIFFITHS, ELIZABETH : 200.
—— REBECCA : 200.
GROOM-GARDENER, Wage of : 102.
GROSS, PETER : 202.
GROVES, ALICE : 205.
GROWTOWN (Co. Wexford) : 149, 172,
    195, 196, 197, 223.
GRUBB, ANN (nee WILLAN) : 74.
—— ANNA : 64.
—— ANNE : 94.
—— BENJAMIN : 69, 73, 79, 94, 96,
    215, (27).
—— —— junior : 93, 105, 107.
—— Brothers (end of partnership) :
    100, 101.
—— Collection : 64 f.f.
—— —— Index : 128-32.
—— ELIZABETH (later Clibborn) : 79.
—— Family of Anner Mills : 74.
—— Family mentioned : 63, 70, 81,
    110, 114.
—— GEORGE : 221.
—— HANNAH : 106.
—— ISABEL : 72, 126, 132, 143.
—— J. ERNEST : 64, 67, 141.
—— JOHN (died 1731) : 71, 72.
—— —— (1737-1784) : 142.
—— —— (1766-1841) : 79, 82, 89, 96-
    106.
—— —— Testimony to : 94.
—— —— Speaks Irish in London 102.
—— —— of Anner Mills : 74, 78, 80,
    92, 215, (21).
—— JONATHAN : 101, 103, 104.
—— —— Instals steam in mill : 105—
    106.
GRUBB JOSEPH (1768-1844) : 82, 92, 96,
    97, 218.
—— —— his will mentioned : 95.
GRUBB JOSEPH (built Anner Mills, 1765)
    72, 74.
—— —— SAMUEL : 88.
—— JOSHUA : 86.
—— LYDIA : 64, 66, 107.
—— —— (diaries of 1846-7) : 94.
—— MARGARET (nee Shackleton) : 21.
    36, 50.

—— —— Testimony to : 94.
—— MARGARET : 113.
—— MRS. (of Anner Mills) : 216.
—— —— Visit to Birmingham : 107.
—— REBECCA : 80.
—— —— (Silhouette) : 69.
—— RICHARD, mentioned : 221.
—— ROBERT : 54, 67, 82.
—— SAMUEL : 21, 44, 216, 221.
—— SARAH (nee Pim) of Anner Mills : 68, 76, 78, 79, 80, 89, 96, 113, 114, 142, 215, (21).
—— SARAH (nee Tuke) : 82, 130.
—— —— (nee Lynes) : 89, 96—107.
—— SUSA : 66.
—— THOMAS (firm of) : 151.
Guardians : 208.
GUELDERLAND : 91.
GUIDES : 5.
GUINNESS'S PORTER : 102.
GUMMERE, AMELIA : 72.
GUNPOWDER, Selling of : 63.
GURNEY Family of Earlham : 77.
—— name mentioned : 29.
—— JOSEPH-JOHN : 105—107.
—— PRISCILLA : 77.
—— RICHARD : 92.
—— R. : 84.

H

HACK, JAMES : 99.
HADDAWAY, WILSON : 202.
HALF YEARLY MEETING : 1, 2.
HALL, DAVID : 33.
HALL, SARAH (later Birbeck) : 33.
HALL name mentioned : 29.
HALLYER, ELIZABETH : 172.
HAM, Arrival from America of : 86.
HAMEL, DR. : 155.
HAMILTON, ESQ., (Newcastle, Co. Limerick) : 136.
HAMILTON, JOSH. : 169.
HANCOCK, JACOB, junior : 216, (8).
—— JOHN (1763 mentioned) : 54.
HANDCOCK, JOHN : 215, (22).
HANDS family : 114.
HANKS, JEREMIAH : 225.
HANNYNGTON'S BANK, failure of : 111.
HARDING, WILLIAM : 217, (15), (20), (24), (26).
HARLEM, near Dublin : 46, 61, 212.
HAROLD'S CROSS, Dublin : 42.
HARPER, AUNT : 58.
—— EPHRAIM : 59.
—— MRS. C. : 59.
HARRIS, HENRY : 168.
HARVEY, ABIGAIL : 63.
—— AMBROSE : 217.
—— EDWARD (1783-1858) : 144.
—— family : 63, 110, 114, 144.
—— FRANCIS : 63.

—— H. L. : 144.
—— MARGARET : 63.
—— MARGARET (nee Boyle), (1786-1832), Journal of : 144.
—— MARGARET (nee Stephens) (wife of William Harvey) : 144.
—— MSS. : 229.
—— REUBEN : 170.
—— RICHARD : 144.
—— THOMAS : 85.
—— —— junior : 63.
—— W. W. : 163.
—— WILLIAM : 144, 174.
HARWICH GREEN, Harwell (place) : 108.
HASLAM, T. J. : 221.
HASTINGS, Grubb children at : 102.
HATHERTON, LORD : 110.
HATS, Price of : 102.
HATTON, BARTH., mentioned : 212.
—— EDWARD : 210.
—— JOSEPH : 73.
—— SUSANNA : 84.
HAUGHTON, BENJAMIN : 160, 215, (38).
—— DEBORAH : 167.
—— ELIZABETH : 167.
—— family : 81.
—— HANNAH : 167.
—— J. B. : 86.
—— JOHN : 167.
—— JONATHAN : 29, 167.
—— MARY : 46, 53.
—— SAMUEL : 167.
—— SARAH : 167.
—— WILLIAM : 54.
HAUTENVILLE, ABIGAIL : 217, (28).
HAVERFOREWEST : 204.
HAWKESWORTH, LYDIA : 22.
HAWKINS, SAML. : 202.
HAYTERS, firm of : AII.
HAYWARD'S HILL, Cork, alias Ballyhernon : 122.
" H, E." : 54.
HEAD, ELIZABETH—see JACOB, ELIZABETH.
HEARTH MONEY, : 21.
HEAS, DAN : 63.
—— DAVID : 63.
—— DENNIS : 63.
—— THOMAS : 63.
HEATHER, family letters : 111, 229.
—— JAMES (d.1827) : 111.
—— JAMES, junior : 111.
—— WILLIAM : 111.
—— WILLIAM, junior : 111.
HEATING, Use of warm air for : 103.
HEAZELTON-DOUGLAS family : 112.
HEAZLETON family letters : 229.
—— JAMES MORTON : 112.
—— WILLIAM : 112.
HELVEDEN : 102.
HEMPHILL, DR. : 107.
HENDERSON, ABRAHAM : 161.

HERITAGE, EPHRAIM : 6.
HERSCHELL, DR., His telescope : 96.
HERSCHELL, SIR WILLIAM : 63.
HETHERINGTON, GRACE : 170.
HEWSON—letters from : 118.
Hibernia, S.S., Sinking of : 100.
HICKSITE MOVEMENT (American) : 103, 105.
HIETT, ELIZABETH : 178.
—— HANNAH : 178.
—— **James** : 178.
—— JANE : 178.
—— MARTHA : 178.
—— MARY : 178.
—— SAMUEL : 178.
—— SARAH : 178.
HIGGINSON, Aunt : 53.
—— JANE : 53.
—— Mrs. : 53.
HIGH COURT OF CHANCERY : 217, (6).
HIGHWORTH, Parish of : 187.
HIGH WYCOMBE, mentioned : 106.
HILL, ELIZABETH (nee Alexander) (wife of James Hill, senior) : 151.
—— HANNAH (nee Strangman) : 145.
—— JAMES of Limerick (1818-1871) Diary of, 1847-1868 : 133, 151.
—— JAMES (of Waterford) : 145.
—— JONATHAN : 205.
—— MARGARET (nee Newsom) : 151.
—— ROWLAND : 82.
—— THOMAS : 189.
—— WILLIAM of Limerick : 215, (26).
HILLARY, HENRY : 166.
History of Friends (SEWELL) : 104.
History of Quakers in Ireland : 122.
HOARE, SAMUEL : 22.
HODGKIN CORRESPONDENCE : 116.
HODGKIN, JOHN : 116.
HODGSON, DOROTHY : 43.
—— HANNAH (later Piper) : 43.
HODSON, ELIZABETH : 13.
—— (Shopkeeper) : 30.
HOEY, JAMES, printer : 39.
HOGS, scalded, Prices of : 86.
HOLLYMOUNT, Co. Wexford : 198.
HOLME, THOMAS, of Bregurteen : 11, 211.
HOLMES, BENJAMIN : 117 168.
HOLYHEAD, Journey to : 100.
—— Hotel mentioned : 106.
HOME, THOMAS : 210.
HOOPE, ROBERT : 24.
HOPPER, ISAAC : 103.
HOPWOOD, SAMUEL : 24, 117.
HORETOWN, (Co. Wexford) : 109.
—— —— : AII 229.
HORNER, TABITHA : 121.
HOROE, GEORGE : 163.
HORSES, Method of travel by sea : 100.
HORSES, Provision of : 5.
HOUNDSDITCH : 105.

HOWELL, CHARLES : 166.
HOWLAND, WALTER : 202.
HOWTH : 100.
HUDSON, SAMUEL : 210.
HUGHES, JOSEPH : 221.
—— WILLIAM : 166.
HUGUENOTS : 107.
HUMPHREYS, ANN : 24.
—— JOSEPH : 28, 52.
—— name mentioned : 53.
HUNTER, PRISCILLA : 178.
HURST, CHARLES : 75.
HUTCHINSON, JAMES : 173.
HYGROMETER CLOSET, Dublin : 39.

I

IDSTON, BERKSHIRE : 187.
INCEST, Dr. Salmon's opinion on : 110.
IMPEY, MRS. E. J. A. : 23, 51.
IMPORTS : 63.
INCORPORATED SOCIETY in Dublin for Promoting English Protestant Schools in Ireland, Legacy to : 168.
INDIANS (Christian teaching) : 54.
INFLUENZA (1775) : 63.
INMAN, I. : 22.
INNOCULATION AGAINST SMALLPOX : 44.
INSTITUTE, Royal Cork : 63.
INSURANCE, Advisibility of : 63.
INSURRECTION of 1798 : 44, 73, 109, 140, 143, 149.
IRELAND, Conditions in : 105.
—— Disturbed state of : 103.
—— Friends visiting : 103.
—— National Library of : 126, 127.
—— History of Southern : 63
—— Political affairs in (1838) : 106.
—— State of trade with England : 96.
IRISH FAMINE : 110.
IRISH LANGUAGE : 102.
IRISH RESIGNATIONS from Religious Society of Friends : 105.
IRISH SEA, Dangerous passage of : 96.
IRON AND STEEL, Importation of : 108.
ISLE OF MAN, Visits in : 134.
ISLEWORTH (Middlesex) : 97.
ISLINGTON, Middlesex, mentioned : 213.

J

JACKMAN, JNO. : 194.
JACKSON, ANNA : 185.
—— ANNA MARIA : 204.
—— ELIZABETH : 204.
—— **Erasmus** : 179.
—— family genealogy : 224, (22).
—— —— mentioned : 20.
—— FRANCES : 204.
—— HANNAH : 204.
—— ISAAC (Printer and Publisher) : 38, 122, 216.

222 INDEX

—— JANE : 202.
—— JOSEPH : 86.
—— —— of Tincurry : 215, (27).
—— MARY : 179, 204.
—— name mentioned : 24.
—— NATHANIEL : 179, 180, 202, 204.
—— Publishers : 38.
—— RACHEL : 205.
—— RACHEL MARIA : 180, 204.
—— REUBEN HARVEY : 185.
—— Robert : 180.
—— ROBERT : 179, 204, 205, 210.
—— R. : 108.
—— THOMAS : 205.
—— WILLIAM : 217, (9).
JACOB, ANNE : 113, 191.
—— Doctor (of Mountmellick) : 61.
—— ELIZABETH (nee Head) : 84.
—— Family mentioned : 63, 84, 130.
—— —— of Waterford and Clonmel : 86.
—— —— Origin : 83.
—— H. : 86.
—— JANE : 94.
—— ISAAC : 86, 87.
—— —— THOMAS : 87.
—— JOHN (Oculist) : 87.
—— JOSEPH, 1675-1722 (Testimony to) 84.
—— JOSHUA : 106.
—— MARY (Her mathematics Book) : 94.
—— RICHARD : 63, 86.
—— ROBERT : 181.
—— SAMUEL : 86.
—— SUSANNAH (see Lecky Susannah).
—— SYBIL NARCISSUS : 87.
—— THOMAS : 85.
—— THOMAS (son of Joseph) : 84.
—— —— STRANGMAN : 83.
—— —— WHITE : 160.
—— JOHN : 166.
JAFFRAY, ABIGAIL : 217, (28).
—— ROBERT : 217, (3), (4), (5), (10), (28).
JAMAICA mentioned : 106.
JAMES II (address to) : 95.
—— Order of, for release of Friends · 224 (19).
JELLICO, JOHN : 221.
—— THOMAS : 221.
JENKEN, CALEB : 180.
JENKINS, A. A. : 77.
JERSEY, West : 123.
—— East, Taking up of land in : 123.
John and Susan, Ship : 85.
JOHNSON, ABIGAIL : 46.
—— DEBORAH (nee Chandlee) : 41.
—— E. : 31.
—— FRANCIS : 41, 53.
—— JANE : 53.
—— JOHN : 53.
—— JOHN F. : 41.
—— PAUL : 168.
—— DR. PAUL : 18.
—— RICHARD : 28.
JOHNSTON, BOB : 30.
—— GERVAIS : 215, (22).
—— PAUL : 217, (1), (2).
JOINT COMMITTEE, for Education : 129.
JONES, ELI : 87.
—— Index : 159
—— ISABEL : 159.
—— SYBIL : 87.
JORDAN, RICHARD : 76.
Journal of Friends Historical Society : 109, 123.
JOYNER, HENRY : 186.
JUBEE, GEORGE (condemned prisoner) : 114.
JUDD, " UNCLE " : 74.
JULY STREET, Southwark, London : 168.

K

KAVANAGH, LAURENCE : 192.
KATHRENS, SAML. : 169.
KELLY, JOHN : 215, (25).
—— WALTER : 176.
KELP, Trade in : 85, 86.
KENDAL : 29, 99.
KENT, DANIEL : 221.
—— Duke and Duchess of : 105.
—— JOHN : 187.
KESWICK : 22.
KENY, ANN : 186.
KILBARRY, Cork : 122.
KILCARBERRY (? Co. Wexford) : 198.
KILCOMMON (Co. Tipperary) : 175.
KILCOMMONBEG (Co. Tipperary) : 16, 17.
KILCONIMORE (Co. Tipperary) : 10.
KILCONNER (Co. Carlow) : 6, 21, 63, 72, 121.
KILCONNER Mansion House : 220.
KILLCONNER MEETING HOUSE : 220.
KILCULLEN BRIDGE (Co. Kildare) : 30, 38.
—— OLD BRIDGE : 38.
—— Road Repair : 24.
KILDARE : 193, 205.
—— County Authorities : 24.
—— Earl of : 215, (6). 220.
KILHAM, HANNAH : 87.
KILKENNY : 182.
KILLABEGS, Co. Wexford : 198.
KILLAGREW, EDWARD : 202.
KILLALOE (Co. Limerick) : 15.
KILMAINHAM JAIL : 31.
KILTEEL, Registration of Meeting House at : 24.
KING, JOHN : 99.
—— WILLIAM (of Subdury) : 105.

KINGSTOWN : 53.
—— Hill : 41.
—— Railway Station, plan for : 225.
KINNEGO, near Dungannon, Co. Tyrone Home of the Heather family : 111.
KINSALE (Co. Cork) : 14.
—— Convent of : 63.
KIRBY STEVEN (Meeting at) : 26.
KIRKWOOD, J. (Printer) : 225.
KNAGGS, ROBERT : 192.
—— TOM : 192.
KNIGHT family mentioned : 226.
—— THOS. : 226.
KNOCKBALLYMAGHER (Co. Tipperary) : 10, 173.
KNOCKFIELD, Co. Kildare, Lease of lands of : 215 (6).
KNOCKGRAFFON (Tipperary) : 13, 16.
KNOCKLANE, Co. Louth : 169.
KNOTT, ABIGAIL, letters of : 118.
—— ELIZABETH (nee Walpole) : 118.
—— JOHN : 217, (15), (20), (21), (22), (24), (27).
—— THOMAS (of Exeter) : 118.
—— WILLIAM : 217, (9).
KYLE (Robert's family home) : 23.

L

LABOISSERS, his almanack : 38, 39.
Lackey, John : 182.
—— alias LECKEY, JOHN : 218.
—— —— —— —— (physician) : 218.
—— MARY (nee Chadwick) : 218.
—— THOMAS : 218.
LAMBETH : 168.
LAMBSTOWN (Co. Wexford) : 11, 196, 214.
LAMPHIER family mentioned : 109.
LANCASTER : 21, 29.
—— STREET, Belfast : AI.
LANE, name mentioned : 64.
LARD, Price of : 85.
LATHAM, GEORGE : 7.
LA TOUCHE, DAVID : 217, (13).
—— The Hon. DAVID : 216.
LAWLESS, ANN : 177.
LAWRY, GAVIN : 123.
LAWTON, JAMES HULL : 201.
LAYER BRETON (Essex) : 102.
LEADBEATER, DEBORAH : 58.
—— ELIZABETH : 53, 55, 56, 58, 61.
—— MARY (nee Shackleton) : 18, 29, 52, 54, 55, 57, 58, 61, 114, 120, 125, 126, 224, (12).
—— MARY (nee Shackleton) Abstract of Diary of : 133, 143.
—— MARY, Publications of : 55.
—— RICHARD : 58.
—— WILLIAM : 53, 59, 92, 127, 143.
Leadbeater Papers, The : 143.

LEADBEATER-SHACKLETON COLLECTION : 55.
LEAGHMORE, Cork : 162.
LEASES, Dublin : 7.
—— Eoenderry : 8.
LECKEY alias LACKEY, JOHN : 218.
—— MARY (nee Chadwick) : 218.
Lecky, Anne, : 181.
—— " the Banker " : 63.
—— family : 63, 84, 110.
—— HANNAH : 181.
—— HARVEY : 86.
—— JAMES : 181, 215, (11).
—— JOHN : 174, 181.
—— JOHN (1764-1839) Journal of visit to London Yearly Meeting, 1794 : 133, 141.
—— JOHN, (1845-1929) Recollections of my life for my Grandchildren (1855-1899) : 133, 155.
—— (of Carlow) : 215, (6), (11).
·—— JOHN (of Cork) : 63, f.f., 83, 84, 85, 86, 87, 88.
—— MARGARET : 63, 113, 141.
—— MARY P. : 54.
—— MARY (nee Newsom) (wife of Robert John Lecky) : 155.
—— name mentioned : 18, 49, 108.
—— ROBERT : 215 (11).
—— ROBERT (of Youghal) : 63, 141.
—— ROBERT (of Carlow) : 135.
— — ROBERT J. : 63, 88, 155, 174.
—— SUSANNA : 174.
—— SUSANNAH, her sketches : 63.
—— —— (of Youghal) : 63, 86, 87.
—— THOMAS (apprenticeship) : 84.
—— —— : 181.
—— WILLIAM : 181.
—— W. J., Montreal : 155.
LECKY AND MARK, Connection with Newenham's Bank : 86.
LECKY'S BANK NOTES, Wood plates for: 86.
LEE, MARY : 216.
LEE STEAM PACKET, Shares in : 208.
LEEDS (Yorkshire) : 121.
LEEDS UNIVERSITY LIBRARY : 123.
LEGACIES (Waterford and Tipperary) : 17.
LEHINCHIE (LEHENSY) : 3.
LEHENSIE, Queen's Co., see also LEHINCHIE : 211.
LEINSTER PROVINCE BOOK : 10.
—— —— Component meeting of : 3.
—— —— : 4, 7.
—— Province Meeting : 3.
—— Provincial Schools : 128.
—— Quarterly Meeting : 3, 8.
LELAND, JOHN : 217, (5).
—— JOS. AND HENRY, Hat Manufacturers : 28.
—— Major General JOHN : 217 (9).

—— RICHARD : 217 (3).
"LE MESURIER," Advice on dealings with : 86.
LETHAM, JOHN : 166.
LETTERS, Men's Meeting : 7, 15.
—— original : 224 (3).
LEVITSTOWN (? Co. Kildare) : 202.
LEWES (Sussex) : 99.
LEWIS, FRANCIS : 220.
LEXDEN (near Colchester) : 103, 105.
LIBRARY MINUTES : 14, 15.
—— REPORTS : 224 (28-34).
LIGHTFOOT, MICHAEL : 173.
—— SUSANNAH : 73.
—— THOMAS : 75.
LIMERICK : 13, 15, 108, 160, 163.
—— Certificates of Friends in : 221.
—— Meeting : 186.
—— Monthly Meeting : 15.
—— Roman Catholic Bishop of (1796): 215 (26).
LIMERICK ALLEY, Dublin : 222.
LINEAGE BOOK : 8.
LINEN TRADE, Decline of : 105.
—— —— with America : AII.
LISBURN (Co. Antrim) : 7.
—— Monthly Meeting : 215 (41).
—— —— —— Records : AI.
—— School, Committee of : 221.
LISACURRAN (N. Ireland) : 188.
LISNAGARVIE, Co. Antrim, mentioned : 211.
LISNANANE (Co. Tyrone) : AII.
LIST OF MEMBERS : 7.
—— —— —— (Edenderry) : 8.
LITTLE HOUSE (or Schoolhouse) at Sycamore Alley Meeting : 217 (6).
LITTLE KILLIANE (? Killean) : 195, 197.
LITTLE KILLIANE and Ballykelly, Co. Wexford : 120.
LITTON, CHARLOTTE : 217 (21).
—— DANIEL : 217 (27).
—— ESTHER CHARLOTTE : 217 (21), (27).
LIVERPOOL : 99.
—— steam coach : 103.
LODGINGS, Cost of : 104.
LONDON, Meeting in : 101.
—— Religious visit to : 97.
—— Truss Society : 102.
—— University Fund Raising : 103.
—— Wall, Rectory House on : 86.
—— Yearly Meeting 1668, Copy of letter concerning : 224 (8).
—— Yearly Meeting 1786, Journal of visit to : 133.
—— Yearly Meeting 1794 Journal of visit to : 88, 133.
—— —— —— 1766 : 78.
LONGFIELD, DR. J. : 63.
LONGFORD, LORD, House of : 225.
LOOBY family mentioned : 215 (27).

LORD, ARTHUR, Viscount of Ely : 219.
LOVELL, EDITH : 54.
LOVER, WILLIAM FREDERICK : 217 (18).
LURGAN, Lease of land at : 215 (41).
—— Monthly Meeting Records : AI.
—— —— —— Trusts : 215 (41).
LYING IN INSTITUTION (Clonmee) : 65.
LYNES, MRS. (mother to Sarah Grubb) : 97, 98.
—— — SARAH : 76, 79, 89, 96.
—— —— marriage of : 97.

M

MACANALLEY, MARRIOTT (nee Conran) : 169.
McDONELL, Rev. THOMAS : 218.
—— WALTER : 202.
McKEOWN, Captain of vessel Active 86.
MACKEY, WILLIAM : 202.
MACMASTER, MAXWELL : 217 (25).
McINTOSH, SIR JAMES : 99.
MADDOCK, JOSEPH : 168, 217 (1), (5), (21), (27).
—— name mentioned : 24.
MAGINSTOWN, in Tipperary George Fennel of : 215 (27).
MAHARG, DR. : 56.
MAHER, ELIZTH. : 182.
MAHONY, MICKEY : 199.
MAIDSTONE : 99.
MAINE, WILLIAM : 7.
MALCOMSON, DAVID : 86, 92, 215 (31).
—— JOHN : 215 (31).
MALCOMSON-BELL, pedigree : AII.
—— name mentioned : 64.
—— family mentioned : 81.
MALDEN (Essex) : 102.
MALLOW (Cork) : 13, 14,
MALLOWLANE, Cork : 63.
MALONE, FRANCIS : 199.
—— JAMES : 215 (11).
—— name mentioned : 23.
Manders, Jonathan : 183.
—— — S. : 210.
MANNA : 24.
MANUSCRIPT DRAFTS : 122.
MARGATE : 99.
MARK, ELIZABETH : 167.
—— JOHN : 167.
MARRIAGE CERTIFICATES, see each Meeting.
——Intentions of : 17, 226.
—— MARY : 99.
—— JOSEPH : 100.
—— Presentments : 3, 7.
—— Procedure : 5.
—— Records (see each Meeting).
—— with two sisters (pamphlet) : 110.

MARSH, JOSEPH : 99.
MARCILLAC, JEAN DE : 92.
MARSTON (Parish of Highworth) : 187.
MARTIN, ABIGAIL : 184, 195.
—— ANDREW : 197.
—— ELEANOR : 184.
—— ELIZABETH : 184, 195.
—— HENRY : 205.
—— ISAAC : 184.
—— JACOB : 184, 197.
—— JOSIAH : 184.
—— MARGARET : 184.
—— MARY : 184.
—— name mentioned : 120.
—— PATRICK : 195.
—— PHILLIP : 216.
—— RICHARD : 217 (12).
—— Samuel : 184.
—— SARAH : 184, 195.
—— THOMAS : 184.
—— WM. mentioned : 213.
MARYBONE LANE, Dublin : 178.
MARYBOROUGH, LORD : 191.
MASON, GEORGE : 220.
—— JAMES : 221.
MASSEY family : 226.
MATHEWS, THO. : 179.
MATTHEW, Rev. Father : 106, 149, 150.
MATTHEWS, THOMAS, junior : 217 (11).
—— —— surveyor : 217 (4).
—— —— WM. : 30.
MAXWELL, Major (1st King's Dragoon Guards) : 108.
MAY, AMOS : 167.
MAYNE, WILLIAM, of Dublin, (carpenter) : 211.
MEATH STREET (Dublin) : 3, 7, 168, 173, 180, 205.
—— —— —— possession of dwelling house : 215 (38).
—— —— —— Quaker Meeting House in : 216.
MEELICK MILL, Queen's Co. : 223.
MEETING HOUSE, first of Quakers in Dublin : 211.
MEETING HOUSES, Care of : 5.
—— —— Registration of : 24.
—— —— Material relating to: 224 (7).
MEETINGS for Discipline : 99.
MEETING PRONOUNCEMENTS : 224 (6).
MEETINGS :
—— National : 1, 2, 14.
—— Yearly : 1, 2, 14, 15.
—— Half Yearly : 1, 2.
—— Provincial : 1 3, 4, 5, 7, 13. AI.
—— Quarterly : 1, 4, 8, 13, 15, 16.
—— Monthly : 1, 5, 6, 7, 9, 10, 11, 12, 13, 16, 17.
—— Women's : 1, 2, 6, 7, 8, 9, 11, 13, 17.
—— Men's : 1, 2, 5, 6, 7, 8, 9, 10, 11, 12, 15.

—— Preparative : 1, 10.
—— Six weeks : 1, 13, 16, 17.
—— Particular : 1.
—— American : 2.
—— Three Weeks : 14, 17.
—— Select : 14.
—— Women's Quarterly : 16.
—— —— Six weeks : 16.
—— —— Monthly : 16.
—— for Worship : 99.
MEETINGS, Monthly, see each Meeting.
MELBOURNE, JOHN : 192.
MELLOR, EBENEZER : 128.
—— LYDIA (later Shackleton) : 49.
—— MARGARET : 49.
MEMBERS, Lists of : 10, 11, 14, 15.
MENAI BRIDGE : 53.
MENDICITY INSTITUTION, Clonmel : 87.
MEN'S MEETINGS, see each Meeting.
MERRYWEATHER, MARY, see DAVIS, MARY.
—— JOHN : 99.
"MESURIEM HOUSE, London," : 86.
METHEGLIN, Cask of : 183.
MEYER, SARAH : 189.
MIDDLESEX and London Meetings, Visits to : 102.
MIDDLESEX QUARTERLY MEETING : 22.
MIDLAND, Great Western Railway Stock : 198.
MILECROSS, (Co. Down) : AII.
MILVERTON, SOMERSET : 60.
MINEHEAD (Somerset) : 60.
MINISTER'S CERTIFICATES (1778-1834) : 2.
—— Deceased, Testimonies to : 2.
—— and Elders, Meetings of : 2.
—— Visits : 14, 17.
MINISTRY and Oversight Meetings : 15. see also each Meeting.
MINUTES, see each Meeting.
MOATE : 3, 9, 110, 217 (10).
—— Birr attached to : 10.
—— Meetings Records : 227.
—— Women's Meetings : 117.
MOGRIDGE, THOMAS : 117.
MOIRA, Co. Down : 132.
MOLLOY, T. : 30.
—— WILLIAM : 194.
MONEY, English and Irish compared : 100.
MONEYMORE, (Co. Londonderry) : AII.
MONMOUTH, Wm. Sinderbee of : 200.
MONTGOMERY, M. A. : 53.
MONTHLY MEETINGS, : 5, see also Meetings.
—— —— Women's, see each Meeting.
MONTREAL, mentioned : 157.
MOONE, Co. Kildare : 58.
MOOR, CONNELL : 205.
—— JAMES : 205.
—— SAMUEL : 205.

INDEX

MOORE, ANNE : 173.
—— CHARLES : 114.
—— Elizabeth : 185.
—— JAMES (Co. Kildare) : 114.
—— LAWRENCE : 173.
—— REBECCA : 173.
MORGAN family mentioned : 109.
—— M. : 186.
MORRIS, ANNE : 181.
—— " Cousin " : 21.
—— family mentioned : 226.
—— JOHN : 181, 206.
—— RICHARD : 192.
—— SARAH : 22.
MORRISON, JOSEPH : 198.
MORTIMER, RUSSELL : 123, 229.
MORTON, SAMUEL AND JOHN, of Philadelphia : AII.
MOUNTMELLICK (Queen's Co.) : 3, 10, 35, 58, 110, 140, 173, 179, 180, 204.
—— Meeting Book of 1667 : 10.
—— —— House, Lease of : 219.
—— Monthly Meeting : 8, 10.
—— School : 3, 128, 156, 180.
MOUNT OPHALY : 27.
MOUNTRATH (Queen's Co.) : 3, 10, 192, 194, 215 (5), (7), (13).
—— Earl of : 215 (7), (13), (19).
—— Lease of land at : 215 (5), (19).
—— Meeting Records : 227.
MOUNT VENUS : 61.
—— WILSON (Edenderry) : 90, 108, 109.
MOWBRAY, ANNE : 185.
—— MARY : 185.
MOYALLEN OR TULLYLISH, Co. DOWN: 215 (4), (12), AII.
MOYALLOW (Cork) see MALLOW.
MOYL ABBEY, Co. Kildare, Lands of : 220.
MUNSTER MEETINGS (times of, 1694-1775) : 95.
—— Province Meeting : 13, 15.
—— Provincial School : 129.
—— Quarterly Meeting : 13, 15, 16.
—— Women's Meeting : 13.
MÜNSTER (Germany) : 82.
MURPHY, MARY : 172.
MURRAY, LINDLEY : 76, 99.
—— WILLIAM : 226.
MUTTON, Price of : 100.

N

NATIONAL INSURANCE CO. : 208.
—— LIBRARY OF IRELAND : 126, 127.
—— MEETING : 1, 13.
—— —— PROCEEDINGS : 227.
—— —— of 1669 : 14.
—— —— HOUSE (Dublin) : 7.
—— WOMEN'S MEETING : 13.
NEALE, ABRAHAM : 96.

—— family genealogy : 224 (22).
—— MARY, Marriage settlement 1812 : 215 (33), 223.
—— MARY (nee Peisley) : 92.
—— RICHARD : 223.
—— SAMUEL : 42, 43, 73.
—— SARAH : 42.
NEEMSTOWN, Wexford : 197.
NEVILL, JAMES : 39.
NEVINS, R. 26
NEWBY, THOS. : 99.
NEWBURY mentioned : 99.
NEWCOMB, GEORGE : 217 (25).
NEWENHAM, DEBBY : 26.
—— SIR EDARDW : 21, 54.
—— GEORGE : 86, 183.
—— and LECKY, Bankers : 63.
—— name mentioned : 24.
NEWFOUNDLAND, Aid for ships from: 84.
—— Bay of Bulls : 85.
NEWGARDEN (Co. Carlow) : 3, 6.
—— map of burial ground, 19th century : 225.
—— — North Carolina : 33.
NEWGATE JAIL (Dublin) : 31.
NEW HAMBRO OR HAMBOROUGH (Dungannon), bleach green : AII.
NEW JERSEY mentioned : 157.
—— —— Friends in : 72.
—— —— Taking of land in : 123.
NEWMARKET (Dublin) : 169, 216.
NEWPORTS BANK (Waterford) : 80.
NEW ROSS : 184.
NEWSOM, CATHERINE (nee Lucas) : 138.
NEWSOM, DENIS : 221.
—— family of Edenderry : 224 (14).
NEWSOM, GEORGE of Edenderry : 145.
—— family mentioned : 81, 90.
—— —— letters : 108.
—— GEORGE (of Cork) : 73, 138, 145, 210.
—— (——) his diary : 133.
—— ISABEL (nee Hill) : 145.
—— JOHN : 138.
—— JOSEPH P. : 108.
—— JOSHUA : 133.
—— —— his journal : 145.
—— LYDIA (nee Wilson) : 138, 145.
—— MARY (nee Unthank) : 151.
—— PHEBE, her diary : 133, 152.
—— THOMAS, of Cork, mentioned : 151.
—— WILLIAM, mentioned : 108, 152.
NEW SOUTH WALES, Governor of : 63.
—— —— Journey to : 109.
NEWTOWN SCHOOL : 80, 85, 86, 94, 129.
—— —— Accounts of : 129.
—— —— Centenary : 129.
—— —— Exclusion of girls : 129.
—— —— Essays : 94.
—— —— law suit : 86.
—— HILL, near Tramore : 185.
—— (Waterford) : 6.

INDEX

NEW YORK, mentioned : 157.
NIALL, JOHN : 160.
NICHOLSON family, Notes on : 224 (12).
—— JOHN, junior : 215 (1).
——PETER : 224 (17).
—— —— Appeal against his disownment by the Society of Friends : 115.
—— THOMAS : 217 (9).
NICKALLS, THOS. : 99.
NIGHTCAPS : 23.
NOREVILLE, Queen's Co. : 209.
NORTH CAROLINA : 33.
NORTHERN COUNTIES, Visits to : 99.
NORWICH : 22.
NOWLAN, ELIZABETH, widow : 220.
—— MARY : 167.
—— PATRICK (deceased by 1756) : 220.
NURNEY, Kildare : 193.

O

OATS, Price of : 85, 108.
O'CONNELL, DANIEL : 88, 103, 104, 229.
O'BRIEN, ANN : AIII.
—— family correspondence : 229.
—— JOHN G. : 208.
—— MARY (nee Wright) : 229.
—— WILLIAM : 229.
O'CONNEL, REV. TIMOTHY : 218.
OHIO, Letters from : 118.
OIL, Newfoundland, trade in : 85, 86.
OLD BAWN, Dublin : 46.
OLD BOOLEY, Co. Wexford : 208.
OLD MELDRUM AND KINMUCK, Old Meeting House of : 97.
OLD TENTER (Roscrea) : 215 (15).
OPIE, AMELIA, of Norwich : 110.
ORAM, WILLIAM : 187.
ORMOND, DUKE OF, property in Clonmel 218.
ORPEN, DR. CHARLES : 28, 52.
OSBORNE, ELIZTH. : 182.
—— RICHARD WILLIAM : 217 (26).
Overseas Trade of Waterford, Louis M. Cullen : 145.
OXFORD, Corpus Christi College, letters from : 86.

P

PALMER, HUMPHREY : 215 (24).
—— JOSEPH : 215 (24).
"PAPIST" ATTORNEY GENERAL, Appointment of : 106.
PARAMATTA : 88.
PARKE, ROBERT : 202.
PARKER, ROBERT : 183.
PARLIAMENT STREET (Dublin) : 41.
PARLIAMENTARY COMMITTEE : 2.

PARR, JAMES : 225.
PARSONS. SIR WILLIAM : 215 (14).
PARTICULAR MEETINGS : 1.
  see also Meetings.
PATRICK STREET, Dublin : 169.
PATRIOTIC SHARES : 191.
PAYTON, CATHERINE : 92.
PEARCE, CHARLES : 187.
PEARCE, family of Limerick, letters of : 119.
—— early meetings in their house: 15.
—— ELIZABETH : 187.
—— FRANCIS : 187.
—— JOSEPH : 187.
—— KATHERINE : 187.
—— MARGARET : 187.
—— MARTHA : 187.
—— MARY : 187.
—— PRUDENCE : 187.
Pearce, Richard : 15, 186, 187.
—— SARAH : 186.
—— **Thomas** : 186, 187.
—— THOMAS : 15.
PEASE, EDWARD : AII.
—— HENRY : 77.
—— JOSEPH, M.P., mentioned : 106.
—— —— —— : 103, 104.
—— —— —— (his travelling map) : 225.
PEDLOW, ANN : 188.
—— EDWARD : 188.
—— HENRY : 188.
—— ISABELLA : 188.
—— James : 188.
—— JANE : 188.
—— JOHN : 188.
—— JOSEPH : 188.
—— MARY : 188.
—— SARAH : 188.
—— SHUSEY : 188.
—— THOMAS : 188.
PEEL MEETING : 22.
PEEL, SIR ROBERT, Resignation of : 103.
PEET, EDWARD : 215 (20).
—— JOSHUA : 194.
PEILE, Surgeon : 56.
PEISLEY, MARY *see* NEALE.
—— SAMUEL : 74.
PEMBERTON, JNO. : 30.
—— name mentioned : 29.
PENINSULAR WAR : 217, (12).
PENKETH SCHOOL, mentioned : 154.
PENMENMAWR : 22.
PENN family, survey of Cork land : 136.
—— GULIELMA MARIA (formerly Springett) : 214.
—— WILLIAM : 123, 224 (19).
—— —— junior : 214.
—— —— Memorial to : 157.
—— —— Transfer of land by : 213, 214.

INDEX

PENNSYLVANIA, 123, Taking up of land in : 213.
PENNY POST : 107.
PENROSE, BILLY : 26.
—— COOPER : 189.
—— family mentioned : 109.
—— FRAN. : 96.
—— GEORGE R. : 204.
—— JACOB, junior : 185.
—— PEGGY : 26.
—— name mentioned : 12.
—— WILLIAM : 96.
PERROTT, JOHN : 224 (9).
PERTH GUILDHALL, Meeting in : 97.
PETERSBURG : 77.
PETTERS, JOHN : 84.
PETTY CASH : 14.
PHELAN, name mentioned : 64.
—— ROBERT : 215 (31).
PHELPS family : 108, 114.
—— THOMAS : 186, 215 (22).
—— W. W. : 86.
PHILADELPHIA : 205.
—— Epistle from : 22.
—— mentioned : 157.
—— Rolls office : 213.
—— Yearly Meeting : 75.
PHILLIPS, CATHERINE : 22, 74.
—— HANNAH : 189.
—— JAMES : 189.
—— JOHN : 187, 189.
—— MARY : 189.
—— SARAH (nee Fawcett) : 48.
—— SUSANNAH : 195.
—— Thomas : 189.
PHOTOGRAPHS, miscellaneous : 226.
PICKOVER, ISAAC : 117.
PIG PRICES : 85, 86.
PIKE, " Aunt " : 92.
—— DEBORAH : 190.
—— EBENEZER : 54, 164, 189.
—— family mentioned : 81, 109, 114.
—— Jo. of Cork : 99.
—— JOSEPH (1698) : 213.
—— —— (1776) : 21.
—— MARGARET (nee Christy) : 25.
—— MARY : 46, 136.
—— MOLLY : 26.
PIKE, name mentioned : 18.
—— RICHARD : 43.
—— SAML. : 170.
—— WIGHT : 21.
—— William (inventory) : 190.
—— WILLIAM : 201.
PIKELAND (Pa.) : 75.
PILKINGTON, JOHN : 178.
PIM, ABIGAIL : 76.
—— ANNE (nee Greenwood) : 148.
—— ANTHONY : 219.
—— Anthony : 191.
—— BETTY : 26.

—— Bros. & Co. Wholesale Drapers : 153, 157.
—— CHARLES, Leases of Kildare land 1738-1774 : 215 (5:7:8-10:13:17).
—— CHARLES, junior, Leases of Kildare land 1738-1774 : 215 (19:20:29: 30:36).
—— —— Leases of Kildare land 1858: 215 (39).
—— Charles of Mountrath : 192.
—— —— (1741) : 193.
—— —— (1794) : 194.
—— —— (1815) : 192.
—— —— A. (1842) : 191.
—— DEBORAH (nee Bewley) : 140.
—— ELIZABETH : 74, 92, 191.
—— family mentioned : 81, 114.
—— —— letters : 110.
—— FRANCIS : 192, 215 (36).
—— FREDERIC WILLIAM (1839-1924), Journal of his visit to America 1864: 133, 157.
—— GEORGE : 191.
—— HANNAH : 22, 63, 77, 215 (30).
—— HENRY (1803-1881) : 148.
—— JAMES of Mountmellick : 74, 91, 140, 192, 215 (30), 219.
—— —— of Rushin : 193, 219.
—— —— of Dublin : 148.
—— JOHN of Belfast : 80, 122.
—— —— of Lackey (Queen's Co.) : 219.
—— —— of Mountrath : 192, 193.
—— —— of London : 99.
—— JOHN of Tottenham (1718-1796) : 22, 92.
—— —— Deed of Annuity 1793 : 215 (23).
—— —— Power of Attorney 1803 : 215 (30).
—— —— T. : 191.
—— JONATHAN of Dublin : 110, 153, 157, 217 (21), (22), (27).
—— —— of Mountmellick : 140, 192, 193, 194.
—— JOSEPH : 63.
—— —— JOSHUA : 219.
—— MARY, letter from R. Shackleton 1752, : 54.
—— —— of Mountmellick : 61.
—— —— of Mountrath : 194.
—— —— of Rushin 1747 : 193.
—— —— —— 1781 : 215 (20).
—— MOSES of Lackey : 219.
PIM's DISCOUNT HOUSE, London : 100.
PIM, SAMUEL : 191.
—— SAM : 26.
—— SARAH (later Grubb) : 22, 74, 92.
—— —— of Ballitore : 90.
—— SARAH (nee Robinson) : 140.
—— SUSANNA (nee Todhunter) : 153, 157.

—— SYLVANUS : 191.
—— THOMAS, Journal of tour in Italy 1852 : 133, 153.
—— THOMAS : 110, 193, 194.
—— THOMAS THACKER : 191.
—— TOBIAS of Fancroft : 215 (15).
—— —— of Rushin : 193.
—— W. HARVEY : 153.
—— WILLIAM H. (French passport for) : 110.
PIM, WILLIAM, Journal of European tour : 133, 148.
—— name mentioned : 18, 23, 24, 29.
PIPER, HANNAH : see Hodgson.
—— CAPTAIN JOSEPH : 43.
PITTSBURGH, Grocery business in : 112.
—— mentioned : 157.
PL(E)ADWELL, TOBIAS of Mountmellick : 219.
PLAIN DRESS : 76.
—— LANGUAGE : 22.
PLEADWELL, ELIZABETH : 205.
POETRY EXTRACTS : 94.
POLEGATE (Dublin) : 7.
POLL TAX : 10.
POOLE, DEBORAH : 195.
—— DOROTHY : 196.
—— Dorset Co. : 99.
—— ELIZA. : 195.
—— ELIZABETH : 196.
—— —— of Growtown Wexford, : see Addey, Lizzie.
—— HANNAH (nee Leckey) : 181.
—— Jacob : 195.
—— JACOB : 120, 124, 184, 197, 223.
—— JEANE : 196.
—— JOHN LECKY : 181.
—— Jonathan : 196.
—— Joseph : 197.
—— —— : 172, 184, 195, 196, 203.
—— Letters of family : 120.
—— MARGARET : 196.
—— MARY : 195, 196.
—— —— (nee Sparrow) : 120.
—— RICHARD : 120, 181, 184, 196.
—— SARAH : 184, 195, 196.
—— SARAH (nee Martin) : 197.
—— THOMAS : 196.
—— WILLIAM : 196.
POOR, Care of : 3.
—— Committee of : 7, 14.
—— Distress among : 106.
—— Friends : 180, 186.
—— Fund Accounts : 17.
—— Laws : 106.
—— Relief of : 5, 7,
—— Women's Committee for : 7, 14.
POPHAM, —— : 210.
PORK, Selling prices of : 85.
PORRIDGE, from Indian meal : 64.
PORTARLINGTON : 58, 167.
PORT ROYAL, America (? Pikeland) : 75.

POSTAL SERVICES : 104.
—— CHARGES : 105.
POTASH, Trade in : 85, 86.
POWELL, DANIEL : 214.
—— MARY : 193.
POWER, ROGER : 200.
—— THOMAS GODFREY : 94.
PREPARATIVE MEETING (Cork City) : 14.
—— —— Mountmellick : 10.
PRICE, WM. : 183.
PRICES AND CUSTOMS, Comparisons between England and Ireland : 99.
PRICES OF BEEF : 100.
—— —— CATTLE : 84.
—— —— CLOTHING : 28.
—— —— FISH : 100.
—— —— FOOD : 53.
—— —— FURNISHINGS : 53.
—— —— GRAIN AND PROVISIONS : 63.
—— —— MUTTON : 100.
—— —— PRINTING : 55.
—— —— SOAP : 85.
—— —— TURKEYS : 101.
PRINCE AND PRINCESS OF WALES, Visit to Dublin, 1868 : 156.
PRINTING : 1, 55.
PRINTERS AND PUBLISHERS, c.1810 : 55.
—— CARRICK : 55.
—— COLLIS : 55.
—— DUGDALE : 55.
—— KEENE : 55.
—— JOHNSON : 55.
PRIOR PARK SCHOOL : see Suir Island School.
PRISON REFORM : 99.
PRIVATEERS, American : 43.
"PROGRESS OF TRUTH," Record of : 1, 2.
PROVINCE MEETING : 3, 5, 7. see also Meetings.
PROVINCE MEETING MINUTES : 14.
PROVINCIAL MEETINGS, Dating of settlement of : 3.
—— SCHOOL (Leinster) : 3, 54, 172.
—— —— COMMITTEE : 129.
PROVISIONS, Export of : 63.
—— Prices of : 63.
PUBLIC RECORD OFFICE, Dublin : 229.
—— —— —— Belfast : 226, All.
PURVES, SARAH : 198.
—— Thomas : 198.
PYKE, JOSEPH : see Pike.

Q

QUAKER BIBLIOGRAPHY : 33.
Quakers Dublin Weekly Oracle, The : 123.
QUAKERS, *History of in Ireland* : 1, 122, 136.
Quakers in Ireland, Grubb : 132.
Quaker Wills (Eustace and Goodbody): 159, 203.

230 INDEX

QUARTER SESSIONS, Attendance of Friends at : 24.
QUARTERLY MEETING : 4, see also Meetings.
—— —— Women's (Edenderry) : 8.
QUEBEC, Journey from, to Toronto (1823) : AII.
—— mentioned : 157.
—— and New York, Aspects of life in : 111.
QUEEN'S PALACE (Buckingham House) : 1775 : 22.
QUERIES, for serious consideration : 1, 14.
—— Answers to : 2, 3, 13.

R

RABBIT AND HARE SKINS, Export of : 102.
RAILWAY, proposed, to Achill Sound : 110.
RALLINS, Barnaby : 121.
RANCOCAS (America) : 72.
RANDALL, FRANCIS : 11.
—— GEORGE : 162, 177.
RANDALL'S MILLS (Wexford) : 11, 195.
RANSOME, REBECCA : 22.
"RANTERS" (White Quakers) : 106.
RAPE MARSH, Cork, common name of south marsh : 200.
RAPHAEL CARTOONS (at Buckingham House) : 22.
RATE IN AID (letter of John Bright) : 110.
RATHANGAN (Co. Kildare) : 8, 10, 29, 118, 140.
RATHBONE, WILLIAM : 21.
RATHCORMICK (Cork) : 63.
RATHDOWNEY (Queen's Co.) : 215 (24).
RATHFRY(I)LAND, formerly Balliachien, (Co. Down) : 215 (3), (16).
RATHRONAN (Tipperary) : 72.
RAYNOR, ELIZABETH (nee Shackleton) : 42, 147.
—— MAURICE : 42, 147.
—— name mentioned : 18.
—— WILLIAM : 42.
—— —— Diary of : 133, 147.
READ, MARY : 217 (12).
—— RICHARD : 217 (12).
—— WILLIAM, senior : 217 (12), (13).
—— —— junior : 217 (12).
Recollections (Addey) : 149.
RECORDS, Keeping of : 5.
—— National : 2.
—— of Meetings, see each meeting.
—— of Friends travelling : 14.
REDCASTLE, Queen's Co., Lease lands at : 215 (9).
REEVES, JOHN : 221.

—— LAWSON : 221.
—— WILLIAM : 221.
REFORM QUESTION, mentioned : 103.
REGISTERS, see each Meeting.
RELIEF, Letters concerning : 15.
—— to poor Friends : 95.
REMOVAL, Certificates of : 7, 8, 10, 11, 12, 14, 15, 16, 17, 224 (1), (23-26).
RENOOGNAN (?) : 24.
REPORTS, Yearly, from London and from Provincial Meetings : 2.
RESEARCH WORK, Aids to : 159.
RETREAT (Donnybrook) : 7, 87.
Retreat Journal : 2.
REYNOLDS, MARTHA : 182.
RHEUMATIC GOUT : 49.
RIALL, CHARLES : 86.
—— MARTHA : 66.
RICHARDSON ANNA (nee Grubb) her letters : 113.
—— DEBORAH : 204.
—— family mentioned : 81.
—— JAMES N. : AII.
—— JOHN, of Mountrath : 215 (35).
—— —— S. W. : AII.
—— JOSEPH, of Antrim : 215 (22).
—— MARY, of Dublin : 215 (35).
—— MURIEL : AII.
—— RUTH : 113.
—— SARAH : 113.
—— AND SONS, Almanac 1856 : 154.
RICHHILL MONTHLY MEETING RECORDS: AI.
RICKMAN, JOHN : 99.
—— NATHANIEL : 224 (11).
—— WM. : 99.
RIDGWAY, ELIZABETH : 152.
—— HENRY (of Mountmellick) : 219.
—— —— (of Waterford) : 152.
—— JOHN : 219.
—— JOSHUA : 204.
—— name mentioned : 49, 108.
—— WILLIAM : 219.
RIGG, SAMUEL of Clonmel : 215 (27).
—— THOS. : 166.
RINGWOOD, Hants. : 60.
RISING OF 1798 IN IRELAND : 44, 73, 109, 140, 143, 149, 224 (11), AII.
RIVERVIEW, Limerick : 160.
ROBERTS, ABIGAIL : 51.
—— DOROTHY : 51.
Roberts family, A : 23, 51.
—— family of Queen's Co., mentioned : 23.
—— GEORGE : 51.
—— ISAAC : 178, 216.
—— MARY : 23, 192, 194.
—— NELLIE : 23.
—— RICHARD : 215 (17).
—— SAMUEL : 225.
ROBINSON, ANN : 61.
—— ELIZABETH : 22.

—— ISAAC : 206.
—— JOHN, of Dublin : 212, 217 (10), (11), (14), (23).
—— JOSEPH (1793) : 215 (23).
—— MARY : 191.
—— WILLIAM : 191.
ROBSON, ELIZABETH, mentioned : 106.
ROBSON MSS. : 229.
ROCHESTER : 99.
ROGERS, JOHN : 182.
—— THOS. :182.
ROOKE, GEORGE : 117, 134, 173, 216.
ROPER, SAMUEL : 216.
ROPER'S REST (Dublin) : 61.
ROSBARNAGH, near Newport, Mayo : 110.
ROSCREA, Tipperary : 10, 215 (15).
—— —— Abbey Street, : 215 (15).
—— —— Castle Pleasure Gardens : 215 (15).
—— Meeting House : 215 (15).
ROSE, GRIMES : 30.
—— MARY, her cure for dropsy : 108.
ROSENALLIS, Queen's Co. : 3, 10, 211.
—— plan for burial ground : 225.
ROSS, (on Wye), Religious visit to : 97.
ROSS, FORBES : 180.
ROSS (Wexford) : 11, 85.
ROUTE, from Cumberland to London : 139.
ROUTH, LAURENCE : 3.
—— name mentioned : 49.
ROWE, DENNIS : 53.
ROWSOM, JAMES : 199.
—— (Mrs.) : 199.
—— **Samuel** : 199.
ROYAL COLLEGE of Surgeons in Ireland: 212.
ROYAL EXCHANGE Co., Insurance policies made with : 215 (21).
RUDD, THOMAS, visit to Ireland, 1706 : 134.
RUSHIN, Queen's Co. : 192, 193, 215 (20), 219.
RUSSELL, ANNE : 168.
—— FRANCIS : 168 193.
—— GREGORY : 220.
—— HUGH : 202.
—— JAMES : 95.
—— SAMUEL : 217 (9).
—— THOMAS : 168.
RUSSIA, Emperor of : 28, 224 (11).
—— Empress of : 39.
—— PRIME MINISTER : 77.
RUTTY, JOHN : 1 11, 15, 17.
RUTTY JOHN, *History of Quakers in Ireland* : 7, 15, 122, 136.

S

SADLEIR, MR. BURKE : 110.
ST. GEORGE, Melesina : 143.

ST. GEORGE STEAM PACKET COMPANY : 174.
SAINTHILL, R. : 86.
—— RICHARD, junior : 63.
ST. JOHN, Lands of (? Kildare) : 202.
ST. LEGER, HAYWARD : 122.
ST. STEPHEN'S GREEN, Dublin : 212.
SALLINS : 30.
SALMON, DR., Provost of Trinity College, Dublin : 110.
SALMON, Price of : 104.
SALT, Price of : 85.
SAMPSON, MARY : 135.
—— DR. THOMAS : 135.
SAMUEL, GEORGE : 160.
SANDERS, JOHN : 24.
SANDS, DAVID : 75, 76.
SANTIAGO DE CUBA : 118.
SARGINT, RD. : 210.
SAUL, JOHN : 117.
SAUNDERS, GEORGE : 161.
SAVAGE, ABRA. : 226.
SCANLAN'S ALMANAC : 38.
SCARBOROUGH, Journey from : 105.
SCARR, JOHN : 160.
SCATTERGOOD, THOMAS : 76, 140.
SCHOOL, Ackworth (Yorks.) : 229.
—— Ballitore : 54, 88, 132, 143, 147.
—— Brookfield : 132.
—— Camden Street, Dublin : 4, 131.
—— Edenderry : 88, 128.
—— Greenrow (Cumberland) : 58.
—— Mountmellick : 3, 128, 156, 180.
—— Newtown : 80, 85, 86, 94, 129.
—— SUIR ISLAND : 13, 67, 87, 94, 113, 130, 225.
—— Tottenham (London) : 101.
—— COMMITTEE, Munster Provincial : 13.
SCIENCE MUSEUM, South Kensington : 63.
SCOTLAND, Religious visit to : 97.
SCOTT, JOB, mentioned : 140.
SCURVY, Cure for : 46.
SEA BATHING : 26, 41.
SEALE, ELIZABETH : 173.
—— GREGORY : 173.
—— HINDRANCE (nee Edmundson) : 173.
—— JAMES : 173.
—— JANE : 173.
—— MARTHA : 173.
—— THOMAS : 173.
—— WILLIAM : 173.
SEA ROBBERS, Escape from : 224 (11).
SELECT MEETING : 14.
SEPARATIONS IN SOCIETY OF FRIENDS : 106.
SEVENTEENTH century letters and documents : 228.
SEVERN STEAM PACKET, from Cork to Bristol : 208.

SEVILLE, College at : 63.
SEWEL, (WILLIAM), Copy of his *History of Friends* asked for by the King (William IV) : 104.
SHACKLETON, ABRAHAM (1696-1771) : 33, 50, 132, 143, 147.
—— ABRAHAM, junior : 44, 49, 132, 143, 215 (28 and 34).
—— DEBORAH : 21, 25, 26, 32, 43, 46, 167.
—— —— (later Chandlee) : 22, 34
—— EBENEZER : 58.
—— ELIZABETH : 167.
Also see RAYNOR, ELIZABETH.
—— ELIZABETH (nee Carleton) : 21, 50, 54.
—— ELIZABETH (nee Fuller) : 21.
—— family mentioned : 18, 74, 143.
—— MARGARET (later GRUBB) : 21, 44.
—— MARY (later Leadbeater) : 32, 46, 51, 57, 92, 167.
—— —— —— her childhood letters : 62.
—— RICHARD : 18, 21, 22, 42, 48, 50, 60, 61, 63, 82, 92, 114, 132, 143, 167.
—— —— his views on teaching : 54.
—— —— Letters of : 54.
—— SARAH : 36, 46, 56, 62, 167
SHAFTESBURY : 99.
SHANNON, ANN : 42, 58.
—— ELIZABETH : 42.
—— JANE : 194.
—— JOHN : 28, 180.
—— WILLIAM : 194.
SHARP, ANTHONY : 123, 216, 224 (9).
—— HESTER : 123.
—— ISRAEL : 205.
—— MANUSCRIPTS : 123.
—— THOMAS : 224 (9).
SHEARES, HENRY : 57.
SHELDON, ELEAZAR : 173.
—— SUSANNA : 173.
SHELLEY, ALEXANDER, junior : 54.
—— JANE : 54.
SHIELDS mentioned : 99.
SHILLITOE, THOMAS, *Journal of* : 106.
—— —— mentioned : 76, 103.
SHIPLEY, JOHN : 99.
SHIPS' CHANDLERS : 63.
SHOE LANE, London : 168.
SHOVELS, Price of : 108.
SIMMONS, ALICE : 194.
—— ISAAC : 217 (10), (23), (26).
—— OLIVER : 166.
—— THOMAS : 212, 217 (10), (11), (14), (23).
SIMPLE WATERS : 30.
SINDERBEE, FRANCIS : 200.
—— GEORGE : 200.
—— **Richard** : 200.
SINDERBY, CHARLES : 200.
—— WILLIAM : 200.

SINGLETON, EDWARD : 213.
SINTON-CHRISTY Pedigree : 229.
" SIRIUS " (Steam vessel) : 106.
Six Generations in Ireland : 149.
SIXSMITH, ANN : 205.
SIX-WEEKS MEETING (subsidiary to the Province Meeting) : 16.
SKELTON, PETER : 3.
SKIBBEREEN : 13.
SKIPTON (Yorkshire) : 33.
SKINNER'S ALLEY, Liberties, Dublin : 169.
SKINNER'S Row, Dublin : 28, 118.
SLAVERY, Anti- : 57, 100, 102, 150.
—— Abolition of : 103, 104.
—— Dr. Salmon's opinions on : 110.
SLAVE LABOUR : 82.
—— TRADE, Controversy : 96.
SLAVES, Traffic in : 97.
SLEIGH, RICHARD : 201.
Sleigh, Sarah : 201.
SLOUGH, Herschell's Telescope at : 96.
SMITH, FREDERICK : 76.
—— HESTER : 108.
—— JOHN : 162.
—— JOSEPH, *Catalogue of Friends' Books* : 135.
—— SAMUEL : 76.
SNAKE, live, sent to Clonmel : 104.
SMITHFIELD, in Oxmantown, Dublin : 169.
SMYTH, JAMES : 181.
—— MARY ANNE : 181.
SOAP, Price of : 85.
SOMERSET : 83.
SOUP KITCHEN ACCOUNTS (Clonmel) : 94.
SOUTH AMERICA, Journey in : 91.
SOUTHERN IRELAND, Bank failures in : 100.
SOUTH GATE GREEN (Bury St. Edmunds), House at : 98, 99.
SOUTHAMPTON : 99.
SOUTH MARSH (Cork), commonly known as Rape Marsh : 200.
SOUTH SEAS : 104.
SPALDING (Lincs.) : 99.
SPARKES, ANSTIS : 19.
Sparrow, Alexander : 202.
SPARROW, DEBORAH : 120.
—— family mentioned : 109, 120.
—— JAMES : 202.
—— JANE : 195.
—— JOHN : 120, 184.
—— JONATHAN : 208.
—— MARTHA : 195.
—— R. : 166.
—— REBECCA : 202.
—— RICHARD : 202, 215 (27).
—— SAMUEL : 202.
—— **William** : 172, 203.
SPAWELL ROAD, WEXFORD : 198.

INDEX

Spectator : 208.
SPEECH TRAINING SCHOOL : 46.
SPRINGETT, H. : 213.
SPRINGMOUNT, Cork : 42.
STAFFORD, HANNAH : 189.
STAMP OFFICE, Dublin, Old site : 7.
  see also : 217 (8).
STANTON, EDWARD : 202.
STANSTEAD (? Essex) : 102.
STEAMBOATS (1824) : 100.
STEARNES, HENRY : 168.
STEPHENS, ANNE : 54.
—— PENELOPE : 195.
—— —— (Uncle to Edward Harvey) : 144.
STEPHENSON, JOHN : 22.
—— SARAH : 76.
STEVENS, JOHN : 217 (1).
STEVENSON, SALLY : 30.
STEWARDSON, THOMAS : 76.
STOCK, HENRY : 217 (17).
STOCKTON : 99.
STOKE NEWINGTON : 82, 96, 103.
—— —— Growth of : 104.
STONEY, R. VESEY : 110.
STOREY, THOMAS : 213.
STORTFORD : 102.
STRAMORE, near Moyallen (Co. Down) : 25, 46, 167.
STRANGMAN, ELIZABETH *see* Gatchell.
STRANGMAN family mentioned : 84, 91.
—— JAMES PIM : 91.
—— JOSEPH : 80, 91.
—— JOSHUA : 54, 173, 219.
—— —— junior : 219.
—— J. W. : 116.
—— LOUISA (later Conran) : 61.
—— MARY : 91.
—— name mentioned : 64, 108, 145.
—— SAMUEL : 91, 179.
—— THOMAS : 168.
—— SUSANNA : 173.
STRANGMAN'S, of Waterford, Butter Merchants : 100.
STRATFORD, ANTHONY : 118.
STRATTON, T. : 187.
—— WM. : 187.
STRETTLE, ABEL : 217 (13), 220.
—— AMOS : 7, 24.
—— ROBERT : 217 (3).
STRETCHES *alias* STRITCHES ISLAND : 218.
STRITCHES *alias* STRETCHES ISLAND : 218.
STURGE, JOSEPH : 77.
SUDBURY, (Suffolk) : 96, 99, 105.
SUEGEMIA, E. (?) : 213.
SUFFERINGS, Bundles of original papers of : 224 (18), 227.
—— for Bandon, Co. Cork, : 226.
  see also each Meeting.
SUFFOLK : 79.
SUFFIN, near Parsonstown, lease of lands of : 215 (14).

SUGAR, cessation of purchase from West Indies : 82.
—— Government duty on : 82.
—— Price of : 97, 104.
—— Proposed bounty on : 97.
—— Restrictions on use of : 97.
SUGHRUE, TIMOTHY : 183.
SUIR ISLAND SCHOOL : 13, 67, 87, 94, 113, 130.
—— —— —— Prospectus of : 130.
—— —— —— Map of : 225.
SULLY, DR. JOHN : 24.
SULPHUR : 24.
SUMMERHILL, Cork : 34.
SUMNER, WILL : 168.
SUNDAY'S WELLS (Cork) : 200.
SUNDERLAND : 99.
SURGEON-APOTHECARY, Treatment by : 101.
SUTTON, FRANCIS : 204.
—— **Mary** : 204.
SWARTHMORE, Collection of letters of early Friends : 224.
SWINNEY'S FARM, near Mountrath : 215 (29).
SWEENEY, PATRICK, mentioned : 218.
SYCAMORE ALLEY MEETING HOUSE, Dublin : 7, 140.
SYRIA (Trustees of Schools) : 198.

T

TABINET : 28.
TALLOW, Trade in : 85, 86.
TANNAGHMORE LODGE (Tyrone) : 188.
TANNER'S END (Tottenham) : 22, 92.
TASMANIA, Letters from : 105.
Tatler (magazine) : 208.
TAYLOR, JOSHUA : 217 (21), 226.
—— WILLIAM : 212, 217 (10), (11).
TEA, Prices at auction of : 105.
TELEGRAPH SYSTEM, in Cuba : 118.
TESTIMONIES : 1, 13, 224 (2).
—— Bundles of original : 227.
—— of disunity : 17.
THACKER, MARY : 204.
—— ROBERT : 204.
—— WILLIAM : 191.
THAXTED : 102.
THEOBALD, ELIZABETH H., mentioned : 144.
THOMAS COURT, Dublin, service in Courthouse : 38.
THOMAS STREET, Dublin : 28, 88.
THOMPSON, Abigail : 46, 167.
—— ANDREW : 123.
—— ELIZABETH : 167.
—— JOHN : 167.
—— JOSEPH : 116.
—— name mentioned : 49.
—— THOMAS : 154.

—— WM. : 183.
THREE WEEKS MEETING, Cork : 14.
see also Meetings.
TIMAHOE (Kildare) : 7.
—— —— Registration of Meeting House at : 24, 215 (2).
TIMBER YARD : 191.
TINEEL (Queen's Co.) (William Edmundson's farm) : 173.
THOMPSON, ANDREW : 123.
—— ELIZABETH : 167.
—— JOHN : 167.
—— JOSEPH : 116.
—— name mentioned : 49.
—— THOMAS, of Enniscorthy : 154 167, 195.
—— WM. : 183.
TIPPERARY, Co. : 13, 16, 174.
—— Meeting Houses : 95.
—— —— Records : 227.
—— Militia, release of Apprentice from : 86.
—— Monthly Meeting : 13, 16, 71.
—— Six Weeks Meeting : 1.
—— Women's Monthly Meeting : 16.
TITHE LISTS : 7.
TITHES, Motion in Parliament respecting : 21.
TOBACCO, growth of : 88.
TOBERHEAD MEETING HOUSE (Co. Antrim), Lease of : 215 (22).
TODHUNTER, WILLIAM : 110, 116.
TOLBOTS, ELIAS : 183.
—— THOMAS : 183.
TOMA(O)LOSSETT, Co. Wexford : 215 (32, 33), 223.
TOMEY, ELIZA. : 73.
TOTTENHAM : 22, 29.
TOTTENHAM FRIENDS'S SCHOOL, Fees at: 101.
—— mentioned : 139.
TRADES, Union of : 63.
TRAFFORD, THOMAS : 12.
TRAMORE (Co. Waterford) : 185.
TRANSIT INSTRUMENT : 63.
TRATTLE, MARMADUKE : 86.
TRAVEL, Documents concerning : 224 (1).
—— Speed of : 100, 106.
TRAVELLING RECORDS OF FRIENDS : 14.
TRAVEL, Fatigue of : 20.
TRAVELLING, Certificates for : 224 (23-26).
TREASURER'S ACCOUNTS : 224 (28-34).
TRENCH, CHENEVIX, Archbishop : 143.
——DR. R. CHENEVIX : 110.
—— MELESINA : 55.
TREVELYAN, SIR CHARLES : 110.
TREVOR, PATRICK : 217 (12).
Trial of Pennsylvania, 100 ton ship : 123.
TRINITY COLLEGE, Dublin : 86, 122.
TROTTER, JOHN BENJAMIN : 57.

TRUST Property, Northern Ireland : AI.
TUCKER, RICHARD : 217 (28).
TUCKETT, JAMES (Ship's Captain) : 85.
TUKE, ELIZABETH : 114.
—— JAMES, HACK : 116.
—— SARAH : 46.
—— WILLIAM : 46, 99.
TULLAMORE : 10.
TULLOW : 6.
TULLYLISH (i.e. MOYALLEN) Meeting House, Lease of : 215 (4) (12).
TURKEYS, Price of : 101.
TURNER, MARY : 229.
—— ROBERT (of Dublin) : 123, 211.
—— —— (of Grange) : AI.
—— SAMUEL : 186.
TURNPIKE ROADS, : 24, 30.
—— —— Cost of : 30.
TYRELL, ADMIRAL (impressed by Samuel Fothergill) : 29.
TYTHES : 103.
—— Testimonies against : 2.

U

ULSTER as part of Ireland : 110.
—— Province Minutes : 159.
—— —— —— : AI.
—— Provincial School Schedule of Legacies for : 215 (41).
—— Quarterly Meeting Records : AI.
UNEMPLOYED MEN Relief of : 64.
UNION OF TRADES : 63.
UNITED STATES Economic situation in 1864 : 157.
UNTHANK ROBERT : 222.
USHER WILLIAM : 215 (14).
UXBRIDGE mentioned : 106.

V

VACCINATION : 28.
VALENTIA ISLAND : 155.
VALENTINE JOHN : 217 (15) (20).
VALLENLING JOHN : 171.
VALLINTINE HANNAH : 172.
—— THOMAS : 172.
VALU O. : 210.
VAN DIEMENS LAND Journey to : 106.
—— —— —— Future of Quakerism in : AII.
VENUS Transit of 1769 : 38.
—— —— —— 1874 : 157.
VERGENNES COMTE DE : 75.
VICTORIA, QUEEN : 105 106.
VINCENT Dame MARY : 213.
—— SIR MATTHIAS : 213.
—— THEODORE : 213.
—— VINCENT : 213.
VINEGAR HILL Battle of : 75.

INDEX

VISITING FRIENDS Lists of : 94.
VISITS: Ministers, Narrative of : 14.
VOLUNTEERS (1782) : 30.
VOTING, power of proprietors in East Jersey : 123.

W

" W." JOHN : 54.
WADE, PETER : 180.
WAGINIGEN : 91.
WAKEFIELD, C. : 106.
—— family mentioned : 109.
WAKEFIELD, PRATT & MEIRS (London) : AII.
WALDENFIELD SAMUEL : 117.
WALES, Visit to : 96.
Walks through Ireland : 57.
WALKER, JOHN : 61.
WALPOLE, BRIDGET : 215 (25).
—— ELIZABETH : 161.
—— JOSEPH, mentioned : 118.
—— name mentioned : 23, 120.
—— T. : 221.
—— THOMAS : 215 (25).
—— WILLIAM : 209.
W(ALPOLE), M., query concerning will of : 118.
WALSH, MRS. : 63.
—— WM. : 63.
WALTER, JOHN : 215 (1).
WARBURTON : 191.
WARD, DOROTHEA : 205.
—— RALPH : 217 (8).
WARING, ANNE (nee White) : 208.
—— ELIZABETH : 208.
—— HANNAH : 208.
—— JOSEPH : 208.
—— MARIA : 208.
—— SAMUEL : 215 (16).
—— THOMAS : 208.
—— —— WHITE : 208.
Warning to England, A—Fox, George :1.
WATERFORD : 17, 21, 42, 83, 145, 129, 147, 160, 161, 172, 185, 207, 208.
—— Butter trade of : 145.
—— Customs at : 84.
—— Gas Company : 208.
—— Monthly Meeting : 17.
—— Plan of burial ground at Parliament Street : 225.
—— Six Weeks Meeting : 17.
WATER MARKS : 38.
WATERTON, CHARLES : 105.
WATSON, ABIGAIL (nee Craven, then Boles) her letters : 121.
—— family of Carlow, letters of : 18.
—— —— —— intermarriage with Lecky family : 63.
—— JANE : 29.
—— LAURENCE : 196.
—— name mentioned : 24, 49.

—— SAMUEL : 24, 121, 166, 220.
—— SOL. : 165, 166.
—— SOLOMON : 215 (27).
——'s Almanac : 38.
WEBB, ALFRED (compiler Irish Biography) : 149.
—— DEBORAH (her reminiscences, 1905) : 133, 149.
—— —— (nee Davis) : 150.
—— EDITH (her diary, 1868) : 133, 156.
—— GERTRUDE : 156.
—— H. : 156.
—— HANNAH (nee Waring) : 149.
—— JAMES, of Dublin : 120, 150, 156, 195, 217 (15), (20), (22), (24), (27).
—— JOHN : 217 (21), (27).
WEBB, MR. : 216.
—— RICHARD, DAVIS (publisher, of Dublin) : 149.
—— —— his sketch of visit to Erris, Co. Mayo, in 1847 : 133, 150.
—— SUSANNA (wife of James) : 156.
—— THOMAS HENRY, compiler of Quaker Pedigrees : 159.
WEBBER, GEORGE of Cork (merchant) : 211.
Webster, Elizabeth : 205.
WEBSTER, ELIZABETH : 180.
—— JOS. : 167.
—— JOSHUA : 180.
—— MARY (alias Tuite) : 180.
—— ROBERT : 180.
WELLINGTON, DUKE OF : 82.
—— Letter from : 110.
WELDON, WILLIAM : 84.
WELLINGHAM, near LEWES, mentioned : 99.
WELLINGTON (Somerset) : 99.
WESLEY, JOHN : 140.
WESTBURY, Parish of : 200.
WEST, ROBERT, original signature to indenture, 1708 : 214.
WEST INDIES, (J. Gurney's book on) : 107.
—— mentioned : 117.
—— Trade with : 85.
—— Slavery in : 106.
WEST, MATTHEW : 28.
WESTMINSTER MEETING : 104.
WEXFORD : 3, 11, 84, 134, 140, 195, 196, 197, 198, 203.
—— (" drinking the waters at ") : 24.
—— Establishment of Meeting in : 107.
—— Monthly Meeting : 71, 172.
—— —— —— Legacy to : 198.
—— (rising of 1798 in) : 140.
WHEAT, Price of : 85.
WHEATSHEAF (INN), Dublin : 30.
WHEELAN, Co. Kildare : 205.
WHEELER, DANIEL : 104, 105.
—— —— his voyage to Russia : 106.
—— EDWARD : 99.

INDEX

WHITE, A. : 221.
—— Ann (Cork) : 206.
—— Ann (Waterford) : 207.
—— ANN : 208.
—— BENJAMIN : 207.
—— CHARLOTTE : 215 (39).
—— DANIEL : 166, 206.
—— **Dinah** : 208.
—— —— : 206, 207.
—— ELIZABETH : 208.
—— EMLYN SYMON : 186.
—— GEORGE : 208.
—— HANNAH : 206, 207, 208.
—— —— ELIZABETH : 208.
WHITEHAVEN, (Cumberland) : 21, 58, 139.
—— —— Attack by American privateers : 43.
WHITE, HENRY : 199, 206, 207, 208.
—— JAMES : 132, 215 (34), 206, 208.
—— JOHN : 206, 208.
—— —— TAYLOR : 208.
—— JOSEPH, of Pennsylvania : 54.
—— WALTER : 207.
—— WM. : 201.
—— JOSHUA : 206.
—— LYDIA : 208.
—— MARIA : 208.
—— MARY (letter to) : 110.
—— MIRIAM : 206.
—— PATT : 184.
WHITE QUAKERS : 106.
WHITE, SARAH : 172, 206, 208.
—— THOMAS : 207, 208.
—— —— (JAMES) : 206.
—— THOS. : 221.
WHITLEY, LOUISE : 182.
WHITNELL, ARTHUR : 202.
WHITSITT, SARAH, daughter of John and Ruth Whitsitt : 112.
—— WILLIAM : 24.
—— —— junior : 24.
WHITSUNTIDE, Yearly Meeting might be disassociated from : 22.
WHITWORTH, JOHN : 54.
WICKLOW : 3, 12.
—— " drinking the waters at " : 21.
WIDDOWS, ELIZABETH : 167.
WIGHAM family : 97.
WIGHT, DEBORAH (nee Abell) : 136.
—— JOSHUA (1678-1758) Diary of : 133, 136.
—— AND PIKE, Merchants, Cork : 136.
—— THOMAS : 1, 7, 11, 15, 17, 136, 138, 226.
—— —— History of Quakers in Ireland: 15, 17, 122.
WILBERFORCE, WILLIAM : 100.
WILBUR, JOHN (from America) mentioned : 103.
WILEY, T. : 73.
WILKINSON, MARGARET : 33.

—— name mentioned : 64.
WILKISON, THOMAS : 173.
WILLAN, ANN : 71.
—— MARY : 71.
—— WILLIAM : 71.
WILLIAM III, Statue of : 88.
—— —— —— Blowing up of : 105.
WILLIAMITE WARS : 13.
—— —— (conditions during) : 123.
WILLIAMS, BEN : 223.
—— JANE : 184, 195.
—— JOS. : 46.
—— JOSEPH : 112, 195, 217 (9).
—— SAMUEL : 196.
WILLIAM STREET, Limerick : 163.
WILLS AND INVENTORIES, Books of : 6, 7, 8, 10, 11, 12.
WILSON, ALEX. : 96.
—— BENJ. : 197.
—— ELIZABETH : 109.
—— family letters : 117, 224 (3).
—— ISAAC : 22.
—— JAMES, his descriptions of birds : 105.
—— JOHN : 217 (9), 221.
—— MARY (nee Bewley) of Cumberland : 117.
—— MARY (nee Unthank) : 138.
—— name mentioned : 29, 108.
—— SAMUEL : 221.
—— THOMAS : 108, 117, 138.
WILY, THOS. : 162, 200.
WINE, High price of : 41.
WINSLOW, THOMAS : 173.
—— WILLIAM : 166.
WOMEN'S NATIONAL MEETING : 2. see also Meetings.
WOMEN'S MEETING, Waterford : 17.
WOOD, MARY : 161.
WOODCOCK, ——, of Wexford : 26.
—— **Francis** : 209.
—— —— : 215 (32), (33), 223.
—— MARY : 209, 215 (18), 222.
—— ROBERT : 172.
—— SAMUEL : 222, 223.
—— WILLIAM : 222, 223.
WOOD ENGRAVING, cost of : 55.
WOODHOUSE, Tipperary : 121, 165, 166.
—— —— Burial Ground : 165, 215 (37).
WOOLLEN TRADE, Decline of : 105.
WORCESTER mentioned : 106.
—— Religious visit to : 97.
WORKINGTON mentioned : 139.
WORMWOOD GATE (Dublin) : 7.
WORRELL, name mentioned : 64.
WRIGHT, ANNE (d.1670) : 95, 135.
—— —— (A Brief and true relation of): 135.
—— CATHERINE (formerly Despard) : 218.
—— family letters : 118.

INDEX 237

—— JAMES S. : 118.
—— JOHN : 118, 199.
—— Jonathan : 210.
—— —— (of Waterford) : 118.
—— NATHAN : 118.
—— NEHEMIAH : 118.
—— MARTHA : 118.
—— WILLIAM (of Grahamstown, South Africa) : 118.
WYLY, JOHN : 194.
—— T. : 210.
— — THOMAS : 43.

Y

YEALAND : 99.
YEARLY MEETING : 1, 2, 14, 15.
—— —— connection between London and Dublin : 95.
—— —— Legacy to : 198.
—— —— Committee : 2, 198.
—— —— —— Letterbook : 2.
—— —— London : *see* London Yearly Meeting.
YORK : 99.
YORK, FREDERICK, Duke of : 217 (9), (10).
YOUGHAL : 13, 14, 58, 63, 84, 121, 141, 181, 199.
YOULGROVE, Co. Wexford : 184.
YOUNG, RT. REV. JOHN, Roman Catholic Bishop of Limerick : 215 (26).
YOUTH, Care of, 1680 : 95.
—— Education of : 5.
—— Meeting of : 28.

Z

ZODIAC, Signs of : 40.

www.ingramcontent.com/pod-product-compliance
Lightning Source LLC
Chambersburg PA
CBHW051056230426
43667CB00013B/2316